CRICUT MAKER

4 BOOKS in 1 - Beginner's guide + Maker Guide + Design Space + Project Ideas. The Unofficial Written Guide That You Don't Find in The Box is Finally Here!

KAYLA ARORA

BOOKS

CRICUT FOR BEGINNERS:

Cricut for beginners: Cricut beginner's written guide is Finally here. Through this cricut art guide you will discover the basics of cricut machines, design space and a first guide to new design ideas.

KAYLA ARORA

Table of Contents

Introduction

Speaking of machines that make for all the amazement, functionality, and effectiveness, the Cricut cutting machine is undoubtedly one of them. This, in part, is because of the underlying Cricut Design space, a free of charge mobile application that makes things magical happen.

Cricut cutting machines look and work a bit like a mini plotter. However, instead of drawing or plotting, they cut out intricate craft designs on a host of different materials. These materials range from paper to vinyl, with the new Cricut Maker even able to cut wood and some metal.

Other machines of this kind can cost you several hundred or even thousands of dollars. They can require design majors. They come with complex proprietary software, offering only a fraction of Cricut's design choices, as well as the proprietary, user-friendly Cricut Design Room. In campaigns, tips, tricks, guides, and new materials to use with your Cricut tool, Cricut's massive user base is always sharing the latest and greatest. As a Cricut computer crafter, the abilities are almost unlimited.

Suppose you have recently bought, or are thinking about purchasing, a Cricut machine. In that case, you are indeed looking for an easy how-to guide that can help you get started with this wonderfully creative machine. As such, this guide has been created for your enjoyment and education.

The following chapters will discuss the basic concepts of various "Cricut" machines and how they can be used to create beautiful artwork.

No matter what end of the spectrum is, it would be best if you read this book because it will give you step by step instructions on how to use them, as well as some ideas for exciting projects.

Yet, you may not be entirely familiar with the way the Cricut machine works. Thus, this book is intended to provide you with the necessary groundwork for you to use the machine like a real pro. After all, there is no need to struggle to try to figure out this innovative device. Everything you need to get started is contained within this book clearly and concisely.

In the following pages, you will find out everything you need to know to get started creating innovative projects using the Cricut machine. Each chapter has been designed to help you get the most out of the Cricut machine. This is especially true if you are thinking about using it as part of a business venture. In that regard, you need to master the use of this seemingly magical machine right away. We'll be looking at how you can use the Cricut machine to make some of the most imaginative and creative projects that you can think of.

With that in mind, the only prerequisite for the Cricut machine is imagination. Try to make the most of your ideas by putting them into practice. There is no need to hold back. You already have everything you need to make some of the most creative and imaginative designs. As a result, you will be able to produce more complex designs progressively. Soon, you'll be making professional-quality designs that will certainly impress everyone around.

By choosing this book, you are taking a step in the right direction. It is also satisfying to know that you appreciate the hard work that has gone into creating this guide.

And there's lots more that you can do with Cricut! Let us help you get started.

Chapter 1: What Is and What Can I Make with Cricut

What is a Cricut machine?

A Cricut machine (also known as a craft plotter or die-cutting machine) is a personal cutting machine. It is similar to a desktop printer; Images and designs printed on a computer are sent to the machine. Except that instead of printing the design, the machine moves a blade around to cut out the desired material.

The Cricut machine works automatically and can cut through materials such as paper, vinyl, craft foam, fabric, metal, faux leather, sticker paper, and even adhesive sheets.

There are models of the machine that allow users to use a pen rather than cutting to write texts and draw images. It can be used to produce wedding and party invitations that look handwritten.

The designs are digitally stored; thus, users can select and edit different patterns on their personal computer or mobile devices. Furthermore, there is a Cricut Image Library with over 50,000 images, fonts, and projects that users can choose from.

How does the Cricut machine works?

First of all, Cricut machines are electrical appliances and as such, require power to work. Similar to the workings of the ink nozzle in a printer, they have a tiny computer located within the machine that controls a cutting blade. They use digital cutters that can be connected to a computer through Bluetooth and wireless.

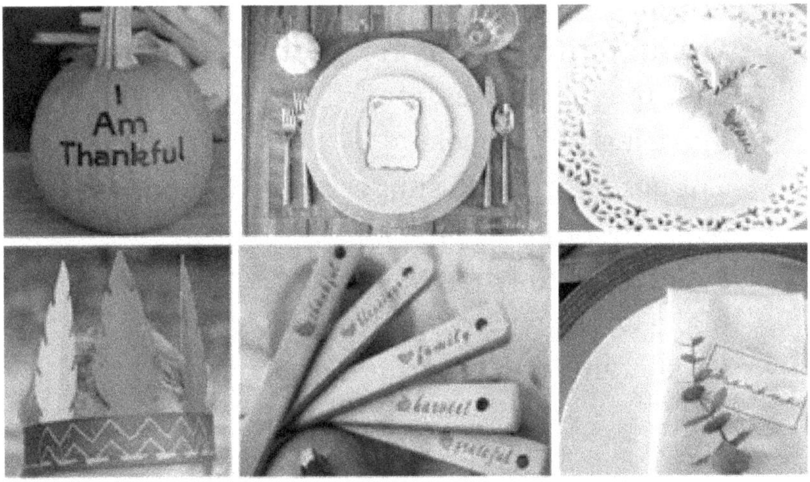

What can I make with a Cricut machine?

There is a lot that can be done with a Cricut machine. The possibilities are limitless; however, the following are a few examples;

- Make custom bags, shirts or hats using iron-on (heat transfer) vinyl.
- Cut quilt square and appliqués

- Create and produce customs cards for events like holiday cards, party invitations, and thank you notes, etc.
- Make window clings using static cling vinyl.
- Make and address envelopes
- Print and cut out stickers
- Etch glass
- Make stencils for etching and spray painting
- Create Christmas ornaments
- Produce Wall decals
- Produce vinyl decals for shot glasses, mugs and champagne glasses, etc.
- Make leather bracelets
- Cut out letters and shapes for scrapbooking
- Make monogram pillows
- Make painted wooden signs
- Make window clings
- Label items in a playroom or pantry

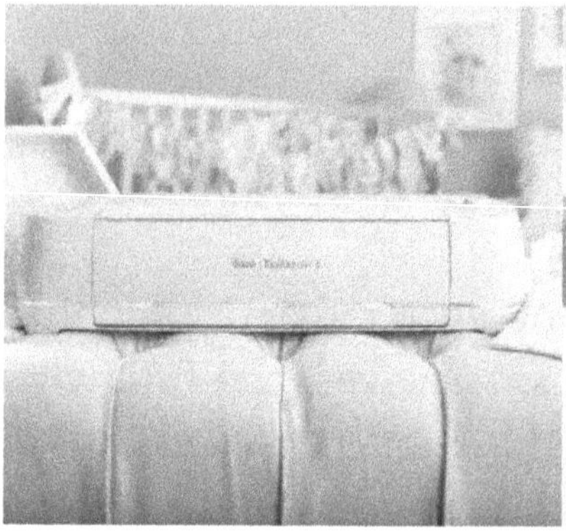
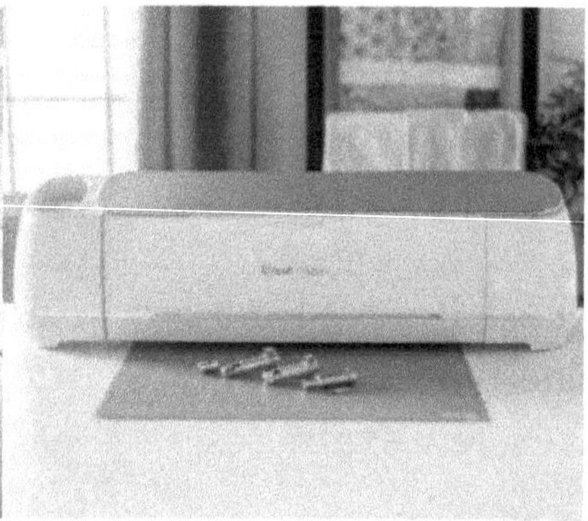

What is a Cricut Machine and How Would I Use One?

Perhaps you know what a Cricut machine is; nevertheless, you need to do slightly more research. Or then again, maybe you need one as a gift, but have to understand what it can do so the "gift provider" knows what they are getting you.

In any case, this post is about Cricut machines and what they can be used for.

Consider them little paper (and now a wide range of other material) CNCs. They are crafter's best friend relative to the immense metal or wood cutting factory— it is portable as well as convenient to travel or move about with.

A Cricut History

If you have been in the crafting scene for some time, you might have an idea or used the older version of Cricut that requires cartridges. You would have to choose a cartridge for your font or shapes, dial in the size you need, type the corresponding button on the keypad, then cut out your design.

Compared to the QuicKutz or Sizzix cutting systems, Cricut was VERY innovative. It takes less room, which makes a lot of sense in the long run. Furthermore, it was flexible as you can change the size of an alphabet or image in seconds and have it cut out.

The issue with the first Cricut machine was that it only cut 8.5 x 11 papers, and you are stuck using those empty cartridges. You couldn't modify the design and make it increasingly unique except if you did some imaginative "particular cutting" after it was off the cutting mat.

Move over Cricut Machines

That is the point where the Silhouette hit the market and had an immediate impact on the market. You could design your samples and use various fonts to cut out. If you were using the Sure Cut 3 program, you have all the opportunities on the planet to adjust your designs.

It was fabulous if you were a paper piecer for scrapbooking. You could break every one of those little characters separate, add various kinds to your cutting mat and afterwards let the machine do all the work.

My cutting device history went this way:

Bought a Sizzix and the most famous letters and shapes I intended to use over and again.

Bought a QuicKutz and all the delightful letter sets as well as new and inventive shapes that they brought to the table (store them in a cute cover with the smart gator device that in the end had various types).

Sold the QuicKutz (other than a couple of passes on that I was unable to leave behind like the chicken and turtle) and used that money to purchase a Cricut.

Learned how to design using Adobe Illustrator and offer the Cricut to purchase a Silhouette Cameo.

Pampered and purchased another Cricut Maker that allowed me to use iPad or PC to design cuts in the Design Space with more varieties of materials.

I've been one-sided towards a Silhouette for many years. Yet, the crafty breezes are changing, and I can see that the potential for a Cricut machine may be way superior to a Silhouette Cameo now. It could be a decent Cricut versus Silhouette discussion.

The Process

You will start by designing your project in design programming.

- Add your material to your cutting mat.
- Cutting mats are 12 inches by 12 inches (except if you purchase a longer tangle like a 12 x 24-inch tangle).
- Load the tangle and material into the machine.
- Press cut.
- Watch as the machine does all the complicated work.
- Unload the tangle from the machine.
- Cautiously lift off your design.
- Get rid of any undesirable pieces.
- Assemble if required.

The Types of Projects You Can Make with a Cricut?

Remarkably, the potential outcomes are only constrained by your imagination. You can mix designs. Use odds and ends of one project to add to another. Work with only paper. Do projects with mixed materials. Here is a rundown of potential projects to kick you off. From that point forward, simply observe where the machine and the materials take you!

- Cut out fun shapes and letters and use them on your scrapbooks.
- Create paper piecings for your scrapbooks.
- Make carefully assembled cards for all occasions.
- Design shirt or dress appliques
- Make adornments
- Make party decorations
- Create your stencils for artistry projects and painting
- Make window stickers and sticks.
- Label all the things!
- Design Monograms
- Create Christmas decorations
- Draw shading pages
- Decorate a cup, mug, or wine glass with vinyl
- Etch glass
- Home stylistic theme (like these honey bee quote tea towels)
- Make a wooden sign.
- Cut quilt squares or fabric shapes

Chapter 2:
Cricut Machine Models

CRICUT EXPLORE ONE

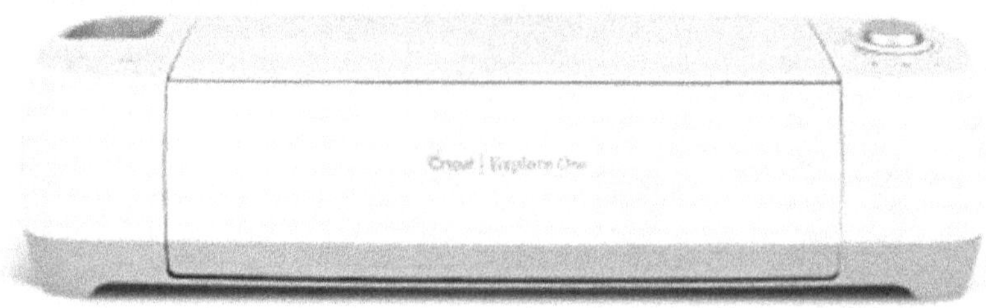

Explore One is ideal for beginners and inexperienced users who want to get into die-cutting, craft cutting, and plotting. The machine isn't advance like the other Explore models, and it is also the cheapest Cricut machine you can get.

Capability:

The machine is also highly capable, even if it's an old model. The system can also handle scoring and writing smoothly.

Materials:

Cutting Force

Even if Explore One is recommended for beginners, it is very professional. The blade is also highly durable.

As for the cutting width, the Explore One can cut sizes that range from 23 ½” tall and ¼ to 11 ½” wide.

Even though the Explore One seems excellent, there are some activities that you can't do on the Cricut Design Space if you're using this model.

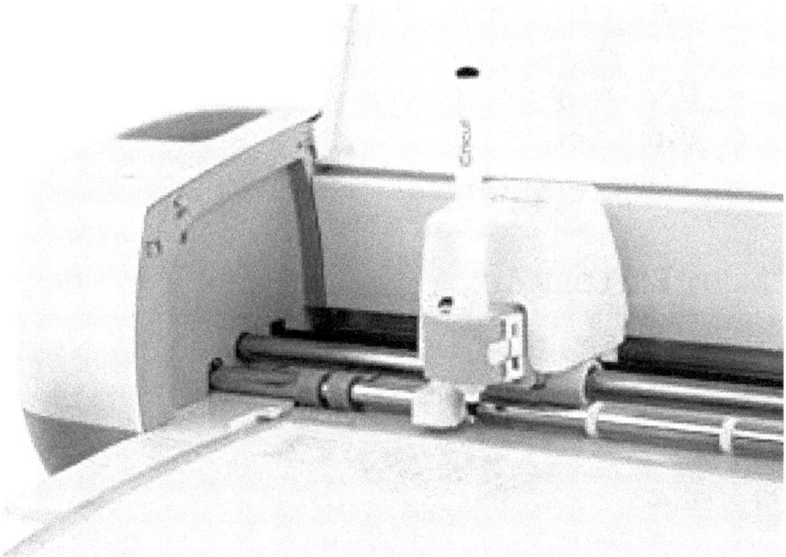

Cricut Design Space is very user friendly when using it for Explore One. It accepts .jpg, .png and .bmp files.

Also, the Cricut Explore One cannot function wirelessly. Suppose you want to add convenience to it and you don't mind the cost. In that case, you can buy a Bluetooth adapter and use it to transfer images or files wirelessly.

The Explore One also comes with one head clamp or carriage only. Because of this, if you want to draw and cut, you have to buy an adapter.

These are the tools that are in a newly purchased Explore One box:

- 24 x 9.5 x 9.5 sized Cricut Explore One machine.
- German carbide premium blade.
- Over 50 free images
- Over 25 free one-click projects.
- 12" x 12" Standard Grip cutting mat.
- USB and power cords.
- Vinyl sample.
- Welcome guide.

Cricut Explore Air

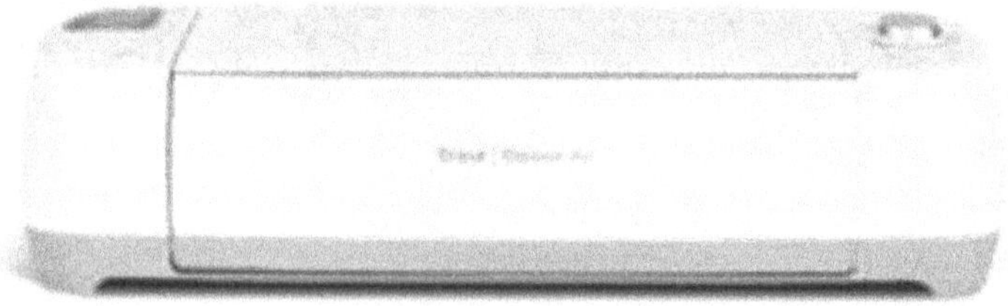

While this is quite similar to the Explore One model, it also comes with some additional features. The main difference between them is the presence of the inbuilt Bluetooth adapter. Suppose you don't enjoy seeing cables and wires all around your workplace, especially with the danger of tripping over them. In that case, this model solves that problem.

Capability

The Explore Air is also different from Explore One because it features a double carriage. This means that you can draw, write or score while you cut because it has two clamps to hold both tools. This saves you money because you don't have to purchase a tool adapter.

Materials

Explore Air is quite liberating when it comes to materials. It features a dial that can allow you to choose the material that you're about to cut. That way, you don't have to guess the blade depth and mess up the material.

The machine will know how deep it will have to cut for felt and how gentle it has to be for paper or vinyl. This feature is especially great for beginners who are not well versed with the blade depths.

For experienced users, the Cricut Explore Air also features several custom settings that allow the user to customize the cutting of their design.

This model can cut more materials than the Explore One, including fabric, poster board, vellum, and about 70 more.

Cutting Force

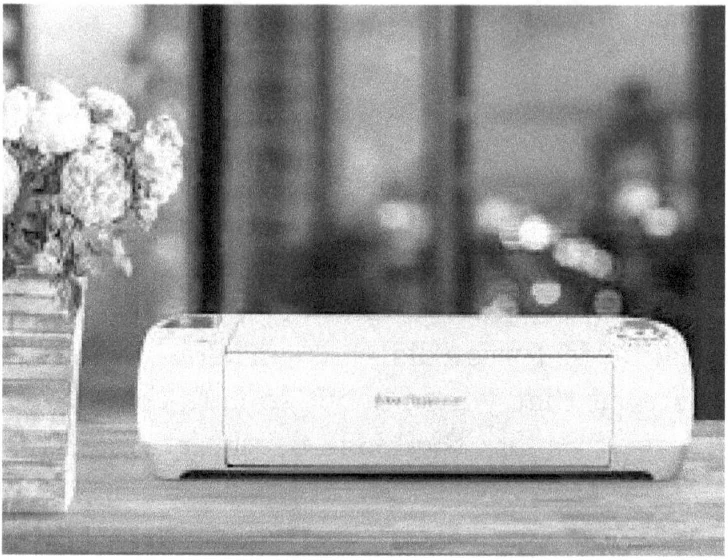

The system is more powerful than the older model when it comes to the cutting force. It features a Cut Smart technology made by Cricut, which enhances the blade control of the system and gives your creations a more professional look. It can cut anything that is as wide as 23.5 inches accurately and precisely.

It also has the Smart Set dial, which increases the control you have over the cutting of your project.

The features of the Cricut Design Space are very similar. But, when using Explore Air, you get more freedom, and you are allowed to use .svg, .gif, and .dxf files in addition to the standard files allowed with the Explore One.

Sadly, Explore Air does not have either a knife or a rotary blade. Because of these two types of blades, the Explore Air is recommended for more light crafts and scrapbooking. It does have an inbuilt blade, though.

A brand new Explore Airbox comes with these tools:

- A 25.4 x 10 x 9.2 inches Cricut Explore Sir machine with inbuilt Bluetooth technology.
- It has an inbuilt accessory adapter.
- Inbuilt blade.
- USB and power cord.
- Metallic silver marker.
- Iron-on sample.
- Cardstock sample.
- Over 100 images,
- Over 50 ready-to-cut projects.
- 12" x 12" Standard Grip cutting mat.
- Welcome guide.

Cricut Explore Air 2

This is the youngest sibling of the Cricut Explore line. It is the best of the machines in this line. Explore Air 2 is as efficient as the other ones, but it does its work even better. It even has a better design, and it comes in different colours than you can do.

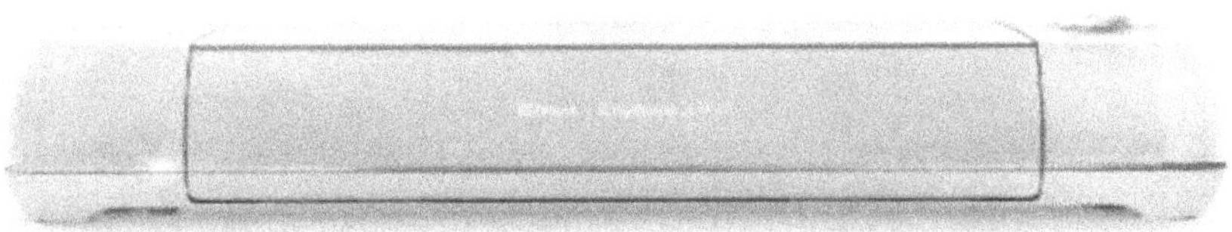

Capability

Capability

The model features a Fast mode that speeds up the cutting process, primarily if you work with deadlines.

It also has the features in the other systems like the German carbide premium blade, inbuilt Bluetooth adapter, dual carriage, and auto-settings.

The great thing about the Explore Air is that it is ideal for both beginners and advanced users.

Materials

This machine can cut through a hundred materials or even more. This includes and is not limited to cotton, silk, tissue paper, corkboard, foil, foam, aluminum, leather, clay, chipboard, burlap, and even birch wood.

It also has the Smart Dial, which helps you manage the cutting width depending on the materials.

Cutting Force

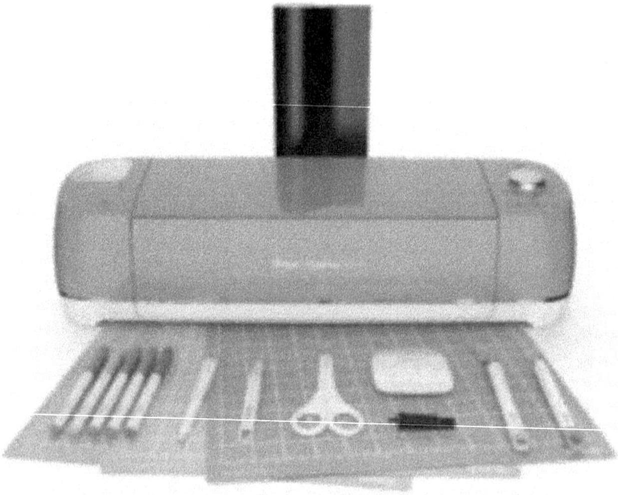

The model is highly potent, and it makes use of the German carbide premium fine point blade, which comes with precision and speed. It is also able to cut any material with a width of 11.5 x 23.5 inches.

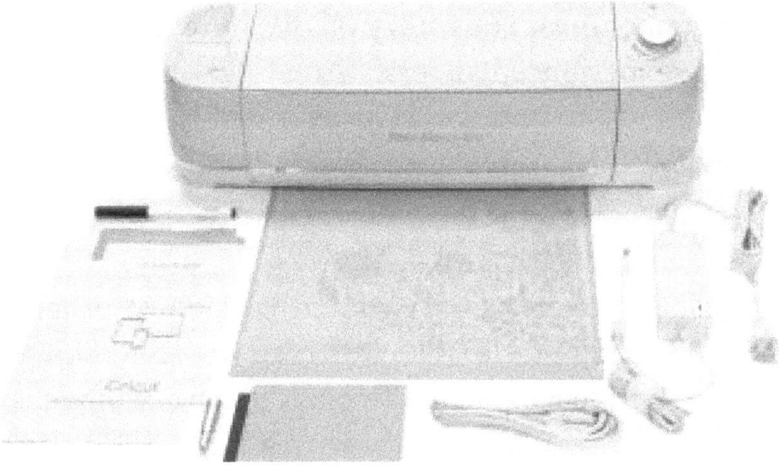

When you first purchase a Cricut Explore Air 2, you get a three months free subscription with access to premium features offered by Cricut!

The Cricut Design Space is also cloud-based for those using iOS devices. With this, you can work offline!

Cricut Maker

The newest Cricut die-cutting machine is the Cricut Maker. If you thought that the Explore Air 2 was a great model, then you should get ready to be blown away.

The Cricut Maker is a rare unit amongst other die-cutting machines. The rotary blade is already enough to attract experienced users. And, for beginners, it provides an avenue for improvement and unlimited creativity.

Capability

The Cricut Maker, as an updated version of others, is very powerful and flexible. It comes with a toolkit that includes a rotary blade, knife blade, deep cut blade, and fine point blade. It also comes with a single and a double scoring wheel, as well as a collection of pens. The pens include a fine point pen, a washable fabric pen, a calligraphy pen, and a scoring stylus.

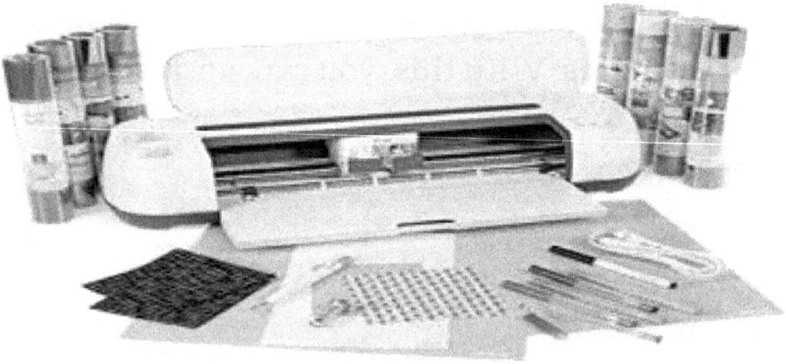

The machine also improves its efficiency by adding some unique features. We have the adaptive tool system, which means that the device can adjust the angle of the blade and the pressure of the blade automatically depending on the material. It doesn't need the Smart dial feature because the Cricut Maker determines your cutting force for you, and its decisions are usually accurate.

It has two clamps, one for the pen or scoring tool and the other for the cutting blade. This system is also unique because of its fast mode and precise mode. This works for any paper, cardstock, and vinyl.

Materials

As expected, the Cricut Maker will be able to handle more and thicker materials than the machines in the Cricut Explore series.

From light materials to basswood and leather, this machine will exceed your expectations.

Cricut Design Space also provides a lot of benefits for Cricut Maker users/. It allows .jpg, .gif, .png, .svg, .bmp and .dxf files.

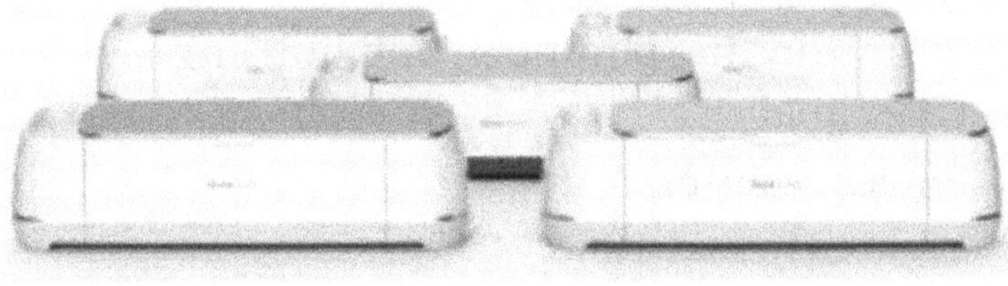

The system also supports wireless Bluetooth adapter. You can also enjoy the Sewing Pattern Library if you own a Cricut Maker. The library contains 50 ready-to-cut projects, and it is a result of a partnership between Cricut and Riley Blake Designs.

Another great benefit you get when using Cricut Maker with Design Space is that you get free membership of Cricut Access for a trial period.

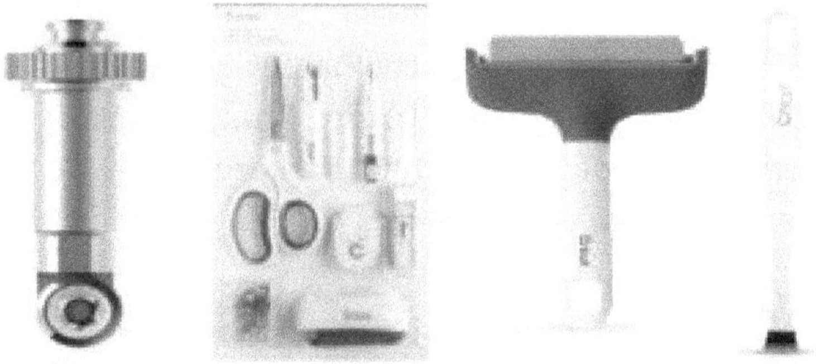

The only downsides to this model are that it is relatively slow when working with very thick materials, although that is expected. It also produces a lot of noise because of the fast mode.

This is what comes in the new Cricut Maker box.

- Cricut Maker machine.
- Rotary blade and drive housing
- Fine point pen.
- Premium fine point pen and housing
- USB cable.
- Power adapter.
- LightGrip Mat 12” x 12”.
- FabricGrip Mat 12” x 12”.
- Fifty ready-to-cut projects, which includes 25 sewing patterns
- Materials for the first project.
- Welcome guide.

WHICH CRICUT MODEL SHOULD YOU USE?

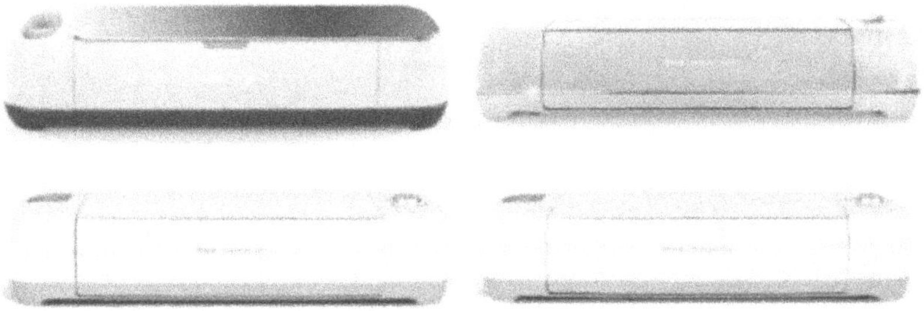

Although all Cricut models are great, the Cricut Maker or Explore Air models are highly recommended, whether you're a beginner or an advanced user. These two machines are usually ideal for most people, no matter the type of craft you use.

For the person who is looking to go into serious crafting, woodworking, sewing, and quilting, then the Cricut Maker is highly recommended. It is highly professional, and it can work for any craft that you're getting into. The system has a lot of benefits, especially on Design Space.

Suppose you're a beginner who is looking to go deep into crafting. In that case, you should also get the Cricut Maker because it will make no sense to purchase an old model, and then buy a new one when you have gained some experience.

You might be planning on using your Cricut machine for business purposes. This will mean that you will be repeating the same action occasionally. For this use, you can use the Cricut Explore Air 2 because it has a fast mode and many other advantages.

Beginners, leisurely crafters, and those who have a tight budget will work better with the Cricut Explore One and Explore Air.

Chapter 3:
Materials used in the Cricut and how they are used

WHAT MATERIALS CAN YOU USE WITH YOUR CRICUT?

As you have already read in this book, Cricut boasts being able to work with over 100 materials to bring your creations to life like never before. Due to the vast array of media that Cricut will carry to your crafting station, the sky is the limit for what you can do with your Cricut computer, irrespective of the model you want to purchase.

Here are 100 materials which your Cricut can use without any problems.

Fabric

- Polyester
- Linen
- Printable Fabric
- Silk
- Cotton Fabric
- Wool Felt
- Canvas
- Metallic Leather
- Oil Cloth
- Felt
- Faux Suede

- Flannel
- Denim
- Burlap
- Duck Cloth
- Leather
- Faux Leather

Foam

- Glitter Foam
- Craft Foam

Foil

- Aluminum Foil
- Embossable Foil
- Aluminum Sheets
- Foil Poster Board
- Foil Embossed Paper
- Adhesive Foil
- Foil Iron-On
- Foil Acetate

Paper

- Poster Board
- Contact Paper
- Metallic Paper
- Glitter Cardstock
- Solid Core Cardstock
- Flocked Cardstock
- Printable Sticker Paper
- Notebook Paper
- Parchment Paper

- Photo Framing Mat
- Metallic Vellum
- Vellum
- Freezer Paper
- Metallic Cardstock
- Flocked Paper
- Metallic Poster Board
- Corrugated Paper
- Peal Cardstock
- Glitter Paper
- Paper Board
- Tissue Paper
- Rice Paper
- Cardboard
- Shimmer Paper
- Pearl Paper
- Craft Paper
- Photographs
- Cardstock
- Temporary Tattoo Paper
- Copy Paper
- Washi Sheets
- Scrapbook Paper
- Post Its
- Construction Paper
- Washi Tape
- Paper Grocery Bags
- Adhesive Cardstock
- Wrapping Paper

Plastic

- Shrink Plastic
- Transparency Film
- Duct Tape
- Window Cling
- Magnet Sheets
- Plastic Packaging
- Stencil Material
- Printable Magnet Sheets

Vinyl

- Holographic Iron-On
- Removable Adhesive Vinyl
- Flocked Iron-On
- Neon Iron-On
- Matte Vinyl
- Metallic Vinyl
- Stencil Vinyl
- Outdoor Vinyl
- Adhesive Vinyl
- Printable Vinyl
- Printable Iron-On
- Glitter Vinyl
- Glossy Vinyl
- Glossy Iron-On
- Chalkboard Vinyl
- Matte Iron-On
- Glitter Iron-On
- Permanent Adhesive Vinyl
- Dry Erase Vinyl

- Holographic Vinyl
- Metallic Iron-On
- Paint Chips

Wood

- Chipboard
- Wood Veneer
- Adhesive Wood
- Corkboard
- Balsa Wood
- Birch Wood

Chapter 4:
How to Use Cricut Machine

SETTING UP STEP BY STEP

Opening the Box

When you purchase a bundle from Cricut, you will receive a few boxes, but the most significant box amongst them will hold the Cricut Maker. To recognize it, you'll see the picture of the Maker on the box.

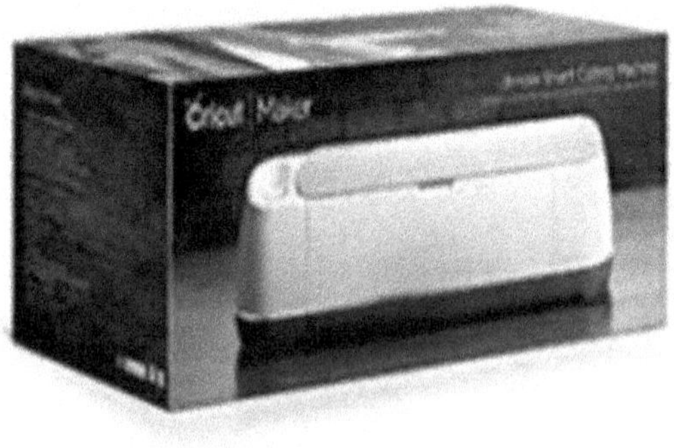

When opening the Cricut box, the first thing you see is the welcome packet placed on the machine. The welcome package contains a welcome manuscript, a rotary blade with cover, a fine point pen, a USB cable, and a packet with your first project.

When you take the Cricut machine out of the box, the power cord will be underneath along with the cutting mats. You will also see half of the settings on the dial between the fabrics. This is for when you need a little less or a little more force than is given by the programmed settings. If you cut a light cardstock, for example, but the knife doesn't completely cut the design, you can pick the half setting between Light and Cardstock. Or if you cut poster board and the blade exerts too much pressure by slicing your pad, simply select the arrangement between the cloth and the poster board. If you use another product and face it, you can use this tool well over a hundred different materials, so why wouldn't you? All that you need to do is just to change the dial to the setting' Custom.' You can then pick the exact product you are using from the massive dropdown list in Design Space. And again, the Cricut changes its blade settings automatically so that you don't have to.

Unwrapping

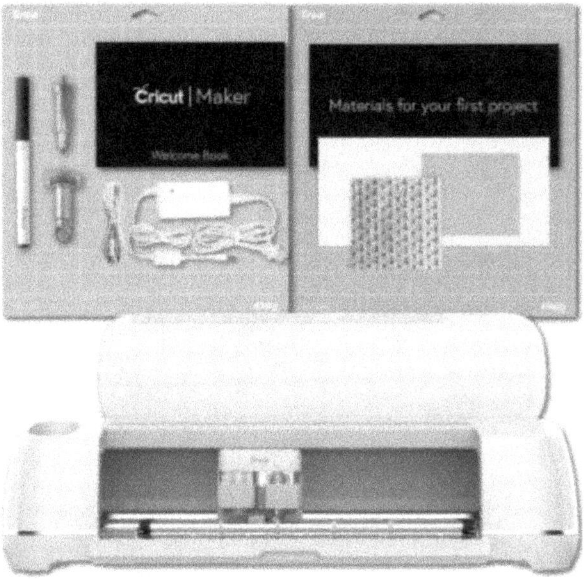

The Cricut machine is wrapped with a layer of cellophane and a protective wrapper. Before setting up the device, you have to remove the wrappings.

Some Styrofoam protects the in-housing of the machine, and that has to go too.

Your Cricut Maker will also come with some supplies, and you should unwrap them and check them out. Lucky for you, the fine point blade is already installed in the Cricut Maker, so you don't have to bother with that.

Visit cricut.com/setup

The following step in setting up your machine lies in the technical aspects. Cricut has a webpage dedicated to walking you through this process, which makes it super easy.

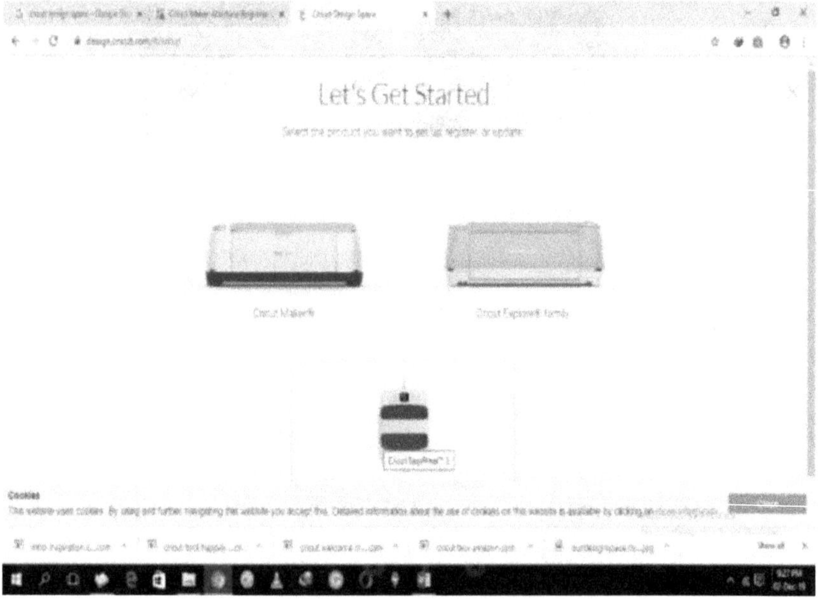

Open cricut.com/setup on your device. You can use any device that is compatible with Cricut like a smartphone, tablet or computer. When you do that, you will be asked to install Cricut Design Space and also sign up. Then, you'll be given your Cricut ID.

If you have been using a former Cricut machine before, then you can carry on with your former ID.

Plugging It In

Then, you need to take your USB cord and the power cord to power up your Cricut machine.

This will be shown on the setup wizard of the webpage.

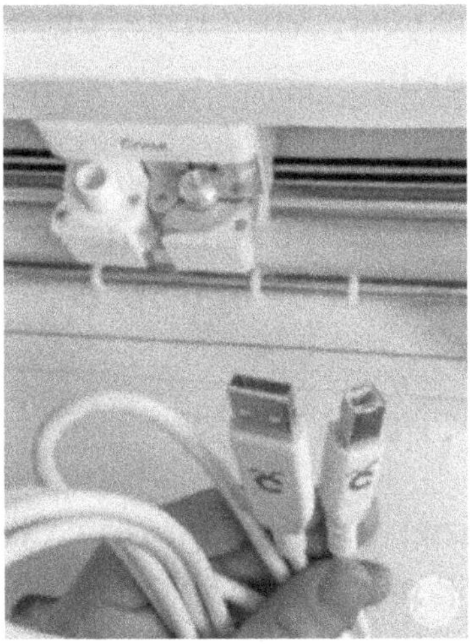

For the USB cord, you connect the square end to the Cricut Maker device and the other end to the computer. And, the power cord is easy to connect the Cricut Maker to the power outlet.

Claim Your Bonus

After plugging in your Cricut, you will be able to claim a free welcome bonus from Cricut, which is a free month of Cricut Access. This means that you get to enjoy access to projects, fonts, and Cricut Cut Files.

Begin Your Project

If you need a little something to practice with before starting on your intended project, Cricut Maker machines usually come with a little project in the welcome pack to help you get acquainted with the tools.

The Maker comes with all the tools that you need to complete the project, which is usually the task of making a little card.

After this, then you can begin using it. The thing is, when you want to use your Cricut Maker, you need to learn how to use Cricut Design Space.

Using Cricut Software

So, Cricut machines use a program called Cricut Design Spaces, and you'll need to make sure that you have this downloaded and installed when you're ready. Download the app if you plan to use a smartphone or tablet, or if you're on the computer, go to http://design.cricut.com/setup to get the software. If it's not hooked up already, make sure you've got Bluetooth compatibility enabled on the device, or the cord plugged in. To turn on your machine, hold the power button. You'll then go to settings, where you should see your Cricut model in Bluetooth settings. Choose that, and from there, your device will ask you to put a Bluetooth passcode in. Just make this something generic and easy to remember.

Once that's done, you can now use Design Space.

When you're in the online mode, you'll see a lot of projects that you can use. For this tutorial, I do suggest making sure that you choose an easy one, such as the "Enjoy Card" project you can get automatically.

So, you've got everything all linked up – let's move onto the first cut for this project.

Imputing Cartridges and Keypad

The first cut that you'll be doing does involve keypad input and cartridges, and these are usually done with the "Enjoy Card" project you get right away. So, once everything is set up, choose this project, and from there, you can use the tools and the accessories within the project.

You will need to set the smart dial before you get started making your projects. This is on the right side of the Explore Air 2, and it's the way you choose your materials. Turn the dial to whatever type of material you want, since this does help with ensuring you've got the right blade settings. There are even half settings for those in-between projects.

For example, let's say you have some light cardstock. You can choose that setting or the adjacent half setting. Once this is selected in Design Space, your machine will automatically adjust to the correct setting.

You can also choose the fast mode, which is in the "set, load, go" area on the screen, and you can then check the position of the box under the indicator for dial position. Then, press this and make your cut. However, the fast mode is incredibly loud, so be careful.

Now, we've mentioned cartridges. While these usually aren't used in the Explore Air 2 machines anymore, they are helpful with beginner projects. To do this, once you have the Design Space software, and everything is connected, go to the hamburger menu, and you'll see an option called "ink cartridges." Press that Cricut, and from there, choose the Cricut device. The machine will then tell you to put your cartridge in. Do that, and once it's detected, it will ask you to link the cartridge.

Do remember, though, that once you link this, you can't use it with other machines – the one limit to these cartridges.

Once it's confirmed, you can go to images, and click the cartridges option to find the ones that you want to make. You can filter the cartridges to figure out what you need, and you can check out your images tab for any other cartridges that are purchased or uploaded.

You can get digital cartridges, which means you buy them online and choose the images directly from your available options. They aren't physical, so there is no linking required.

Loading and Unloading Your Paper

To load paper into a Cricut machine, you'll want to make sure that the paper is at least three inches by three inches. Otherwise, it won't cut very well. You should use regular paper for this.

Now, to make this work, you need to put the paper onto the cutting mat. You should have one of those, so take it right now and remove the attached film. Put a corner of the paper to the area where you are directed to align the paper corners. From there, push the paper directly onto the cutting mat for proper adherence. Once you do that, you just load it into the machine, following the arrows. You'll want to keep the paper firmly on the mat. Press the "load paper" key that you see as you do this. If it doesn't take for some reason, press the unload paper key, and try this again until it shows up.

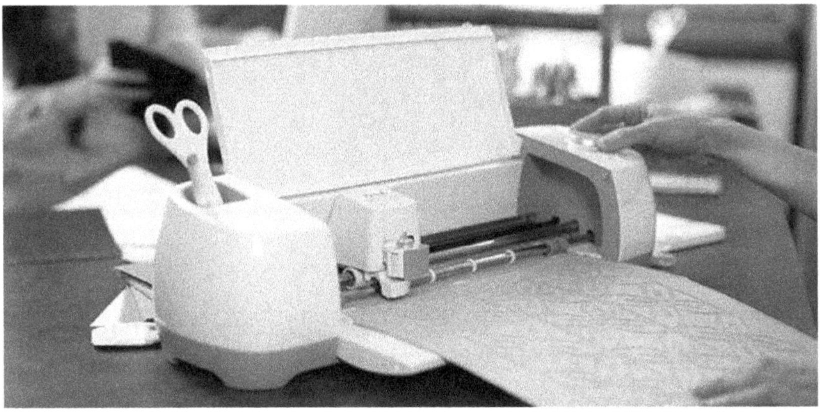

Now, before you do any cutting for your design, you should always have a test cut in place. Some people don't do this, but it's incredibly helpful when learning how to use a Cricut. Otherwise, you won't get the pressure correct in some cases, so get in the habit of doing it for your pieces.

SELECTING SHAPES, LETTERS, AND PHRASES

When you're creating your design in Design Space, you usually begin by using letters, shapes, numbers, or different fonts. These are the basics, and they're incredibly easy.

To make text, you just press the text tool on the left-hand side and type out your text. For example, write the word hello, or joy, or whatever you want to use.

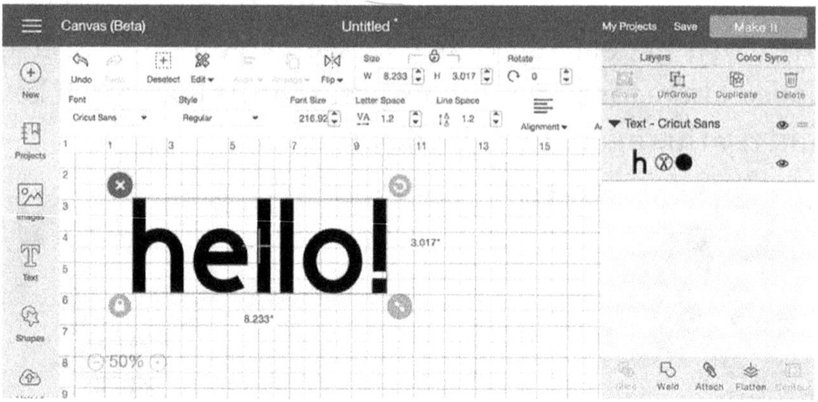

You can choose different Cricut or system fonts, too. Cricut ones will be in green, and if you have Cricut Access, this is a great way to begin using this. You can sort these, too, so you don't end up accidentally paying for a font.

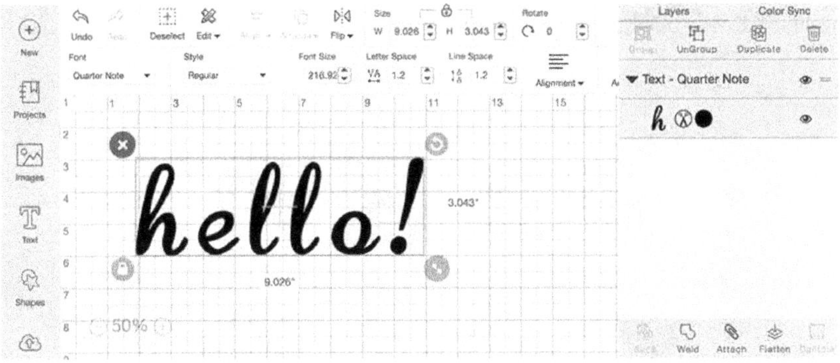

The Cricut ones are supposed to be made for Cricut, so you know they'll look good. Design Space also lets you put them closer together so they can be cut with a precise cut. You can change this by going to line spacing and adjusting as needed. To fix individual letters, you go to the advanced dropdown menu to ungroup the letters, so everything is separate as required.

Cricut also offers different writing styles, which is a great way to add text to projects. The way to do this is to choose a font that's made with a specific type and choose only the Cricut ones, and then go to writing. This will then narrow down the choice, so you're using the right font for writing.

Adding shapes is pretty easy, as well. In Design Space, choose the shapes option. Once you click it, the window will then pop out, and you'll have an incredible array of different shapes that you can use with just one click. Choose your shape, and from there, put it in the space. Drag the corners to make this bigger or smaller.

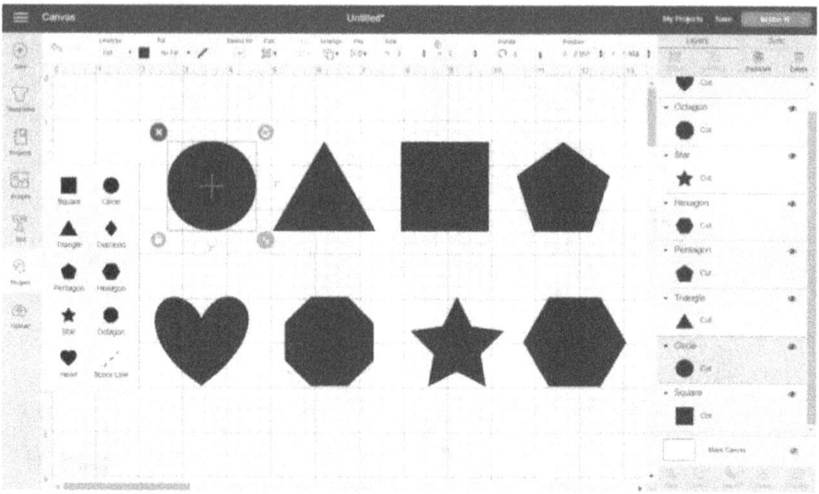

There is also the score line, which creates a folding line for you to use. Personally, if you're thinking of trying to make a card at first, I suggest using this.

You can also resize your options by dragging them towards the right-hand side, and you can change the orientation by choosing that option, and then flipping it around. You can select exact measurements as well, which is suitable for those design projects that need everything to be precise.

Once you've chosen the design, it's time for you to start cutting.

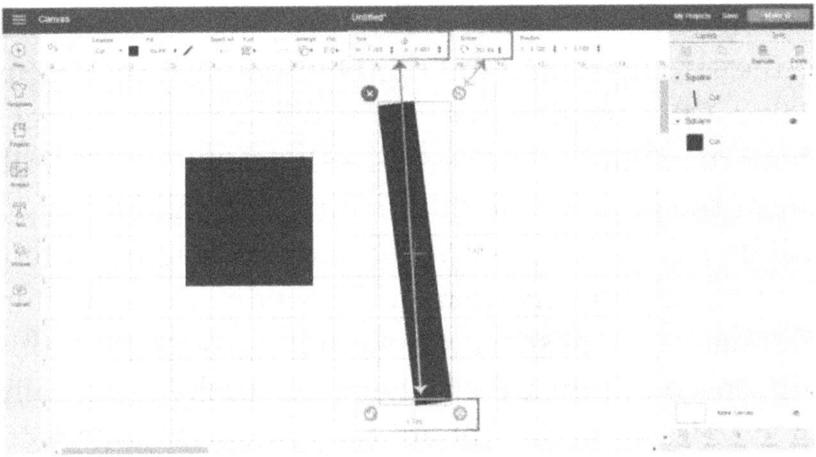

How to Remove Your Cut from The Cutting Mat?

Removing your cut from the mat is easy, but complicated. I ran into the issue of it being more complicated with vinyl projects since they love to just stick around there. But we'll explain how you can create precise cuts and remove them, as well.

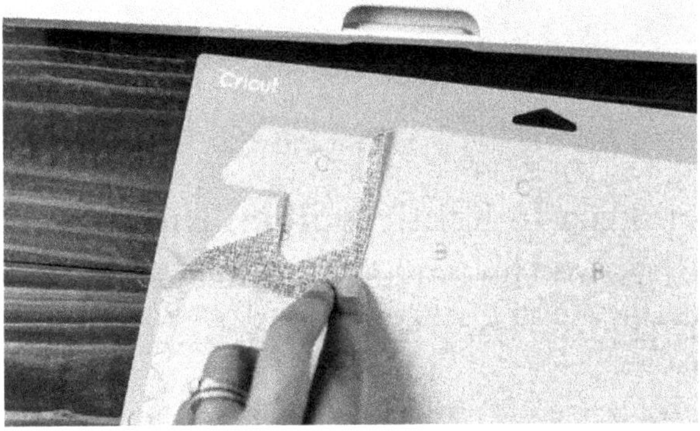

The first thing to remember is to make sure that you're using the right mat. The light grip ones are good for very lightweight material, with the pink one being one of the strongest, and only to be used with the Cricut Maker. Once the design is cut, you'll probably be eager about removing the project directly from the mat. Still, one of the problems with this is that often, the project will be ruined if you're not careful. Instead of pulling the project from the mat itself, bend the mat within your hand, and push it away from the project, since this will loosen it from the mat. Bend this both horizontally and vertically, so that the adhesive releases the project.

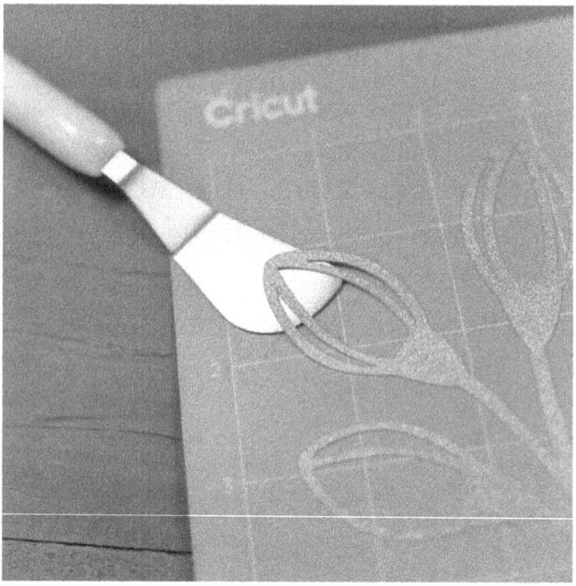

Use this spatula to lightly pull on the vinyl, until you can grab it from the corner and lift it. Otherwise, you risk curling it or tearing the mat, which is what we don't want.

Now, with the initial cuts, such as the paper ones, this will be incredibly easy. Trust me; I was surprised at how little effort it took. Still, one of the biggest things to remember is that with Cricut machines, you have to go slow when removing the material. Do this slowly, and don't get rushed near the end. Taking your time will save you a lot of problems, and it will even save you money and stress, too!

You will notice that Cricut mats are incredibly sticky. If you don't have a Cricut spatula on hand or don't want to spend the money, metal spatulas will work, too. You can put the paper on a flat surface and then lightly remove it. But always be careful when removing these items.

Cricut machines are pretty easy to use, and the beauty is that with the right understanding and ideas, you can make any items you want to.

Chapter 5: How to Use Cricut Machine: Advanced Step

How to Perform Linetype from Windows/Mac

Place your text or images onto the design screen.

From the Edit bar, select the Linetype dropdown. Note that the current Linetype is highlighted. Of course, you can change at once Linetype of multiple layers by selecting the layers to be changed and then choose the desired Linetype from the dropdown. The image of the canvas will change to reflect your selection once this is done.

You can use the Print Then Cut feature by selecting the Fill dropdown. From there, select Print. To add color, or pattern fill to the layer, select 'Color' or 'Pattern' from the Fill swatch dropdown.

It is important to note here that if the line type is set to write or score and there are multiple layers to your project, then there is the need for the image to be attached to another layer. This is done by selecting both layers in the Layers panel and clicking the Attach button.

How to Perform Linetype from Android/iOS

Place your text or images onto the design screen.

At the bottom of the screen, tap on the “Layers” to access the Layers panel.

Click on the arrow that is next to the layer to obtain the Layer Attributes Panel. The current Linetype will always be highlighted.

Tap on the desired Linetype, which will change to reflect your selection.

If you are done with your selection, tap on the ‘Layers’ to close it.

CUTTING INSTRUCTIONS FOR MATERIALS

Now that you have organized your Linetype, it is time to prepare the material for cutting using the Cricut Maker machine. The instructions for preparing the material are stated in a simplified and easy-to-understand way for the user.

The first thing is to place the craft foam on the mat with the smooth side down.

All the four edges of the material should be taped to the mat about 1” from each corner.

Move the White Star Wheels on the Cricut Maker machine to the right. This is to ensure that the Star Wheel will not leave any imprint on the material.

Ensure that you clean the front metal bar if you intend to cut thicker craft foam and also ensure that no part of the material goes under the rubber rollers because it can cause the machine to jam.

Test a cut to ensure that the edges come out fine else replace the blade before cutting the original material for the project.

After loading your mat for a Knife Blade project and selecting the cut setting of your choice, the Design Space of the machine will inform you of the expected cut time.

Note that thicker materials will take more time to cut than thinner materials for obvious reasons. First, thicker materials will require multiple cut-passes; secondly, the cut pressure will be increasing gradually.

How to Prepare Balsa Wood Material for Knife Blade?

Cut the size of the material that is needed for the project and protect your work surface.

Clean the surfaces of the wood by removing any stickers or package that can obstruct work. Then, wipe the surface with a cloth or spray with compressed air to remove dust and other particles on the surfaces.

Mirror the images in the Design space.

Create a firm bond between your material and the mat's adhesive surface with a brayer.

Use tape to hold all the edges of the wood.

Move the White Star Wheels on the Cricut Maker to the right.

Before you start cutting, ensure that: no part of the material goes under the rubber rollers. It can cause a jam.

You test a cut before cutting your main project.

All cuts are within ¼” from the edge of the wood.

How to Change True Control Knife blade

Twist the handle to unlock.

Push the button to remove the used blade. The used blade should be stored in the cartridge.

Align flats on the handle with the new blade.

Again, push the button to attach the handle to the blade without removing the blade from the cartridge.

Release the button and pull the blade out of the cartridge.

Twist to lock it.

Step by Step Instructions for Calibration of Knife Blade

Calibration is the first thing to do before you begin your first cut using Knife Blade. This will assist the Cricut Maker machine in recognizing what is called the Knife

Blade Drive Housing as well as deliver the best cut on your material. These instructions are as follows:

Select the account menu and after that select Calibration.

Choose Knife Blade.

Place a sheet of plain printing paper onto the machine, insert your Knife Blade and select Continue.

Carefully choose your machine from the drop-down menu and then load into the machine the mat along with the paper.

Press the Go button to start the Calibration. The machine will cut seven sets of lines that will overlap at the center.

Check on your mat to find the set of lines with the best overlap and then select them from the drop-down menu.

Select Continue to complete your Calibration.

You are done with the calibration. All you need do is navigate back to your canvas and show your creativity.

Keys and Buttons on Keypad

Do not hold the shift button; it is only necessary to select the button then select the key with the shape or letter on the upper right corner that you would like. That shape or letter should then appear on the LCD screen. When the shift key is activated, it will light up.

The Shift lock key does the same thing as the Shift key except the Shift lock key allows for the repeated selection of upper right corner shapes and letters without having to keep selecting the shift key. Space and backspace keys work the same as space and backspace keys on a keyboard on a computer or other digital device. The space key puts a blank space between the two letters, shapes, or words. The backspace key deletes the last letter, figure or word selected from the LCD screen. Most Cricut users do not use the space key as they cut one word at a time. It is recommended to use the space key when negative space in the cut is desired.

The Clear Display key, unlike the backspace key, will delete all selected shapes, letters, and phrases from the LCD Display screen. The Reset All key erases all settings on your Display screen, returning all the settings to the factory default.

When selecting letters, shapes, and phrases, you can choose the Repeat Last button to repeat the previously selected item on the LCD screen. This means that if you choose a triangle, then a circle and then the repeat last button, the Cricut Cutter will cut one triangle and two circles. Each time when the Cricut Cutter machine cuts, it will make a sound mimicking a cricket chirp. Select the Sound on/off button to eliminate this noise. Selecting this will become the setting for the machine, and when you turn the machine off and back on, the setting will still be turned off. To turn the noise back on, select the Sound on/off button.

Finding Awesome Fonts

The Cricut Design Space has plenty of fonts that you can use for your craftwork, and the great thing about this app is that it also uses the fonts that you upload to the app. Is there a specific font that you love to use, but you can't find it in the Design Space? Here are some places where you can find some awesome, cool, and best of all—FREE fonts!

- – dafont.com
- – 1001freefonts.com
- – fontsquirrel.com

Blade Navigation and Calibration

The blades that come with a Cricut machine are essential to understand, and you will need to calibrate your blades every single time you use your machine.

Each blade needs this because it will help you figure out which level of depth and pressure your cut needs to be. Typically, each blade needs to be calibrated only once, which is great, because then you don't have to spend time doing this each time. Once you've done it once, it will stay calibrated, but if you decide to change the housings of the blades or if you use them in another machine, you'll need to calibrate it again.

So, if you plan on using a knife blade and then a rotary cutter, you'll want to make sure that you do recalibrate – and make sure you do this before you start with your project. It is incredibly easy to do this, though, which is why it's encouraged.

To calibrate a blade, you just launch the Design Space, and from there, you open the menu and choose calibration. Then, select the blade that you're going to put in. For this explanation, let's say you're using a knife blade.

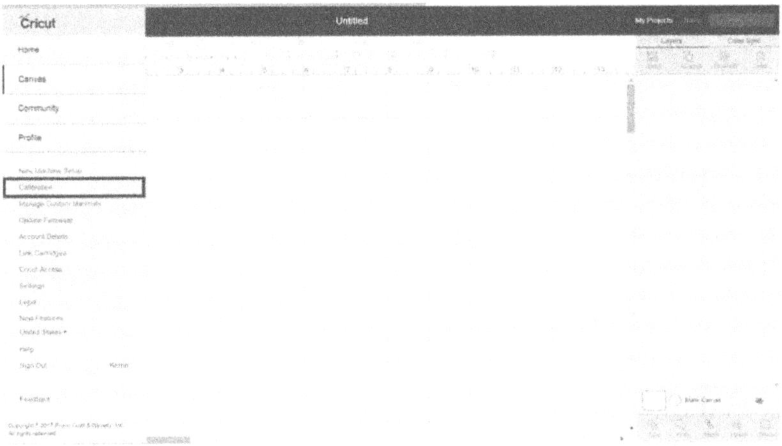

Put that blade in the clamp B area and do a test cut, such as with copy paper into the mat, and then load that into the machine.

Press continue, then press the go button on the machine. It will then do everything that you need for the item itself, and it will start to cut.

You can then choose which calibration is best for your blade, but usually, the first one is good enough.

You can do this with every blade you use, and every time you use a new blade on your machine, I highly recommend you do this – for best results, of course.

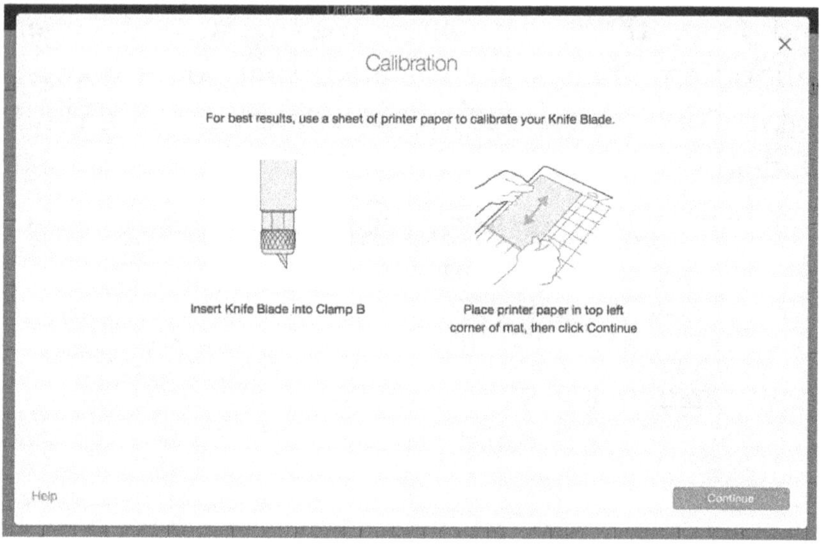

Set Paper Size

Setting paper size in a Cricut machine is pretty simple. You will want to use this with either cartridge or with Design Space for what you'd like to make. This also comes with a cutting mat, and you'll want to load this up with paper so that you can use it.

To do this, you'll want to make sure that you have it plugged in, then go to the project preview screen. Suppose you choose a material that's bigger than the mat size. In that case, it will automatically be changed, and it'll be adjusted as necessary based on the size of the material that you select.

You can choose the color, the size of the material, whether or not it'll mirror – and you can also choose to entirely skip the mat, too, if you don't want that image printed just yet.

Note that the material size menu does offer sizes that are bigger than the largest mat available.

If you're planning on using the print then cut mode, do understand that it's limited to a print area of 8.5x11 inches, but again, you can choose these settings for yourself.

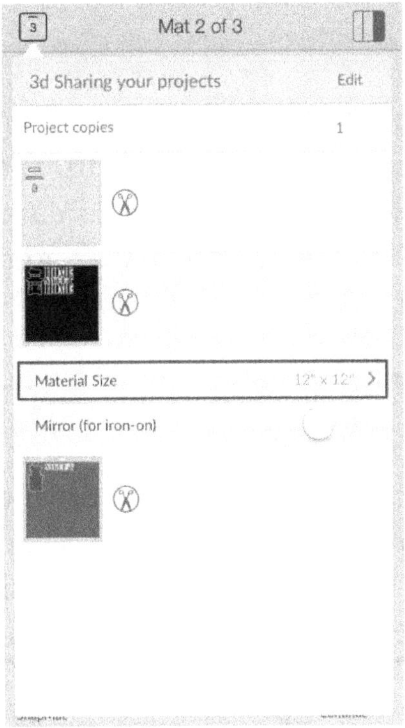

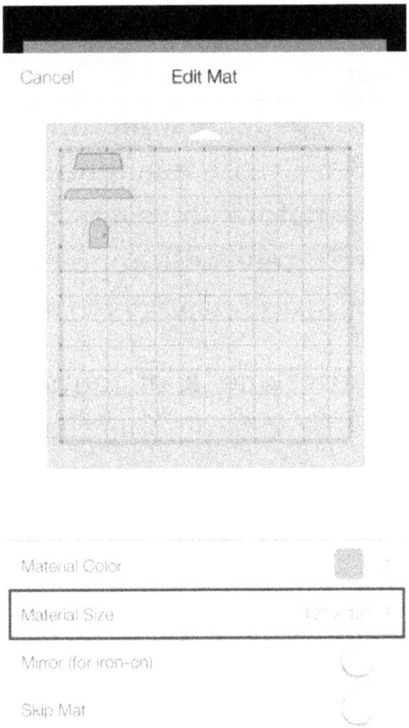

Load Last

To load that paper and image last is pretty simple. Remember the preview we discussed in the previous section? Remember that "skip this mat" step? Press that, and then go. You'll be able to skip this quite easily. It's one of those operations that's a little different from what you may be used to, but if you want to skip design and don't want to work with it just yet, this is probably the best option for you to use. If you're worried about forgetting it, don't worry – Cricut will remind you.

Paper Saver

Saving paper is something you'll want to consider doing with a Cricut machine because it loves to eat up the paper before you even start decorating. The Explore Air 2 definitely will appreciate it if you save paper, and there are a few ways to do so.

The first one is, of course, to halve your mats. But you don't need to do only that.

You can also go to the material saver option on the machine, which will automatically adjust and align your paper as best it can. Unfortunately, on newer machines, it's not directly stated, but there is a way to save paper on these.

You'll want to create tabbed dividers to organize your projects and save them directly there.

The first step is to create a background shape. Make sure that the paper looks like a background. Go to shapes, and then select the square to make the square shape.

Next, once you've created squares to represent the paper, arrange this to move to the back so that the shapes are organized to save the most space on each mat. Then organize the items that are on top of where the background is and arrange them, so they all fit on a singular mat.

Rotating is your best friend – you can use this feature whenever you choose objects, so I do suggest getting familiarized with it.

Next, you hide the background at this point, and you do this by choosing the square, and in Design Space, literally hiding this on the right side. Look at the eyeball on the screen, and you'll see a line through the eyeball. That means it's hidden.

Check over everything and fine-tune it at this point. Make sure they are grouped around one object and make sure everything has measurements. Move these around if they're outside of the measurements required.

Once they're confirmed, you then attach these on the right-hand side of Design Space, which keeps everything neatly together – they're all cut from the same sheet.

From here, repeat this until everything is neatly attached. It will save your paper, but will it save you time? That's debatable, of course.

Speed Dial

So, the speed dial typically comes into play when you're setting the pressure and speed. Fast mode is one of the options available on the Explore Air 2 and the Maker machines, which make the machine run considerably quicker than other models. You can use this with vinyl, cardstock, and iron-on materials. To set this, go to the cut screen. You'll have a lot of speed dials here, and various settings. If you have the right material in place when choosing it, you'll be given the option to do it quickly with fast mode. From there, you simply tap or click on that switch to toggle this to the position for on. That will activate fast mode for that item.

It will make everything about two times faster, which means that if you're creating intricate swirl designs, it will take 30 seconds instead of the 73-second average it usually takes.

However, one downside to this is that because it's so fast, it will sometimes make the cuts less precise – you'll want to move back to the regular mode for more refined work.

This is all usually set with the smart-set dial, which will offer the right settings for you to get the best cuts that you can on any material you're using. Virtually, this dial eliminates you having to check the pressure on this manually.

To change the speed and pressure for a particular material that isn't already determined with the preset settings, you will need to select custom mode and choose what you want to create. Of course, the smart-set dial is better for the Cricut products and mats. If you notice that the blade is cutting too deep or not profound enough, there is a half-settings option on each material that you can adjust to achieve the ideal cut.

Usually, the way you do this with the pre-set settings is to upload and create a project, press go, and load the mat, then move the smart-set dial on the machine itself to any setting. Let's select custom and choose the speed for this one.

In Design Space, you then choose the material, add the custom speed, and you can adjust these settings. You can even adjust the number of times you want the cut to be changed with the smart-set dial, too. Speed is something you can adapt to suit the material, which can be helpful if you're struggling with putting together some right settings for your items.

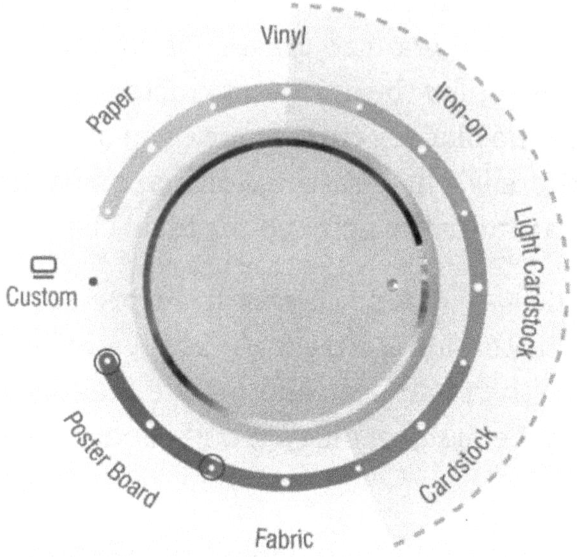

Pressure Dial

Now, let's talk about pressure. Each piece of material will require different pressure settings. If you're not using enough pressure, the blade won't cut into the material, and if you use too much pressure, you'll end up cutting the mat, which isn't what you want to do.

The smart-set dial kind of takes the guesswork out of it. You simply choose the setting that best fits your material, and from there, you let it cut. If you notice you're not getting a deep enough cut, then you'll want to adjust it about half a setting to get a better result. From there, adjust as needed.

But did you know that you can change the pressure on the smart-set dial for custom materials? Let's say you're cutting something very different, such as foil, and you want to set the pressure to be incredibly light so that the foil doesn't get shredded. What you do is you load the material in, and you choose the custom setting. You can then select the material you plan to cut, such as foil – and if it's not on the list, you can add it.

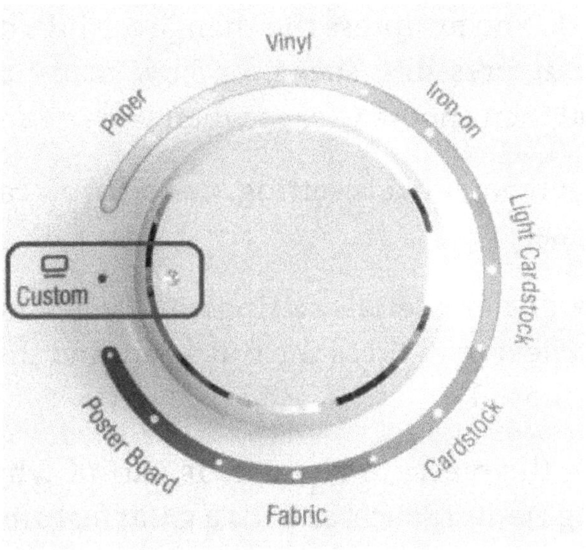

From here, you're given pressure options. Often, people will go too heavy with their custom settings, so I do suggest that you go lighter for the first time and change it as needed. Several draggers go from low to high. If you need lots of pressure, obviously let it go higher. If you don't need much pressure, make sure it's left lower. You will also want to adjust the number of times the cut is done on a multi-cut feature item.

This is a way for you to achieve multiple cuts for the item, which can be incredibly helpful for those who are trying to get the right cut, or if the material is incredibly hard to cut. I don't suggest using this for very flimsy and thin material, because it'll just waste your blade and the mat itself.

That's all there is to it! This is a great way to improve on your Cricut designs. I love to work with custom cuts, and you can always delete these if you feel like they don't work. You just press the change settings button to adjust your pressure, speed, or how many cuts you want, and then choose to save when you're done.

What if you don't like a setting, period? You can delete it, of course!

To delete, go to materials settings, and you'll see a little trash can next to it. Press the trash can, and the setting will be removed.

Adjusting the pressure and cuts is part of why people love using Design Space, and it's a great feature to try.

Cricut Design Space

Design Space lets you do many things with your Cricut machine. Here are a few things you can do with this convenient app:

- Aligning various items right next to one another.
- Attaching items to hold images in place, and lets you use score lines.
- Arranging these to make them sit on the canvas in different layers.

- Canvas, a tool that lets you arrange prints and vectors so you can use the various instruments with them.
- Contouring, which is a tool that lets you hide image layers quickly, so they're not cut out.
- Color sync, which lets you use multiple colors in one project to reduce the material differences.
- Cut buttons, which will start cuts.
- Make it button: this is the screen that lets you see the designs being cut.
- Draw lines: lets you draw with the pen to write images and such.
- Fill: lets you fill in a pattern or color on an item.
- Flipping items flip it horizontally or vertically by 180 degrees.
- Group: puts different text and images on a singular layer, and everything is moved at once so that it doesn't affect the layout.
- Linetype: an option that you can do with your piece, whether you want to cut a line, draw a line, or score a line.
- Mirrored image: reverses it, which is very important with transfer vinyl, so everything reads correctly.
- Print then Cut: it's an option that lets you print the design, and from there, the machine cuts it.
- Redo: does an action again and reverses it.
- Reverse Weeding: removes the vinyl that's left behind, and it's used mostly for stencil vinyl
- Score lines: helps you make creases in the papers so you can fold it.

- SVG: this is a scalable vector graphic that allows you to cut a file that's scaled to be larger or smaller so that the resolution is kept, and made up of lines that consist of infinite white dots.
- Texts and fonts: let you use put specialized fonts and words within Design Space.
- Weeding: lets you remove the excess vinyl from designs. Press this when you're cutting vinyl.
- Welding: a tool you use when you want to combine two line shapes into one shape, and it's used to make seamless cursive words.

These are most of the functions you can do in Design Space. To use these, simply choose an image or font that you want to use and put it in Design Space. From there, you can do whatever you need to do with it – within reason, of course – and then place the image onto the material that you're using. For learning, I suggest not getting in too deep with vinyl just yet, and get used to using these tools. You also have pens, which can be implemented to help you write images with a tool that looks sharp and crisp. We'll go over the purpose of pens and what you can do with them in the next section.

Cricut Pens

Pens for your Cricut machine are essentially another way to get creative with your projects. I love to use them for cards, handmade tags for gifts, or even fancy invites and labels.

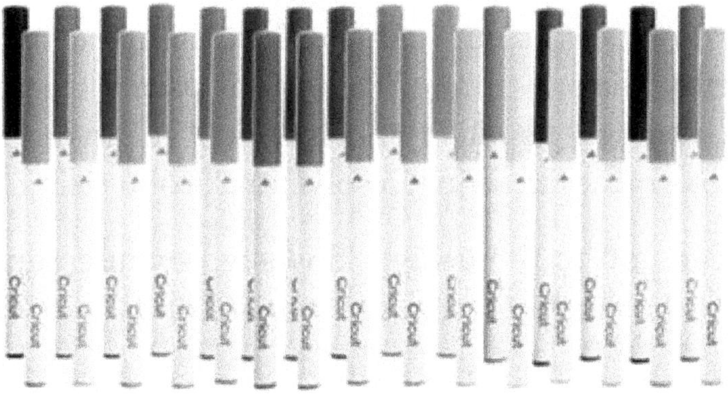

Now, each pen offers a little different finish and point size. They aren't toxic, and they are permanent once they're dried. You've got the extra-fine points for small lettering, up to a medium tip for making thicker lines. There are also glitter and metallic pens, so you have a lot of options to choose from!

But do you have to use them? Well, the answer is no. You can use different pens, but test them on paper first and get adapters to use with them. Cricut pens are your best option.

To use these, choose the wording or design, or whatever you want to do. You want to go to the layers panel that's on the right-hand side, and select the scissors icon – change that to the write icon. From there, you'll want to choose the pen color that you would like to use.

You can then have the design printed out on the material you're using.

Some people like to use different fonts, whether it be system fonts or Cricut fonts, or the Cricut Access fonts. However, the one thing with Design Space is that it will write what will usually be cut, so you'll get an outline of that font rather than just a solid stroke of writing.

This can add to the design; however – you essentially change the machine from cut to write, and there you go.

You can also use the Cricut writing fonts, which you can choose by going to a blank canvas, and then selecting the text tool on the left-hand side, along with the wording you'd like for this to have.

Once you're in the font edit toolbar, you are given a font selection. You choose the writing font filter, so you have fonts that you can write with. From there, choose the font, and then switch from the scissors to the pen icon, and then select the pen color. That's all there is to it!

You can also use this with Cricut Access – if you're planning on using this a lot, it might be worth it.

To insert the pens into the Cricut machine, you want to choose to make it, and from there, you'll then go to the prepare mat screen. It will say draw instead of writing in the thumbnail this time around, so you press continue in the bottom right-hand corner, then put the pen into clamp A – you just unlock it and then put it in. Wait until it clicks, and that's it!

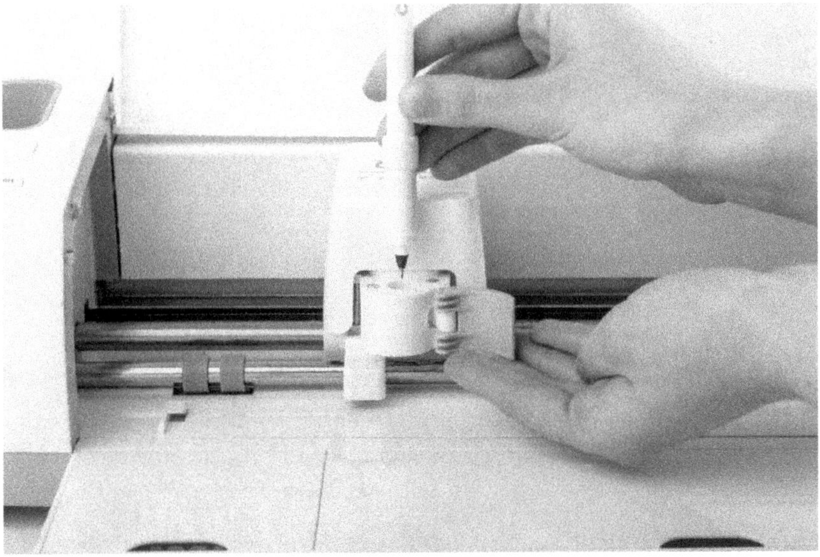

Cricut pens are super easy, and it's a great idea to consider trying these out.

As you can see, there are many different Cricut features and a lot of functions that may seem complicated but are not that hard. There are tons of options for your Cricut projects, and a lot that you can get out of this machine.

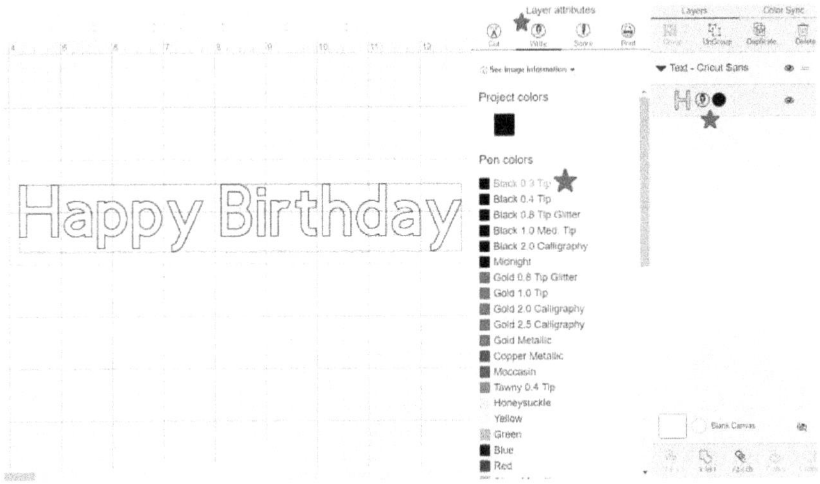

Chapter 6:
Maintenance of the Cricut Machine

Maintaining the Cricut Machine

When using your Cricut machine, over time, it will inevitably collect paper particles, dust, and debris. Also, grease in the device will begin to stick to the carriage track.

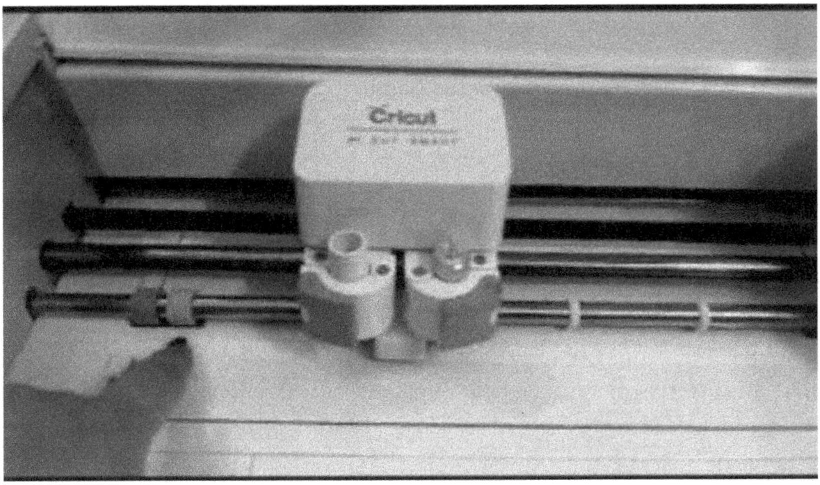

If you want your machine to last long, then you should clean it regularly, or else it can get damaged prematurely. Here are some cleaning tips to help you out when cleaning the machine.

Before cleaning your machine, disconnect it from the power outlet. This will prevent electrocution or any other accident that can damage the device or injure you.

When cleaning your machine, don't use any form of acetone. Acetone, like nail polish remover, will damage the plastic parts of the device permanently.

You can clean the machine using a glass cleaner instead. Spray it on a clean, soft cloth and wipe the device gently.

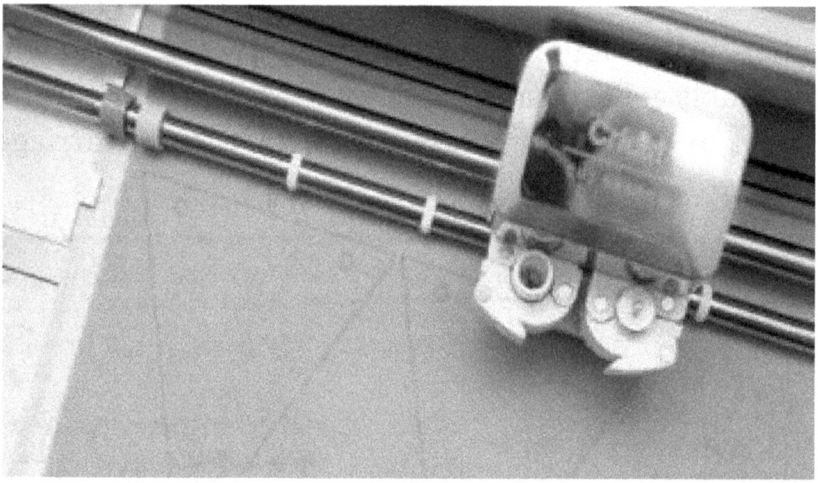

In the case of grease buildup on the carriage tracks, then you should use a tissue, cotton swab, or a soft, clean cloth to wipe it off gently.

There is also the case of a buildup of static electricity on your machine. This can cause dust, debris, and particles to form on the device. This can also be easily cleaned with a soft, clean cloth.

Application of Grease for the Cricut Explore Models

Disconnect the Cricut machine from the power outlet.

Push the Cut Smart carriage gently to the left.

Wipe the entire Cut Smart carriage bar with a tissue. The bar is the surface in front of the belt where the carriage slides on.

Push the Cut Smart carriage gently to the right.

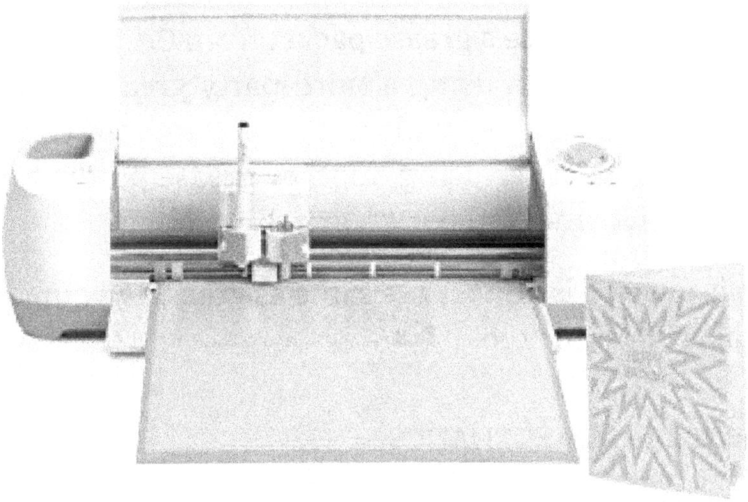

Repeat the cleaning process for the other side by cleaning the bar with a clean tissue.

Then, push the Cut Smart carriage to the center of the bar.

Take a lubrication packet, open it, and squeeze out a little grease. Put the amount of grease on a clean cotton swab.

Apply a small coating of the grease on the two sides of the Cut Smart carriage around the bar so that it will form a quarter inches ring on both sides.

To make the grease become even in the carriage, push the Cut Smart carriage to both sides slowly and repeatedly.

Clean off any grease that stained the bar while you were greasing the machine.

You can purchase a grease packet from Cricut. This will work better than using a third-party grease packet so that the machine will not get damaged. This is especially if, after using another grease product, your Cricut machine is making a grinding sound.

This process is almost the same as greasing your Cricut Maker machine too.

General Maintenance

When your mat isn't in use, cover it with a clear film cover so that dust and hairs won't accumulate on the surface of the mat.

Handle your mats with care. If you want to ensure that the adhesive does not get damaged, avoid touching the sticky surface with your hands.

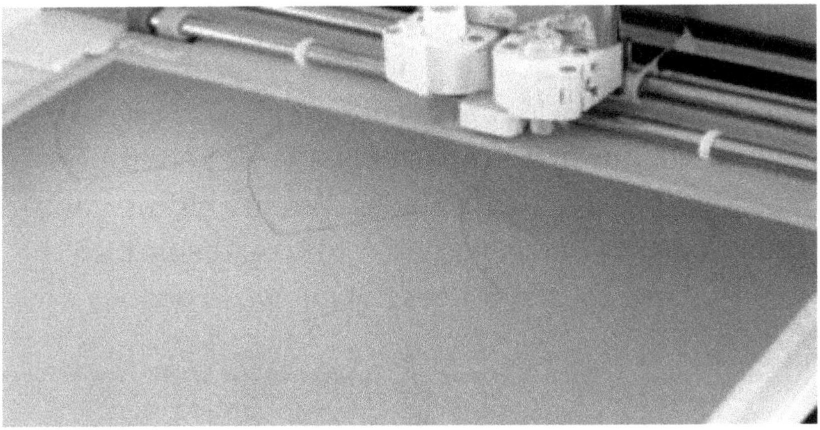

Photo credit: inspiration.cricut.com

Always ensure that your mat dries entirely before using it or covering it up. Don't use heat when drying your mat, but you can place it in front of a fan. Also, ensure that it is drying hanging up so that both sides will dry.

Replacing the Cutting Mat

Nothing lasts forever, and the Cricut Cutting Mat doesn't make any exception from this rule. It takes between 25 and 40 full cuts for a Cutting Mat to get damaged and at that point, it should be replaced. The life expectancy of this spare part depends a lot on the materials you cut and the settings you use. When the paper is no longer sticking to the mat, it needs replacement. It's always better to replace the mat with genuine Cricut Mats, and it's perfect if you can purchase the Cricut Self-Healing Mat. Always remember to rotate the mats to prolong the estimated span of each mat.

Maintaining the Cricut Cutting Blade

You can use your Cricut fine point blade for over a year if you maintain it properly! The same goes for the other types of cutting blades. When holding your Cricut cutting blade, you have to keep it sharp all the time so that it does not get worn out.

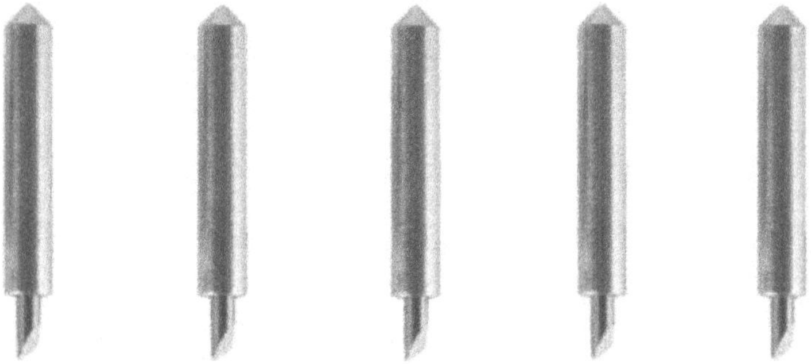

Keeping your blade sharp is essential because if it isn't, it can damage your materials, and cause wastage. Also, if you don't maintain your blades, you will have to replace them often.

Keeping Your Cutting Blade Sharp

Spread a portion of an aluminum foil on a cutting mat. Without removing the blade from the housing, cut out a simple design in the foil. This will sharpen the blade and remove any paper particles, or vinyl stuck on the blade. This can be used for any type of cutting blade.

In the case of heavy-duty cleaning, you should squeeze a sheet of aluminum foil into a ball. You need to remove the blade from the housing of the machine to use this method. Then, depress the plunger, take the blade and stick it into the ball of aluminum foil repeatedly. You can do this 50 times. This will make it sharper and also remove vinyl or paper particles on the blade.

How to Store Your Cutting Blade

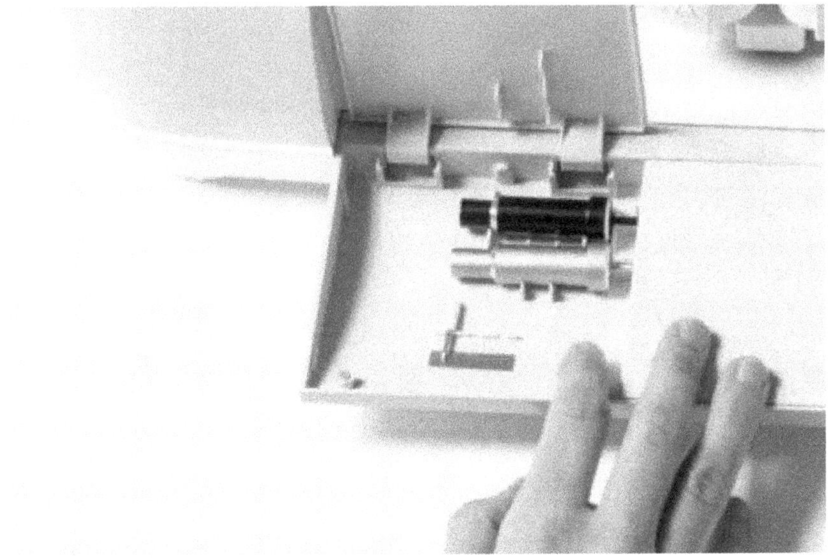

Photo credit: pinterest.com

The best way to store your cutting blade is to leave it in the Cricut compartment. You can place it in the dropdown door that is in front of the machine. That compartment is meant for storing the blade.

As for the blade housing, you can place it on the raised plastic points at the back of the machine. There are magnets in the front of the machine where you can stick loose blades.

When you put your blades in the Cricut machine, you never lose your blades.

Chapter 7: How to Quickly Pay Back Your Initial Investment

Sell and Make Profit -Platforms on Which to Sell Your Crafts

The creativity of your designs and the skill you will develop can allow you to create and start your own business if you wish. For enthusiastic novices, many questions would be faced, such as:

Where do I start?

Like any startup business, initial questions need to be addressed to overcome possible difficulties. For example, addressing issues like defining clientele, the products that might be of interest, where to find them and how to make a profit margin of my sales are essential to tackle from the start. In other words, you will need a useful and well-defined business strategy to start with.

Choosing my clientele

You can target two avenues to sell your products: either by looking at how you can approach the market locally or online. It is advisable to concentrate efforts on one approach to start with as your target is to generate profits as soon as possible. Never forget that your goal is to grow profit and reinvest it so that your business expands. The quicker you increase your sales, the more likely you will reinvest in new tools or new products, making, in turn, more substantial financial turnover. Understanding your marketing strategy is key to your success.

Approaching local markets

You can explore the option of selling your products from 'business to business'. In this configuration, the volume of sales is as important as the size of the production. This is the most challenging balance to reach for a new Cricut based business. The advantage of obtaining contractual work means you can negotiate to buy a large quantity from vendors. However, such 'golden' opportunities are hard to find since such contracts are open to competition. Yet, as a new startup business, you can present your products specifically tailored for business customers. A custom work approach offers positive aspects as businesses always look for originality and useful products. By creating such a relationship, your business is likely to become a point of reference for future contacts, hence launching many opportunities for upselling. However, it is vital to bear in mind that finding such a niche is, hard as competition is very stiff!

Another approach to consider for selling your products is from 'business to customer'. In this model, though the volume of sales remains important, your objective is to present your products to retail customers willing to buy them. Creativity, imagination will be keys to your success, as well as what type of media and medium you want to work in (e.g. T-shirts, mugs). Equally important is a retail space you will need to choose to offer your items. Experiencing different locations and products is all part of the efforts of a new startup business. Also, a custom work approach for local customers will present advantages since the startup cost are the lowest of all the different strategies described so far. However, as a new business in the field, starting can be difficult. Word of mouth can be your first step as well as producing the right products at an affordable price.

Selling Online

Suppose you are an adept of higher technical knowledge. In that case, you can generate significant benefits by providing either quality custom work, bulk offering or informative network. It is advisable to concentrate your efforts on one approach to start with. Suppose you choose, for example, a custom work approach. In that case, you increase the chances to find potential customers looking for your products as they turn to a search engine like Google to see what they are looking for. Websites like Amazon Handmade or Etsy provide an excellent platform to allow to sell custom design services. Equally efficient is the launch of your site. This strategy is worth looking at. Selling online presents advantages such as low startup costs and access to the global market with access to millions of potential customers.

Furthermore, online custom prices tend to be lower than those on the local market. However, access to the global market means that competition is stiff, pushing products to be competitively priced. Selling online requires specific knowledge in logistics as far as shipping and packing your products are concerned, a cost factor that needs to be taken into consideration in your pricing.

Starting a new business requires foremost a business strategy, the foundation for your future success. Asking yourself who your potential customers would be, what kind of products you can sell them and how are the first steps of a future startup business.

Chapter 8:
Cricut Project Ideas to Start Training

BEGINNERS

<u>Fancy Leather Bookmark</u>

Personalized leather bookmarks make nice gifts. They are also straightforward to make with the Cricut.

Material needed:

- Cricut metallic leather
- Cricut holographic iron-on — red for a gold effect
- Purple StrongGrip mat
- Cricut Fine-Point Blade
- Weeding tool
- Pair of scissors for cutting the material to size

- Brayer or scraping tool
- Cricut Knife Blade
- Thin gold string or ribbon

Instructions

1. Cut the leather to the size you want it to be.
2. Each leather holder is approximately 2" wide by 6" high.
3. Cut the holographic paper to the size you want it to be; this will depend on the size of the font and wording you choose for the bookmark.
4. Create a new project in Design Space.
5. Select 'Shapes' from the left-hand menu.
6. Choose the square, unlock it, and set the width to 2" with a height of 6".
7. Choose a triangle from the 'Shapes' menu, and set the width to 1.982" and the height to 1.931".
8. Position the triangle in the rectangle at the bottom. Make sure it is positioned evenly as this is going to create a swallowtail for the bookmark.
9. Select the circle from the shapes menu, and unlock the shape. Set the width and height to 0.181".
10. Duplicate the circle shape.
11. Move the one circle to the top right-hand corner of the bookmark and the other to the left. These will be the holes to put a piece of ribbon or fancy string through.

12. Align the holes and distribute them evenly by using the 'Align' function from the top menu with both circles selected.
13. Select the top left hole with the top of the rectangle and click 'Slice' in the bottom right menu.
14. Select the circle and remove it, then delete it.
15. Select the top right circle with the top of the rectangle and click 'Slice' from the bottom right menu.
16. Select the circle and remove it.
17. Select the bookmark and move it over until you see the other two circles.
18. Select the two circles and delete them.
19. Select the triangle and the bottom of the rectangle, then click 'Slice' from the bottom right-hand menu.
20. Select the first triangle, remove it, and delete it.
21. Select the second triangle, remove it, and delete it.
22. Save your project.
23. You will now have the first part of your leather bookmark ready to print.
24. Place the leather on the cutting mat, and use the brayer tool or scraper tool to flatten it and stick it properly to the cutting mat.
25. Position the little rollers on the feeding bar to the left and right, so they do not run over the leather.
26. Set the dial on the Cricut to custom.

27. Load the knife blade into the second Cricut chamber.
28. In Design Space, click on "Make it."
29. Set the material to Cricut metallic leather.
30. Load the cutting board and leather into the Cricut and hit 'Go' when the Cricut is ready to cut.
31. Unload the cutting board when the Cricut is finished printing and use the spatula to cut the leather bookmark form out.
32. Use the weeding tool to remove any shapes that should not be on the bookmark.
33. Place the holographic paper on the cutting mat, and put the wheels on the loading bar back into their position.
34. Create a new project in Design Space and choose a nice fancy font. Do not make it any bigger than 1.5" wide and 3" high.
35. Save the project.
36. Click on 'Make it,' and choose the correct material.
37. Mirror the image.
38. Switch the blade in the second chamber back to the fine-point blade.
39. Load the cutting board and click 'Go' when the Cricut is ready to cut.
40. Gently peel the back off the design, heat the leather, and place the name on the bookmark where you want it positioned.
41. Use the same iron-on method as the method in the "Queen B" T-shirt project above.

42. Your bookmark is now ready to use or give as a personalized gift.

Personalized Envelopes

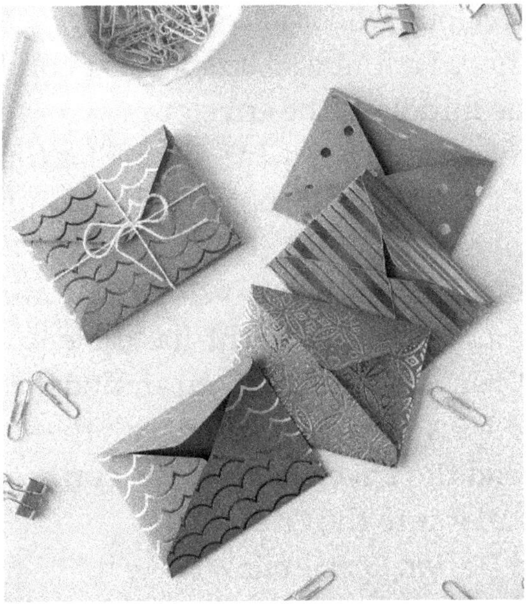

Making personalized envelopes for those personalized greeting cards adds that extra touch.

Material needed:

- Envelope 5.5" by 4.25"
- Cricut pens in the color of your choice
- Green StandardGrip mat
- Spatula

Instructions

1. Create a new project in Design Space.
2. Choose the square from the 'Shapes' menu.

3. Unlock the square, set the width to 5.5" and the height to 4.25".
4. Choose 'Text' from the right-hand menu.
5. This will be the name and address the envelope will be addressed to.
6. Choose a font and size it to fit comfortably in the middle of the envelope.
7. You can choose a different color for the font.
8. Move the text box to the center of the envelope.
9. Select the entire envelope and click 'Attach' from the bottom right-hand menu.
10. When you move the card around the screen, the address text will proceed with the envelope.
11. Load the envelope onto the cutting board and load it into the Cricut.
12. In Design Space, click 'Make it.'
13. Choose the material like paper.
14. Check to see if the pen color you need is loaded into the first compartment of the Cricut.
15. When the project is ready, press 'Go' and let it print.
16. Flip the card over and stick it onto the mat.
17. Use a piece of tape to stick the envelope flap down.
18. Load it into the Cricut.
19. Change the text on the envelope to a return address or 'regards from.'
20. Change the color of the pen if you want the writing in another color.
21. When you are ready, click on 'Make it.'

22. Make sure the material is set to the correct setting.
23. When you are ready, press 'Go.'
24. Once it has finished cutting, you will have a personalized envelope.

INTERMEDIATE

Chipboard puzzle

- Material needed:
- Chipboard
- Adhesive vinyl
- Ruler
- Masking or painter's tape

Instructions

Open Design Space and upload the image you want for your project. Make sure to create your canvas to the size of the puzzle you want to make and adjust your image to fit accordingly. There is a puzzle canvas in Design Space that you can use for the project, or you can develop your puzzle cuts if you want. If this is your first time creating the project, try out the preset cut file to get used to the process.

Send your file to print and cut. This will first print on your vinyl and then cut the square out for the project.

Next, you will want to place your chipboard on your cutting mat. To make sure it is secured well, use a few strips of tape to hold it on your mat for cutting. Make marks on the chipboard before cutting one inch in on all sides. This will help you when placing your vinyl. Also, if you have a Strong-Grip mat, use it for this part of the project.

Before sending your project to cut, transfer your vinyl to the chipboard, aligning it with the marks you just made, so it is in the center of the board. Go over your vinyl with your scraper tool to make sure it adheres properly.

Adjust your cutting blade for chipboard and then send the puzzle file to cut. This will make sure the chipboard and vinyl are cut at the same time and are seamlessly aligned. If the project does not cut away the outside one-inch margin, consider painting it a corresponding color. Still, it should be trimmed out in the process.

Shoes Pouch

Material needed:

- ½ yard of the desired fabric
- Ribbon
- Thread for stitching, needle if you are doing it by hand, or another "sewing" method like liquid stitches or fusible hem tape.
- Iron-on vinyl
- Sewing materials: scissors, rotary cutter, clear quilting ruler, pins, fray check, fabric marking pen
- Iron

Instructions

Use your ruler and rotary cutter to cut the fabric in the size you want. For soft shoes, consider a rectangle like 12" by 9". For larger shoes, use maybe a rectangle about 24" by 12." Apply fray check to the edges of your fabric.

Use your ruler to mark two spots on your fabric, 1 ½ inch from the top on each side.

Open Design Space and prepare the image and words for your bag. Make sure your canvas is set to ½ the width of your fabric to account for the fold in the material. This means you do not want anything that is larger than 9" or 12" or wider than 6" or 12," depending on the size of your fabric rectangle. Once you have your image laid out, make sure to mirror your image before sending it to cut.

Cut your vinyl and make sure to weed away any small parts you do not want.

Lay out your vinyl on your fabric, sticky side down on the print side of your fabric. Do not lay your design about ½" from the bottom or sides of your fabric to account for the seam you are going to create. Also, keep it about one inch from the top to account for the ribbon loop you are going to develop. Once you have it laid out, use a pressing cloth and your iron to attach your vinyl to your fabric.

After you adhere your vinyl to your project, fold your fabric in half and align the edges, pinning them in place. Sew along the edge to secure the bag shape. If you are using another means of making the bag, follow the directions on the packaging. Make sure to fold the fabric in ½ inch to enclose the raw edges of the material. Do not sew or close off the top of your bag. Also, do not sew beyond the markings you made with your pen earlier.

Fold the edge of the top of your bag down. You can make a little fold, about ¼ inch, and then fold again at ¾ inch to encase the seam allowance, or just fold it down one inch and sew it closed. Also, if you are not sewing your project, use your closure material to create the ribbon casing for closing the bag. Do not close off the ends of the bag, making a tube for the ribbon to pass through.

Cut a length of ribbon three or more inches longer than the unfinished width of your bag, meaning 15" or "28". Apply fray check to the ends of the ribbon. Thread the ribbon through the ribbon casing or tube you just created. Attaching a safety pin to one end of the ribbon and using that to pass the ribbon through can be helpful in this process. You want the ribbon coming out on one side of the bag for you can clinch it closed and tie a bow to keep the shoes inside.

Consider adding a new pair of shoes or a special treat inside the bag if you are giving it as a gift or simply slide your shoes on and take them with you in their stylish new casing!

ADVANCED

Dinosaur T-Shirt

Material needed:

- T-shirt of your choice
- Green heat transfer vinyl
- Cricut EasyPress or iron
- Cutting mat
- Weeding tool or pick

Instructions

- Open Cricut Design Space.
- Select the "Image" button in the lower left-hand corner and search "dinosaur."
- Choose your favorite dinosaur and click "Insert."
- Select "Image" again and search for "fossils."
- Choose your favorite fossil and click "Insert."
- Copy the fossil once so that you have two of them.
- Place your vinyl on the cutting mat.
- Send the design to your Cricut.
- Use a weeding tool or pick to remove the excess vinyl from the design.
- Place the dinosaur in the center of the t-shirt, and a fossil on each sleeve, with the plastic side up.
- Carefully iron on the design.
- After cooling, peel away the plastic by rolling it.
- Show off the cool dinosaur t-shirt!

Flower Garden Tote Bag

Material needed:

- Canvas tote bag
- White heat transfer vinyl
- Cricut EasyPress or iron
- Cutting mat

- Weeding tool or pick

Instructions

- Open Cricut Design Space and create a new project.
- Select the "Image" button in the lower left-hand corner and search "flowers."
- Choose your favorite flower and click "Insert."
- Continue with a variety of flowers, lining them up together to form a straight edge at the bottom.
- Place your vinyl on the cutting mat.
- Send the design to your Cricut.
- Use a weeding tool or pick to remove the excess vinyl from the design.
- Place the design along the bottom of the tote bag with the plastic side up.
- Carefully iron on the design.
- After cooling, peel away the plastic by rolling it.
- Carry around your new garden tote bag!
- Drawing Project with Your Cricut

Chapter 9:
Most Common Problems for Beginners

Fixing Cricut Design Space Issues

When you put everything into consideration, it is safe to say that the Design Space software is excellent.

No system is perfect, and there's always room for improvements. Still, on the whole, the software works excellently for several projects. However, there are a couple of related issues that are predominant with the software, including; freezing, slow loading, crashing and not opening at all. When you're faced with these issues, there are several things you can do to fix them, including;

Slow Internet Connection

Without saying much, you must understand that a slow internet connection is one of the leading causes of Design Space problems. Poor internet connection translates into problems for the software because it requires consistent download and upload speeds to function optimally.

Several websites only require good download speeds, *e.g.* YouTube, thus users on these sites can do away with slow upload speeds. However, unlike those sites, Cricut Design Space requires good upload and download speeds to function optimally because users are regularly sending and receiving information as they progress with their designs.

Note: If you're using a modem, you're likely to have a more stable connection if you move closer to it.

Run a speed test

You can use a service like Ookla to run an internet speed test.

For Design Space to run optimally, Cricut specifies the following;

- Broadband connection
- Minimum 1 – 2 Mbps Upload
- Minimum 2 – 3 Mbps Download

After running the speed test, if the results are not good, and you are convinced that the connection is affecting to your Design space issues, you should wait until the connection improves or you call your service providers. There is also the option of switching to a new internet service provider with a proper internet connection.

Your computer

If you run a speed test and realize that your connection is sufficient, then your computer, mobile phone or tablet might be the problem. Cricut has specific requirements for Design Space to function optimally. Below are some of the requirements;

Windows Computers

Your computer;

- Must have at least 4GB of ram
- Must be running on Windows 8 or later
- Must have Bluetooth connection or a free USB port
- Must have at least 50MB of free disk space
- Must have AMD processor or Intel Core series

Apple Computers

For Design Space to work optimally in your Mac computer, it must have the following;

- At least 50MB free space
- 4GB Ram
- Mac OS X 10.12 or a later version
- CPU of 1.83 GHz

Background Programs

If you're running too many background programs while using Design Space, it might also be a problem.

Some multitasking crafters are fond of engaging in different activities while designing on Design Space. For example, some simultaneously chat on Facebook, while downloading movies, watching videos on YouTube, and creating on Design Space. These activities will affect your app and make it malfunction badly; thus, it is essential to shut down other projects and focus solely on Design Space.

While it is crucial to close other apps and shut down other activities, there are other things that you should also do;

i. Run a malware check
ii. If you're using windows, you should upgrade you drivers
iii. Clear your history and cache
iv. Defragment your hard drive
v. Check your anti-virus software and update if needed

If you execute these tests, it might speed up the system, or even solve all related problems.

Your Browser

Your Design Space software might be having issues due to your system browser.

For you to access Design Space, Cricut recommends that you use the latest version of the browser you use. Be it Edge, Chrome, Firefox or Mozilla; just make sure that it is up to date. If it refuses to work on a particular browser, open it in another browser to see if it works. Although the reasons are unknown, sometimes its works and even fits perfectly.

Contact Cricut

If you've tried all possible options and nothing works, you may have to call Cricut customer care to look into the issues you're faced with.

The incorrect cartridge name appears on the Cricut screen

Follow the following steps to correct the error:

Sometimes in manufacturing, the cartridge stickers are placed on backwards on the cartridge. Take out the inserted cartridge and reinsert it backward to check if this is the problem. If this does not solve the problem, move to the next step.

Does this happen with all cartridges?

a) Yes-Move to the next step

b) No-Call customer service or chat online with customer service if it still displays the wrong name after putting it in backward.

A hard reset may be required at this point. Follow the directions in the user manual for this. Again, if this does not fix the problem, move to the next step.

Update Firmware, especially if it is not up to date. If this does not fix the problem, move to the next step.

Call customer service or chat online with customer service if none of the above steps solved the problem.

When images are added to the queue the Cricut machine freezes

Before selecting the image keys, always choose the gray feature keys.

Follow the following steps to correct the error if it is still occurring:

Turn off the Cricut and let it rest for up to one hour. Let it rest for at least a minimum of 10 minutes.

Double-check how the characters were entered; Try re-entering the characters in the correct order and allowing the image to show up on the screen before keying in the subsequent character.

"Characters won't fit" appears when the image memory is exceeded in the queue. Try removing images to see if the problem is fixed. If the problem continues, proceed to the next step.

If you insert another cartridge, does this error still occur?

a) YES-Move to the next step.

b) NO-Call customer service or chat online customer service to speak with them about the error.

A hard reset may be required at this point. Follow the directions in the user manual for this. Again, if this does not fix the problem, move to the next step.

Update Firmware, especially if it is not up to date. If this does not fix the problem, move to the next step.

Call customer service or chat online with customer service if none of the above steps solved the problem.

The Cricut Machine keypad has glitches

Two common keyboard errors occur; the buttons do not respond when pressed, and none of the buttons will work despite lights being lit on the keyboard. If this does not explain your problem, call customer service or chat online with customer service about the issue. If your error is one of the two most common problems, follow the steps below for whichever your problem is.

Non-responsive buttons when pressed:

Check that the machine recognizes the inserted cartridge by making sure the screen displays the cartridges name. If this does not fix the problem, move to the next step.

Check that the mat is loaded into the machine properly. If this does not fix the problem, move to the next step.

If you insert another cartridge, does this error still occur?

a) YES-Move to the next step.

b) NO-Call customer service or chat online customer service to speak with them about the error.

A hard reset may be required at this point. Follow the directions in the user manual for this. Again, if this does not fix the problem, move to the next step.

Update Firmware, especially if it is not up to date. If this does not fix the problem, move to the next step.

Call customer service or chat online with customer service if none of the above steps solved the problem.

No buttons will respond despite lights coming on:

Update Firmware, especially if it is not up to date. Lights on the left side of the keyboard, the power button, and the cut button will light up when in Firmware mode. If this does not fix the problem, move to the next step.

Call customer service or chat online with customer service if the above step did not solve the problem.

Unloading or loading the mat makes the Cricut machine freeze

Follow the following steps to correct the error:

Turn off the Cricut and let it rest for up to one hour. Let it rest for at least a minimum of 10 minutes.

Did you switch a cartridge while the machine was on? This is called "hot-swapping" and can result in the machine freezing.

YES-Turn off your machine and switch the cartridge. If this does not solve the problem, move to the next step.

NO-Move to the next step.

If you insert another cartridge, does this error still occur?

a) YES-Move to the next step.

b) NO-Call customer service or chat online customer service to speak with them about the error.

A hard reset may be required at this point. Follow the directions in the user manual for this. Again, if this does not fix the problem, move to the next step.

Update Firmware, especially if it is not up to date. If this does not fix the problem, move to the next step.

Call customer service or chat online with customer service if none of the above steps solved the problem.

During cutting the carriage does not travel along the track

Follow the following steps to correct the error:

Can the carriage car move quickly to the right and left while the machine is on?

a) YES-Move to the next step.

b) NO-Call customer service or chat online customer service to speak with them about the problem.

Look carefully at the belt, roller bars, and carriage car to see if any damage is evident. Take photos of any observed damage and Call customer service or chat online customer service to speak with them about the problem.

a) Belt-Is it lose or broken?

b) Carriage car-Is it on the track? Is it on track straight?

Call customer service or chat online customer service to speak with them about the problem is no damage is evident.

When loaded into the Cricut machine, the mat becomes crooked

Do not hold the corners or sides of the may when loading it. Instead, hold the bottom in the center and position the mat slightly under and against the roller bar's rubber rings. This is easiest when the bottom of the mat is lifted gently.

Follow the following steps to correct the error:

Look carefully at the roller bar to see if any damage is evident. Take photos of any observed damage and Call customer service or chat online customer service to speak with them about the problem. If there is no damage noticeable, move on to the next step.

The correct mat size must be used for the machine. Double-check, it is accurate. If this does not fix the problem, move on to the next step.

Before loading the mat, make sure it is aligned with guides, and the mat's edges are below the roller bar. If this does not fix the problem, move on to the next step.

As the roller bar begins to roll, lightly press the mat underneath with gentle pressure.

Call customer service or chat online with customer service if none of the above steps solved the problem.

During cutting the machine freezes

Follow the following steps to correct the error:

Turn off the Cricut and let it rest for up to one hour. Let it rest for at least a minimum of 10 minutes.

If you insert another cartridge, does this error still occur?

a) YES-Move to the next step.

b) NO-Call customer service or chat online customer service to speak with them about the error.

A hard reset may be required at this point. Follow the directions in the user manual for this. Again, if this does not fix the problem, move to the next step.

Update Firmware, especially if it is not up to date. If this does not fix the problem, move to the next step.

Call customer service or chat online with customer service if none of the above steps solved the problem

Chapter 10:
Some Tips and Tricks for Beginners

Tips and Tricks to Make Cricut Easier and Efficient

We hope you find the following tips and tricks useful for the many projects you indeed will create!

Subscribe to Cricut Access

If you want to get a full range of use out of both your Cricut Explore machine as well as the Cricut Maker machine, we would recommend you subscribe to Cricut Access right away. There are two options for payment. This works out to be slightly cheaper on a month to month basis. This will give you access to thousands of different predesigned projects as well as Cricut Access exclusive fonts, that you would otherwise have to pay to use.

De-tack Your Cutting Mat

The Circuit Explore machine will come with a green 12"x12" Standard grip cutting mat. The Cricut Maker machine will come with a blue light grip mat. As you already know, you will place your cutting material onto this mat before inserting it into the machine to cut. As you will come to find out, the green cutting mat is too sticky when it is brand new.

Keep Your Cutting Mat Covers

The cutting mats that you purchase for your projects will always come brand new with a plastic protecting sheet over it. You will want to keep this plastic cover as long as you have the mat.

Cleaning the Cricut Cutting Mat

It is imperative to keep your cutting mat clean for it to remain sticky and be available for use over and over. Ideally, you would want to clean the mat every time after use if not at least every couple would suffice. All you will have to do is merely wiping down a clean mat with baby wipes to keep it clean.

Adhere Your Materials to Your Mats with Painter's or Masking Tape

You will find that, as your Cricut mats age, they will slowly lose their grip. Before completely giving up on your mat and throwing it out, considering lining the edges of your project with painter's tape or with masking tape. This will hold your materials in place while they're being cut and will save you the expense of a new mat for some time.

Command Hooks from 3M to Hang Your Cutting Mats When Not in Use

Utilizing your wall space for storage can be invaluable when you're storing something delicate and prone to bending, like your Cricut craft mat. Using Command hooks will ensure that your walls won't be damaged by the adhesive and your mats will always be within arm's reach and will never be hidden from you with this method!

Keep the Clear Plastic Sheet That Comes with Your Cricut Mats

When you buy a new Cricut mat, you will notice a semi-rigid sheet of plastic that comes stuck to the grip. After you complete each project, re-adhere this sheet to the front of your mat before hanging them up or putting them away! This will keep the grip from getting ruined by dust, hair, rogue glitter, or animal fur in the air!

Take Care of Your Mat

Many mats have met their ends in my care, and there are multiple reasons for this. If the material doesn't stick to it, the paper, vinyl, and others will all move around while the blade is trying to cut through, and it will end in a disaster.

Don't Be Lazy

Test those projects first! Testing is key to mastering the Cricut even when you feel like you've already gotten the hang of it. It never hurts to assess your projects before doing the final cut or print. Test before you cut. Make it a habit of yours. It should come without a thought. Instead of doing the whole project at once, do a small element of it first. If it doesn't work, you won't need to wait for it to finish before you can fix the settings and cut the new design. It will also save you the pain of losing the material you wanted to use for the project itself.

Try Different Markers

Don't feel limited by the Cricut markers. That's right! When you are using your Cricut machine to write or draw on your project, any marker that will fit will work correctly. Not only are there cheaper options, but the colors and variety of styles are virtually endless. Don't let anyone tell you that you can only use the markers from the Cricut brand. Even though they are of better quality and made for the machine, you are not limited to using them. Just make sure your markers fit.

Double-Check the Settings

Just like the testers, this is annoying, but you have to make sure that all of your settings are correct and that you have selected the right material option. If you are not using the Cricut Design Space, this is easy to forget. When you utilize the software, there is a broad selection of tools to choose from. However, when you are only using a cartridge, the materials are limited. Still, regardless of which set-up you wish to handle the design, you should check your settings twice.

Keep Your Blades in a Good Condition

Preferably, get one for every material that you are going to cut. In the list of materials that are available to add to your Cricut purchase, you may see different kinds of blades available. A dull blade is never a good thing, and it will ruin your project as easily as a sharp one will cut it entirely.

Extend Your Markers' Shelf Life

Keep your markers upside down with the cap-covered tip facing down when you are not using them? Do not leave them in your Cricut when you are not using them. Secure the cap and put them away afterward.

Chapter 11: Realize the project and sell it

How to Make Money with Cricut

Likewise, there are countless things you can make, which are marketable. Independent entrepreneurship is easier than it's ever been thanks to the internet and web platforms that make selling your products a breeze.

You've likely already heard of some of the platforms that make it easy to start a shop of your own.

With the Cricut, making countless items of every type and theme, for any occasions, is the name of the game. Doing these projects can be a huge source of joy for the avid crafter. Still, suppose you're spending the money on the materials for your projects. In that case, it might make sense for you to start generating a return on those, depending on how much you're doing and spending.

We'll cover some of the basics of what it means to go into business for yourself when you're the sole manufacturer of the goods in your store. Without having to provide a brick and mortar space for your shop, overhead can be so much lower than starting a shop or store is viable for people who might not have a lump sum of startup capital ready to hand.

How Do You Know When It's Time to Start a Shop?

If crafting is your passion, if you prefer to spend your time making items with your Cricut than you would going out or any other activity in your downtime, it could be time.

Should I Quit My Day Job and Go All In?

The thing about selling the products you create is that, since there's no brick and mortar location to manage, no store hours to keep to, you can manage your sales and your projects in the spare time that you have. It is best to start your store while you have a stable source of income. This way, as your store grows, you can scale back where it's necessary to do so in your usual work schedule, to allow for more time to spend on your shop.

How Can I Make Sure People Will Buy My Products?

There is a wealth of ways to market a business in today's digital age. Between social media presence, search engine optimization and more, you can put your name everywhere; it needs to be to generate interest. However, you might find that when you're starting, it will be easiest to pick items that are not custom. Make a couple of each type of thing, take stunning product photos, upload them to your store, and then sell those as off-the-rack items.

As you start to generate more business, you may find that taking on the occasional custom order or commissioned item will benefit you. By and large, you will find that custom orders will take you more time and cost more to produce, for less of a return. Be watchful of this, and if you find that making 100 of general design and selling all of those is the best use of your time and resources, stick with that! There's absolutely nothing wrong with going that route.

Do I Need to Make Enough of Each Item in My Shop to Keep and Inventory?

The short answer to this is no. You don't have to make any more of any items that are being ordered at any given time. With the way Etsy works for sellers, you can determine how much time you have before shipping out an order, so you can make the items as they're ordered, so you can be confident you're never wasting product or letting it sit in your craft room for too long.

The only time it would be best to make any sort of inventory would be if you intend to rent a space or booth at a tradeshow or convention. Having a presence at craft fairs, conventions, tradeshows, etc., can generate impulse buys from passing patrons that could be great for your business.

If at all possible, it's best to wait to go to such an event until you're able to narrow down your best sellers. Once you have a smattering of items you can make that are your hottest items, you can make several of each of those, and keep them at your booth or table, ready for immediate purchase!

Do I Need to Create a Shop to Make Money with Cricut?

To be candid, no, you don't need to create a shop if you don't want to. If there is someone else who runs a craft shop, you might ask them to list your items for you in exchange for a share of the profits.

You could create a partnership with a local school, community center, farmer's market, or another establishment to sell your items for you to their patrons.

Making an online store for your Cricut items might be the most direct, hands-on way to generate a stream of income from the things that you make. This does not mean, however, that it's the only way or that it's the best way for you to go about it. Test the waters, see what's available, and pick a path that is most workable for you and the business you're working to create.

How Should I Price My Items?

This, like everything else, is entirely up to you. One method of pricing is to decide on a rate you would like to be paid per hour spent on a project, multiply that rate by how many hours you spent on that project, and add it together with the costs of all the materials you used to do your project.

For instance, I would never take a full-time job that paid me fewer than $15 per hour. We'll use this as our artisan rate to start. You can always adjust your prices as you get better with your craft, as you generate more of a following, and as you get faster at completing each of the projects you sell! So with this $15 hourly rate, we'll put together a little project. Let's say I'm taking a sheet of printable vinyl and printing an image that I own onto it. From there, I'm layering that vinyl onto a cardboard backing. Once that's done, I'm going to run it through my Cricut and make a jigsaw puzzle out of it.

Once I've made my jigsaw puzzle, I'm going to use more cardboard to make a box, which I will then decoupage. The package will be filled with the puzzle pieces, wrapped with a satin ribbon, and sold in my online store. Let's run the tally!

- Cricut Printable Vinyl - $9
- Cardboard Sheets - $6
- Decoupage Glue - $2
- Satin Ribbon - $1
- 1 Hour of Labor - $15.00
- Artisan jigsaw puzzle - $33.00

Do not sell yourself short on your labor costs, and do not charge less than you spend on your materials, ever! That's no way to run a business, and it's no way to live. Value your time correctly and charge every penny that you're worth. With how beautiful your products are, you will find people will pay your rates, and you will get rave reviews every time!

This question is a little bit loaded and, what it boils down to is which platform is the most convenient, workable, and reliable for you. The business you want to create is going to take up a lot of your time and attention, so you must be using a platform that fits all your needs, meets all your expectations, and solves more problems for you than it causes.

We can tend to be forgiving of quirks in new systems when we're learning them. However, take a little extra time to read the experiences and reviews of people who have used that platform for an extended period. This will give you a look into what your future could be like with that platform, and it's the only gauge you have to go by when it comes to how that platform will serve you.

You will want to spend a little extra time looking into which platforms are available, what costs are involved (if any), how they treat their sellers, what percentages of your sales are taken, and what the sellers on those platforms think of them.

Here are some of the top platforms you'll want to check into!

- Etsy
- Amazon Handmade
- Facebook Marketplace
- Folksy
- Artfire
- Craftsy
- eBay
- Craigslist

You will mostly find that there are not any items you can make with your Cricut, which will not appeal to someone who would like to buy one. If you sell even one of each item you ever make, you're still coming out way ahead of the game, right? A lot of the things I'm about to list out for you are ones that can be purchased at a low rate from retailers, then customized using your design expertise, Cricut magic, and beautiful vinyl appliques that have sayings, monograms, or appealing designs on them. The choice is yours!

Are You Ready to Go into Business?

Far too often, people who are incredibly creative jump into a business before they have thought about the business end of the situation. Suppose you are using a Cricut Maker often and people are giving you tons of feedback about your crafts and gifts. In that case, it might be a signal that you should go into business with your Cricut Maker. Hundreds of users are doing just that. But what can make you unique and keep you in business for a much longer time?

You should have a clear idea of why you want to go into business with your Cricut. Make a list. There may just be one apparent reason, or there could be 3 or 4, but regardless of how many reasons, define why you want to be in business.

You might want to be at home with the kids. Have you ever tried to work at home with kids around? Or, perhaps you are making quite a bit with your Cricut Maker already and have so many orders you cannot keep up on evenings and weekends.

Working outside the home is just not your thing. You have always wanted to be in business for yourself. You enjoy marketing. You have a marketing degree, and you are champing at the bit to be your boss and use that degree to market your projects. You think you can take this Cricut business to the top!

Finally, crafting with your Cricut maker feeds your soul. There isn't anything else you would instead do with your life for a job. You can work on projects almost 24/7, and it doesn't bother you. Even when you are not working, you are thinking of projects you could do if you were using. This is your passion. You have found a way to make the world brighter and a better place.

Make sure you are self-motivated. To be in business, any business, you have to be self-motivated. You may be extremely creative using your Cricut. Still, suppose you are not motivated to network and get customers consistently. In that case, that's going to be a problem in the long run. Also, you might have to work on projects when you don't feel like working because people need their purchases. Are you motivated enough to be able to keep up the pace a business sometimes throws your way? Also, are you ready to deal with "that" customer? We are talking about the customer who just is never happy. You need a plan for the bad penny that just will not go away.

Make sure your finances are in order. And then consult with an advisor and an accountant before going into business and take their advice. Make sure, according to the financial advisors; you can weather any storms that come along because of low tides in the business world. You don't want to ruin your love for your Cricut by ending up in financial trouble because you were not financially prepared to go into business in the first place. There is truly nothing worse than thinking you have found your dream and ending up in a daytime nightmare.

A good question to ask yourself is where I will get my clients? Etsy? Pinterest? Word of Mouth? Will you market on Facebook? How are you going to get your customers? Are you planning to go to craft fairs? Think about your options and what marketing is going to cost. Are you ready to beat the pavement? Go to schools, churches, hit up the little leagues and everyone and anyone who needs something done by a Cricut?

Everyone who goes into business should have a solid business plan. A business plan is a road map of where you are and where you are going. How many things might potentially cost and potential income? With a Cricut Maker, you don't have as many outside variables, and most of the success depends on your hard work and persistence. But you still need a business plan and a good one! Let's get started!

Once these five steps have been addressed, you are ready to get started with your new Cricut Maker Business. How exciting

You Need A Business Name and A Logo

Now that you know your machine, and you have decided to take the plunge into owning your own business with your Cricut, you need to think of a name for this business and a symbol of you. Your name for your business needs to identify you and also be a catchy name that tells people what you do. Pick a name you plan to stick with for a long time. It's costly to change a name and logo, *etc.* A logo isn't necessary, but they are fun to design, and you have a Cricut Maker, so play around with your new name and design

What Kind of a Business License Will You Need?

One of the steps you will have to do is to contact your home state because every state is different in how to obtain a state business license. A license or permit gives you the permission you need to open and operate a business. Registration allows you to claim the name of the business and the business itself as yours. Insurance is another matter and is usually not mandatory with a crating business, but it does cover costs in case of an accident.

Website

The next order of business is to work on a website. You will need to find a host—many people like Bluehost. And, while you are at it, print yourself some business cards on your Cricut. How fun is it to design and print your cards on your Cricut Maker?

Business cards are important because they are your little billboard. They are a way to advertise every time you give one out or pin one on a bulletin board in a restaurant or a coffee shop. Your phone number is on the card, and an idea of what you will create for your customers is on your card. You also will put your business email address on your business cards.

Marketing on Social Media

We are all aware of how social media has become a marketing platform for not only established corporations, but also small businesses and budding entrepreneurs. Simply add hashtags like for sale, product, selling, free shipping, the sample included, and more to entice potential buyers. Join "Facebook" community pages and groups for handcraft sellers and buyers to market your products. Use catchy phrases like customization available at no extra cost or free returns if not satisfied when posting the products on these pages as well as your personal "Facebook" page. Use "Twitter" to share feedback from your happy customers to widen your customer base.

Another tip here is to post pictures of anything and everything you have created using "Cricut" machines, even those that you did not plan to sell. You never know who else might need something that you deemed unsellable. Since you will be creating these only after the order has been placed, you can quickly gather the required supplies after the fact and get crafting.

TARGET LOCAL FARMER'S MARKET AND BOUTIQUES

If you like the thrill of a show-and-tell, then reserve a booth at a local farmer's market and show up with some ready to sell crafts. In this case, you are relying on the number of people attending and a subset of those who might be interested in purchasing from you. Suppose you are in an urban neighborhood where people are keenly interested in unique art designs but do not have the time to create them on their own. In that case, you can easily make big bucks by setting a decent price point for your products.

Bring flyers to hand out people so they can reach you through one of your social media accounts or email and check all your existing "Etsy" listings. Think of these events as a means of marketing for those who are not as active online but can be excited with customized products to meet their next big life event like baby shower, birthday party, or a wedding.

Conclusion

The next step is to utilize your newfound wisdom on the cutting-edge craft project designing and creation offered by "Cricut". You are now poised to follow the detailed instructions described in this book to create your own personalized and one of a kind craft projects that reflect your creativity and serve as an exhibit of your expression. All the "Cricut" devices have also been explained in detail with how and what makes them different from one another as well as their usage. You can selectively choose the "Cricut Maker" or "Cricut Explore" line to turn your ideas into reality and subsequently enhance your creations using "Cricut Easy Press" line or "Cricut Cuttlebug". You will be able to turn even the most unlikely and seemingly unrealistic ideas into beautiful craft projects in no time. All the nuances of the "Design Space" application have also been explained in exquisite detail. You have learnt all about the free resources, including images, fonts and projects that are available through the "Cricut" library so you can save money as you know and sharpen your craft skills.

Taking the DIY world by storm, and increasingly gaining popularity among absolutely fascinated by what you can do. From the original Cricut machine, this brand has worked up to the top, listening to its users and adding more features to make these machines last craft investment. It is fair to say that it has created a brand-new generation of DIY enthusiasts on this side of the globe, and it's only getting bigger.

The next step is to use the detailed instructions provided in this book to create your unique craft projects that reflect your personality and will serve as a testament of your creativity. The detail explanation of all the ways you can use and leverage different “Cricut” devices will help you turn even the most unimaginable ideas into beautiful craft projects in no time. All the nuances of the "Design Space" application have also been explained in exquisite detail. You have learnt all about the free resources, including images, fonts and projects that are available through the “Cricut” library so you can save money as you know and sharpen your craft skills.

If you are considering buying a Cricut machine, you are investing in your future to follow their passion. Maintain an active membership, keep on with accessories, the latest tools and sources of trends, and images to remain relevant and improve your skills.

This should act as your instruction manual for using a Cricut, so after reading this book, you should be able to take the next challenge and create your first project or be willing to address the most complex projects.

In this book, we have given you the tools you need to become a better crafter as well as giving you great advice on how to save money with your supplies and making sure that you can use them for as long as possible as well. Originally the Cricut machines were not thought to be that impressive until people actually started buying them and then they saw that these machines had so much merit that it was beneficial and worth the effort and money.

The best part of this book is that we offer you real value and real knowledge about these machines and help you understand why crafting is so much better with them. It saves you from hand cutting and fatigue as well as frustration and the Maker can work twice as fast as others. Imagine what you would get done and how much time you're saving by the speed of this machine! In addition to that, it can cut three hundred materials where others can only do one hundred. We explain the benefits of having this ultimate machine at your disposal and how it can benefit your crafting.

If you use the tips, we have outlined in this book; then you will be better off when trying to use this machine for the first time. It's not a complicated machine, but the information can be a bit overwhelming at first.

With this book, you will be able to understand your crafting on a better level with a machine that is made for simplicity, power and letting you achieve your crafting dreams.

Cricut Vocabulary and Terms

There are various words and expressions you will hear over and again when you start interacting with Cricut owners (and even Silhouette owners) or checking them when you surf the web looking for help and instructional exercises.

Clingy Mat

This is the cutting mat that you will use to hold the material you need to cut. The material shouldn't be allowed to move while the machine is attempting to slice, score, or draw on it. The clingy tangle holds it in place. There are various degrees of "clingy" depending on the material you are working with.

Tools

This usually refers to a pack of tools that are used along with a Cricut machine group or that you buy independently as an accessory. These typically include a sort of spatula for pulling your design off the clingy tangle, tweezers for lifting and pulling, a pick that resembles a dental instrument for "weeding" and scissors.

Weeding

This term is quite confusing lol. It refers to pulling or removing the "undesirable" pieces out of your design, within the "e" or within a shape that you need to be vacant.

Load and Unload

generally simple. It's the process of stacking and unloading your clingy tangle into the Cricut machine.

Pressure

you will have an option to automate your machine that alters the pressure on the sharp edge, pen, or turning edge. You change this depending on the thickness of your material and the speed that you choose to cut your design at.

Speed

The speed to which you set the machine to cut out the design. Often you can use quicker speeds for more simple designs. The more complicated the design, the slower you need your machine to process and cut.

Cricut Design Space

This is the application on software that you will use to change, set up, and eventually send the cut instructions to your machine with the goal that it can cut the materials as indicated by you your design.

Materials

These are a set of things you add to the clingy tangle to be cut. This can include paper, fake calfskin, copper sheeting, fabric, sticker paper, vinyl, slender wood, chipboard, froth center, and the sky is the limit from there!

CRICUT MAKER GUIDE:

A practical guide to the Cricut maker that talks about this machine. You will learn how to use accessories, materials, and tricks to become an expert in its work.

KAYLA ARORA

Table of Contents

Introduction

Many creating fans have begun to look all starry eyed at their electronic kick the bucket cut machine, the Cricut. Another expansion to the effectively well-known item is improving a product program made only for Cricut clients.

Cricut allowed crafting and cutting of challenging designs skillfully and in a presentable manner. It all started with the invention of the Cricut machine. It works like a printer but has better features to beautify it in every field.

You create a sketch and submit the design to the Cricut on your device or phone. What makes the Cricut unique is that it can be used much like a printer too. The Cricut computer also has the tools that you can use for a cartridge library. Just check for the form you like in the library and give the order to the printer to print it out, and you are ready to go. The blade set up in the Cricut is a sharp one that performs its functions exceptionally cleanly. The cutouts are immaculate for each corner, and each edge is cut out precisely, as seen on the screen.

The Cricut machine is one without limits. Your ingenuity, the vision, is beyond expectations. This computer's function is such that you can use it to simply mold anything you want if you know how to do it. So, you do not need to stay away from it simply because you are not an artist. Embrace the imagination inside and build whatever you want. The Cricut is a perfect tool for people who enjoy the craftsmanship and people who need to cut multiple items and all kinds of material.

The good thing about Cricut is that there are wide varieties of cartridges available in the market to meet the demands of any occasion. How you use your Cricut machines to decorate your home with angel shaped cutouts or pine shapes this Christmas, you'll find Cricut Christmas cartridges readily available. From reindeer to an army of snowmen, from Christmas trees to villages, you can have them all with special Cricut Christmas cartridges. Want to make decorative cards for your family or friends this Christmas? Let the Cricut cartridge do that for you. If the birthday of a loved one is coming, there are lots of designs to choose from. Or you want to host a themed New Year party with unique decorations of various patterns to match your theme. You'll be amazed at the wide variety of Cricut cartridges you can find in the market. All of these are possible with the fantastic Cricut machine.

As you become more familiar with your Cricut machine, you will become more creative, and you will soon find yourself coming up with new project ideas all day long. The Cricut website and Design Space are great tools for project ideas to help get you started if you are unsure what type of project you would like to begin. Pinterest is also another great online resource for project ideas at different levels of difficulty.

When starting a new project, you must always keep in mind that you must first have all of the materials necessary to complete it. It is still helpful to review your stock of tools and materials before getting started. The worst feeling is when you sit down and begin working on a complex project to realize you are out of a specific material needed to finish the job. It will save you a lot of time in the long run if you spend a few minutes at the beginning taking stock of your inventory! Working with materials you already have on hand is also a great way to keep your crafting costs low. It will always feel good to know that you made a custom piece of work without spending a ton of extra money just to complete it!

After knowing all these things, maybe you will now want to give it a try. But wait, as beginners, you still need a lot of ideas on what type of machine you need, what are the different features each possesses, and a lot more. Before purchasing any sort of unit, machine, or any kind of device, there are some essential items you need to learn, and the same applies for the Cricut. When buying any of these machines, you need to know about various kinds of Cricut devices. Collecting knowledge of these kinds will help you find a computer that suits your needs. It aims to input understanding to the reader so that when you reach the store, you are no longer naïve. Turn each page of this book, and you will see what and how this machine will make the life of an artist exciting.

Happy reading!

Chapter 1:
Cricut Maker: What It Is And What It Does.

You will presumably make everything with the Cricut Maker. The Cricut Maker has an expandable game plan of devices: a sharp edge, pen, and a scoring instrument. You can cut through any texture quickly and precisely when you use the spinning side that goes with the Cricut Maker. You have the decision to utilize your plans, move these, and use them using the Cricut application.

This Cricut model is one of the most notable in any case. There are two or three damages to its use. The sharp edge cutting edge that allows you to cut even thick materials is sold freely. Not all pictures are liberated from their Image Library, and in reality, you need to pay for the best ones. There are a couple of fights that require some venture to work with an iPad. Consider these cons before you purchase the Cricut Maker.

Features

- With expandable mechanical assemblies: rotational edge, sharp cutting edge, and pens • The sharp turning edge can cut rapidly and unequivocally.
- Knife sharp edge can manage wobbly and thick materials.
- With fine point pen, 12 x 12 inches cutting mats

- Comes with many propelled sewing plans
- With fundamental structure application, load reaches out on a PC or wireless.
- You can use your unique structures.
- With a device docking opening
- With Bluetooth remote development
- With a USB port to charge your device while being utilized

Pros

- Allows you to tackle different materials
- Comes with expandable gadgets
- You can use other plans from its database.
- Use your PC or mobile phone with the Cricut
- Device dock allows you to work personally with the machine.

Cons

- Knife sharp edge is sold autonomously.
- Complaints that it won't work with an iPad

Available Colors Variations of The Cricut Machine

The Cricut Machine colors can come in two ways, one the color for the casing/enclosure and secondly in terms of the ink needed to draw either the shapes, letters, or phrases being cut.

The following are the general variations in color in terms of the enclosure of the Cricut Machine.

- Black
- Blue
- Lilac
- Mint
- Peach Kiss
- Raspberry
- Rose
- Sky

Cobalt.

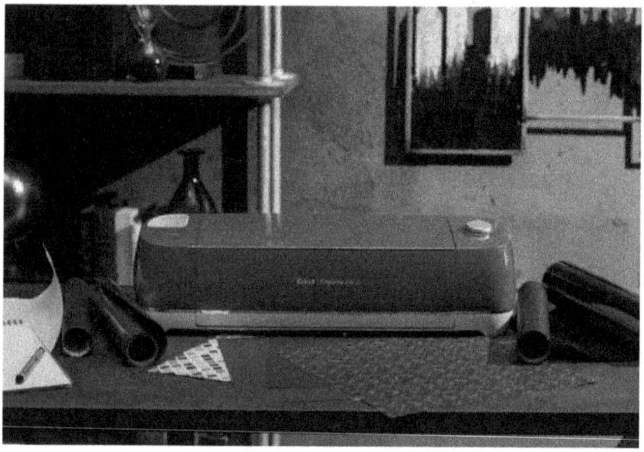

Raspberry.

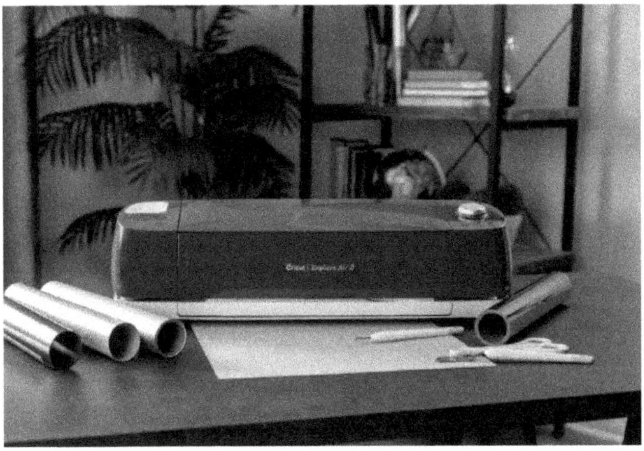

Sunflower.

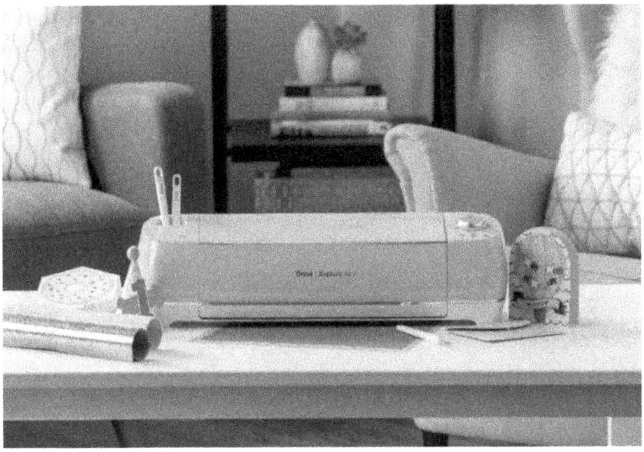

Persimmon.

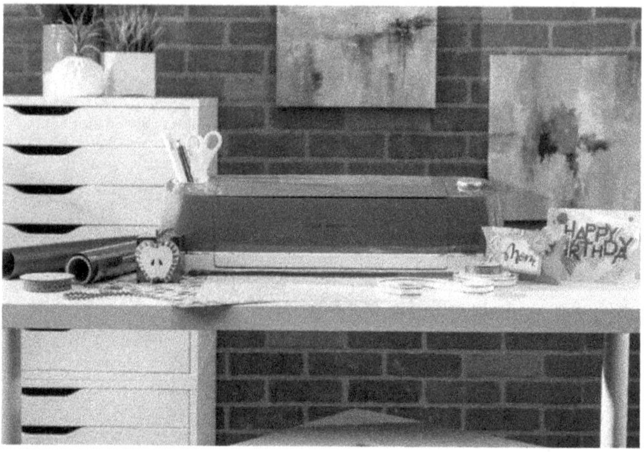

Fuchsia.

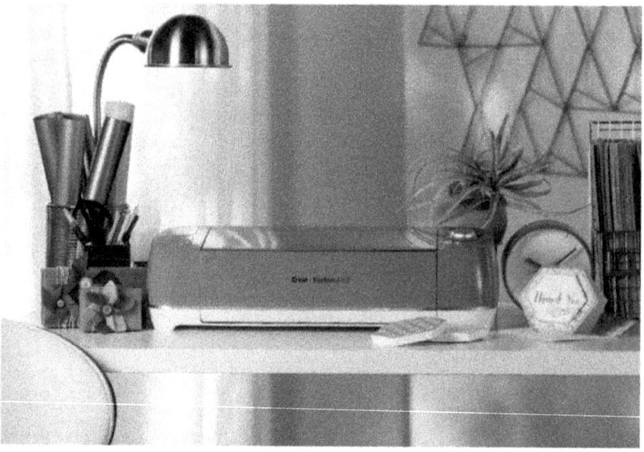

Boysenberry.

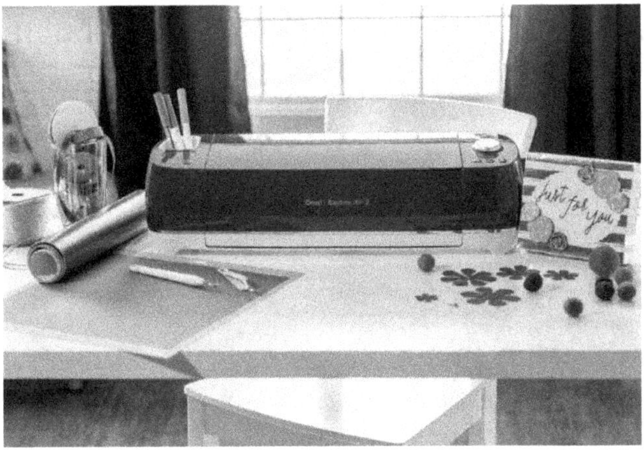

Peacock.

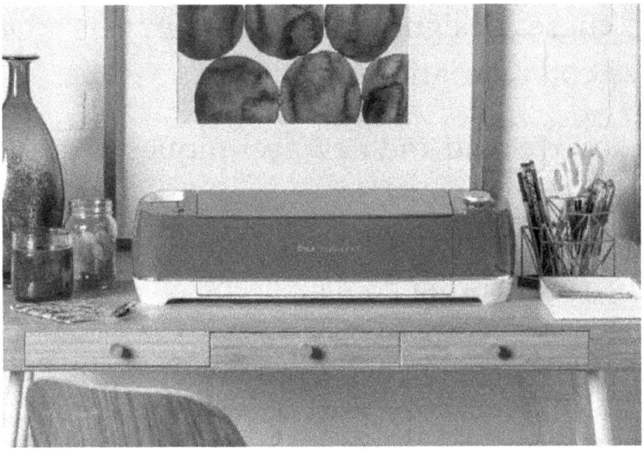

Merlot

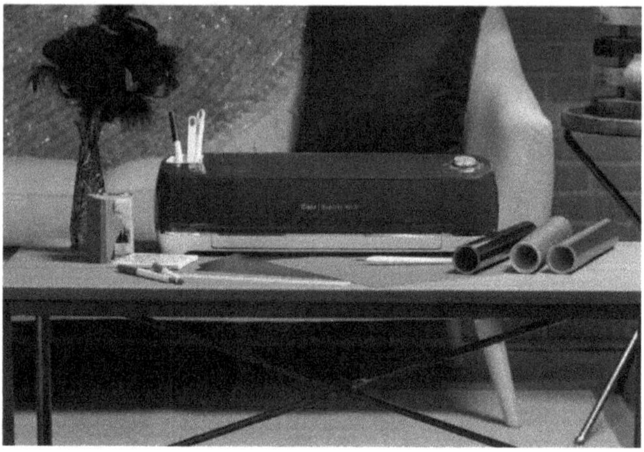

THE VERDICT

Among these designs, the *Raspberry* is the most preferred color variation if;

- You love bold and new techniques to design your craft space/room.
- You craft in color and love making custom T-shirts and other cool projects.

The Raspberry color complements your craft and design space by adding the correct pop amount to the craft room either by cutting, scoring, or pressing. The Merlot design is better suited for late-night crafters seeking to add some color in their design space. However, the Persimmon design has the right hue for highlighting the creative space.

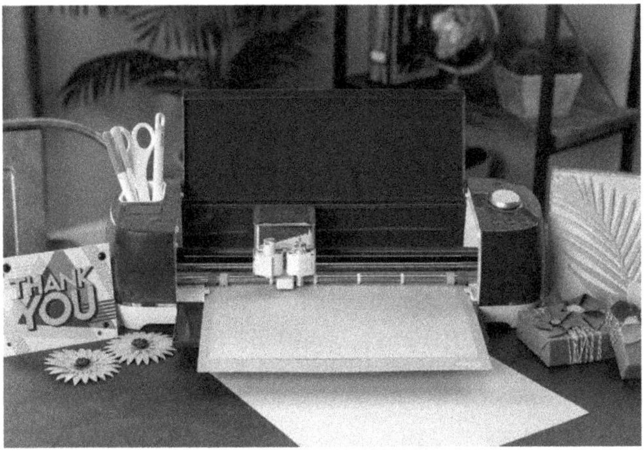

The following table shows some of the shops where you can quickly get the Cricut Machine's different color variations.

S/NO	COLOR VARIATION	WHERE YOU CAN GET IT
1.	Fuchsia	Walmart.com
2.	Persimmon	Amazon
3.	Merlot	Hobby Lobby
4.	Cobalt	JOANN
5.	Peacock	Michaels
6.	Sunflower	Michaels
7.	Boysenberry	Michaels
8.	Raspberry	Cricut.com

Who Can Use The Cricut Machine?

Anyone can go into the store and purchase the machine. Still, there would be no point in using the machine only occasionally. Some of the professionals who may benefit from buying the machine for their business or personal pursuit are;

a) Paper crafter.
b) Woodworker.
c) Sewing enthusiasts.
d) Interior designers.
e) Fashion designers

Chapter 2:
Why Cricut Maker

REASONS FOR CHOOSING CRICUT MAKER

Noise Level

This was the main reason that kept me from choosing the Silhouette. Although Cricut is not a silent machine, the cameo sounds so loud and weird that it bothers me. Some will say it's a matter of habit, but that sound is a BIG NOT to me. On YouTube, there is a video where it shows the speed and sound of both machines.

Use of Vectors (SVG)

Without having to pay an extra cost, I can use SVG files. I am aware of Adobe Illustrator, so the software is a bit limited is not a problem for me. If you don't use Adobe Illustrator, the Cricut software is a limitation.

I Don't Depend On My Pc To Work

Something that caught my attention was the ability to use my machine from my cell phone or iPad. For example, I am in the waiting room for the doctor designing something that I have to work from the comfort of my cell phone. When I get home, I only need to press the GO button without even connecting or having to transfer the file to my PC.

Smart Adjustment Wheel

With a simple turn of the wheel, I can do my projects much faster. This wheel has the settings for the seven most common materials and a fit between two materials that increase my cutting depth if the material is a little thicker than average.

Easy To Use

It has made this machine so simple to use that those who have never done anything creative can use it. It is a simple design, place your mat and press the GO button. The software puts the shapes on each mat, differentiating whether it is something to print, cut, and what color is intended for each design. The most challenging decision is to determine which material to cut each shape.

Capacity with Different Materials

From a line of washi tape, cardboard, foam, balsa wood, fabric, and many more. If it can be placed under the rollers, this machine can cut it. With my engineering mind, I needed numbers and proof that this is true. I found a study done by an independent lab that tested the precision, strength, and cutting ability between the Silhouette Cameo and the Cricut Explore Air.

More Precise Cut in More Detailed Designs

I also decided to use the Cricut because it can make smaller, more precise cuts. In the little time I have with my machine, I have already cut a complete sentence for the cover of an iPhone 8. I distrusted the machine, thinking that I could not make those small cuts. And by surprise, he did it without problems! Below is a picture of how the design looks.

Machine Design

The Cricut design I love how it looks, the colors (although the cameo has some beautiful pastel colors too), strategy, etc. Although we should not judge a machine by its cover, there is no doubt that aesthetics are important, especially if it is something that will be in your work area all day.

Bookmark Adapter

The Cricut marker cart can be used with different markers, not just those of the brand, since they have a traditional design, not like those of Silhouette, which are relatively small and chubby.

Make It Now¨ Proyectos Projects

In Cricut's design space, there is a category where you find complete projects where you only need to get the materials. The software indicates the materials, colors, working time, level of knowledge (whether advanced or beginner) up to the indications. Look at this beautiful detail for Valentine's Day. It's just a matter of looking for the materials, press GO, and follow the instructions.

Chapter 3:
Unboxing The Cricut Maker Machine

The Cricut Maker Machine

In August 2017, Cricut launched the Cricut Maker, adding it to highly efficient cutting machines. The Cricut Maker is designed to work at faster speeds and cut thicker materials. This makes it ideal for both personal and commercial use.

The Cricut Maker allows you to use various tools to work on a wide range of materials like basswood, balsa wood, fabric, leather, vinyl, felt, and paper. The Cricut Maker even allows you to cut patterns on fabrics for your projects. With accessories like embossing tips, a wavy blade, and the rotating blade, every project is made easy. You can also get more accessories depending on what project you are working on.

Unboxing the Cricut Maker Machine

When you buy the Cricut Maker, you get the following in the packaging. While the content may vary depending on which store or country you buy from, the following items are largely constant in every Cricut Maker box.

Each box contains the Cricut Maker machine and the following accessories:

- Rotary Blade and its Drive Housing
- Fine-Point Pen
- FabricGrip™ Mat 12" x 12" for working on fabrics.
- LightGrip™ Mat 12" x 12" for working with other materials.
- Premium Fine-Point Blade and its Housing (this blade comes pre-installed in the B clamp).
- A welcome book
- The Cricut Maker Quick Start Guide
- USB cables
- Power adapter
- Materials to use for your first project.

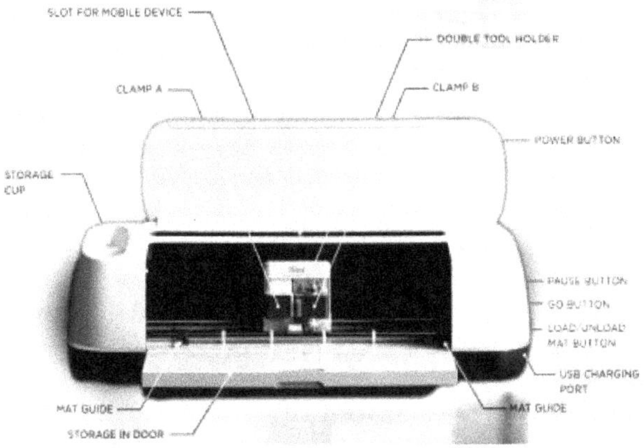

Different parts of the Cricut maker The Tool Cup:

The tool cup is a product of design ingenuity. It provides a place to keep your markers, pens, pencils, and scissors while working. This lets you have an organized workspace that is tidy and uncluttered.

Open Button:

This button opens up the machine to begin loading the cutting mat and cutting operations. It is advisable to close the machine when not in use to protect it from dust and dirt. Just push the Open button, and the machine unfolds like a blooming petal.

Clamp

The clamp works by keeping the blade in place to cut with high levels of accuracy. The Cricut Maker has two clamps, one for each blade housing.

Tray

The tray is where you place the cutting mat and the materials you want to cut.

Mat Guides

The Mat Guides are found on each side of the tray. The guides keep the mat in place. They roll in and out to push the cutting mat to be cut.

Storage Compartments

The storage material provides you with space to store your tools and materials as you work. It allows you to have your stuff handy and within reach.

USB Port:

The USB port lets you charge up your mobile device.

Power Port:

This is where the power adapter is plugged into.

Power Button:

This button powers up the Cricut Maker. You also use this button to shut down the machine.

Smart Device Slot

This is an improvement on previous Cricut Devices. This slot allows you to keep your tablet or smartphone firmly in place as you work. This is especially useful if you are using Cricut Design Space on your phone or iPad.

Features of the Cricut Maker Wide Range of Materials

The new Cricut Maker cuts most of the materials you will work with. It works well with a broader range of craft materials than previous cutting machines.

Expandable Tool Sets

You also have more options when it comes to the tools you can use. There are more tools at your fingertips, and more effects you can create with those tools. With the Cricut Maker, you have tools such as

Rotary Blade

The rotary blade works by carrying complex movements such as gliding and rolling as it cuts. The rotary cutter cuts fast and with high precision. This blade can also cut fabrics.

Knife Blade

This blade is perfect for deep cuts. It easily cuts through stronger materials like mat board and balsa wood.

QuickSwap Tools

Another feature of the Cricut Maker is that it allows you to switch tools easily using the QuickSwap Tools feature.

Adaptive Tool System

The Cricut Maker uses the smart Adaptive Tool System to control the blade direction while adding up to ten times cutting power.

The Cricut Maker also comes with access to a Digital Sewing pattern library with hundreds of different loading patterns. You also get access to practices from established brands such as Simplicity and Riley Blake. Design Space is available to Cricut Maker users, allows for Offline Mode use, and has unique features like the Print Then Cut feature. Other features include the SnapMat feature. Cricut Design Space is available for iOS and Android mobile devices and tablets and Windows and Mac computers.

With the Cricut Maker, you can upload your designs, fonts for use at no cost, and different formats. You also have 50 ready-to-make projects and 25 digital sewing patterns you can use.

Now that you have a good idea of what your machine is capable of, the next thing you need to do is to set it up. Where you set up your machine and how you do it determines how well you enjoy your machine. When setting up, consider placing your machine with adequate lighting, a power socket nearby, and ergonomics. In simple terms, put your machine where you'll be comfortable working with it.

The cartridge slot can be found in the front of the Cricut machine. However, you must ensure the cartridge title is in accordance with the one on the keypad overlay. The first way we will show you how to set up your machine if you're working with an Android or an iOS, we will go step by step to go smoothly and without repeating steps.

You will need to pair your device (either Android or iOS) with your machine. You are going to need to utilize your Bluetooth to do this.

Download the Design Space App. You will need to install it into your machine as well.

Hit the button that says the menu.

Select the button that says machine setup and app overview. Now, you are going to select the button that says a new machine setup. There are going to be on-screen promptings that will help you to complete the setup. Just be sure that you are following them accurately, and if you can't go quickly, that's fine. Go at the pace that you're comfortable with to make sure that you understand what it is they want from you. Going slower will help eliminate mistakes, but if you do make mistakes, don't feel bad. This happens to people every day, and it's easily fixable. You will know that you've done everything right and correctly when telling you that it's time to do your first project. Once this happens, you know that your setup is complete. Once you've done this, it's time to get crafting!

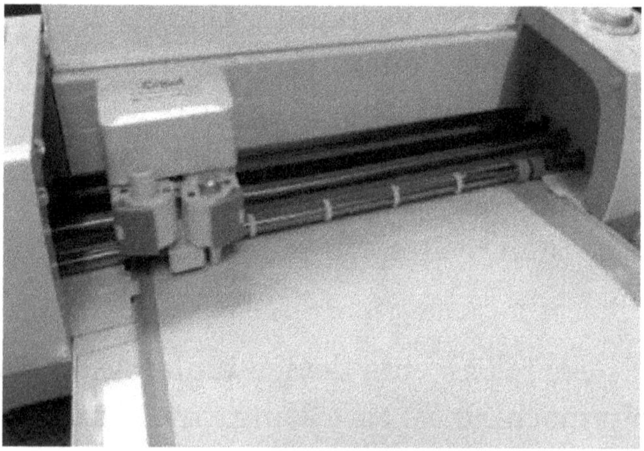

An additional tip for you is that your machine is already automatically registered during the setup. If you don't complete the setup when you connect your device, you need to reconnect it. Because the machine has to be registered, this is something that you can't miss.

If you're working with a Windows or a Mac, you will need to follow these following instructions to make your machine work. This setup is easy as well and offers one less step than the instructions above. Since Macs are considered newer, this will be a little bit different from the instructions above.

Plugin your machine

Don't turn your machine on or try to without plugging it in first.

Power the machine on

Connect your machine to your computer. You are going to do this in two different fashions. This is an excellent option because you can choose which option is the best for you. Either of these ways will work well; it's just whatever you would like it to be.

Go to the website design.cricut.com/setup in your browser because this will be how you are going to finish your set up. From this step, you will complete your setup by making sure you are observing the instructions.

You need to follow the on-screen prompts and instructions to sign in and create your ID. This will be your Cricut ID for the future.

Download the Design Space app and install it on the device. This will have so much benefit for you later as this is where you will gain a lot of benefits.

Don't forget that you will need to plugin when it prompts you to do so.

You will see that you did everything right and correctly when it wants you to do your first project. Once you reach this step, your machine is ready to go, and you can make the practice project so that you can get used to your machine and how it works without wasting materials.

The same tip above about the registration applies here too. If you have a problem setting up on any of the systems, you can come back to this site so that you can be able to set it up without trouble or issues. Having the website tell you what you need to do, and having the prompts is a great helper to new users or older users of the machine as they offer help pages. With simple steps and back up help, starting your device is easy as can be, which greatly benefits the user. These models are made to be as user-friendly as possible to eliminate the issues that other companies have when their items are being set up.

By now, you should have the app installed on your phone or the software already running on your laptop or desktop computer. If you have not yet, you better do so now because things are about to get a lot more serious. It will help if you have Cricut Design Space in front of you to experiment with what we will be discussing.

What's more, you should do this, especially if you are a beginner. Perhaps intermediaries or somewhat experienced users can afford not to have the app or software in front of them right now.

Downloading/Installing

Do you know where to get the Cricut Design Space? Well, if you are on a desktop or Personal Computer, navigate to https://design.cricut.com.

If your smartphone runs on Android OS, enter the Play Store and use the same search term. Remember that downloading or installing this is entirely free of charge. Also, bear in mind that you will need a Cricut ID to sign in. This you can also get for free, even if you do not have a Cricut. Simply follow the prompts provided.

Once you have entered your email and gotten your ID, you will be taken into the Cricut Design Space's primary domain. In this place, all of the magic happens. A quick tip: bookmark this page to your web toolbar so you can find it easily whenever you want to.

The Canvas you will be shown after - similar to a painter's whiteboard - is the ample space where all your designs and progress will reflect - this space has a full grid by default to allow you to see everything about a single work without having to pinch-zoom and un-pinch. Nevertheless, you can choose the appearance and measurements of the grid.

Smart guides And Shortcuts

So you want to try out your first design, and you happen to be stuck while trying to position something on your canvas correctly? This could happen in Cricut Design Space because the Smart Guides are just too smart for their good. Want to know what the guides are about?

Quick one: Smart Guides are a feature of the Android and iOS app version of the product. They are designed to help you when you want to position things in relation to other things. But that could not turn out or position the way you want it to. If you're going to turn this off on the app version, go to Settings - at the toolbar's bottom areas - and toggle the Smart Guides off.

Meanwhile, there's something about the desktop version of Cricut Design Space that makes it somewhat cool - it has some keyboard shortcuts that will come in handy. If you want to see them at any point of use, tap on the question mark key on your keyboard - Shift +. Shortcuts that will prove useful to you include the show hide menu, toggle grid, and select all options.

Other shortcuts also allow you to save and "save project as", undo - this is something you will be thankful for - redo, cut, copy, and paste. What's more, bring forward, send back, bring to front, send to back, and of course, delete.

If you are the kind of technophile who's more used to the keyboard than clicking on a mouse, you will find these shortcuts super useful.

Power ON your Cricut machine

Use the USB cable to connect your computer and your Cricut machine. Alternatively, connect via Bluetooth

Go to your internet browser and go to www.design.cricut.com

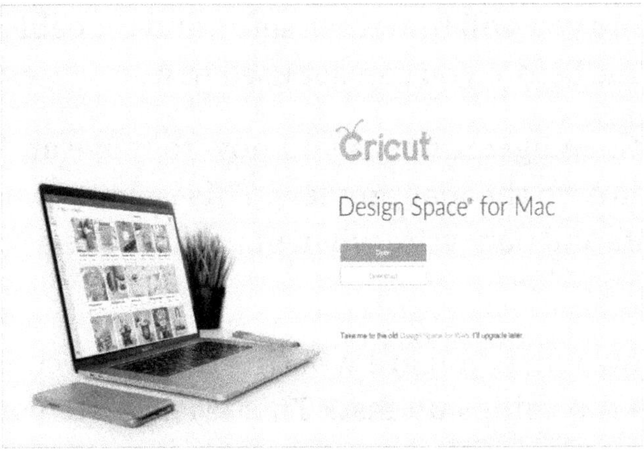

Navigate to setup

Follow to instructions on your screen to create your Cricut ID or sign in if you already have one.

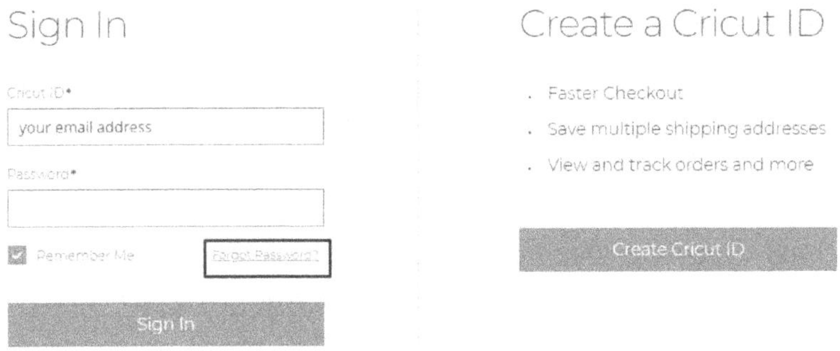

Download the Design Space plugin when you are requested to do so.

How to Position Items on the Cricut Canvas

Not to discourage anyone, but it can take you several months of using the Cricut Design Space almost every day before you will find this useful, and probably a little more time before you can get used to it.

This little nugget informs you how to move and rotate your items on the mat preview. This is done to position your cuts and pen write when you want or feel the need to.

You know when you are working on a project and just want to flip things up fast? This feature lets you do so quickly and effortlessly - well, almost (insert smirk emoticon here).

This comes significantly handy when you want to use up scraps and just spread them all over your canvas. If you are working on an addressed envelope, you can use this tool so that your letters reflect on the "write" side on the envelope. You may also want to reposition - do so by tapping and dragging an item on your canvas to a new location. Simple enough, isn't it?

On the desktop version, move the objects to another mat and conceal them altogether - just click on the three dots. They are not hard to find since they are virtually in your face. So, now you know how to best position those items to make your design all the easier.

Do You Want to Sync Your Colors?

Even a newbie designer knows the essence and impact of colors. In Cricut Design Space, you need to make sure your colors are happy and in harmony, just like every other artwork.

If you have ever worked on a design that had up to five different pink shades that all needed to be cut out on separate pieces of paper or vinyl, you would understand what we are talking about. If not, you will realize soon too.

If you do not know or probably forgot how it feels, it can be very frustrating. It becomes ironic when you develop a red face that matches the moment.

USEFUL TIPS

Always replace Pen Lids after use

When working with pens or markers, always replace the lids after use. This protects the tips of your pens from getting damaged and prevents the ink from being damaged.

Check to ensure your toolset is complete

Before packing up after a work session, ensure that all tools in a toolset are complete. It is vital that before you put away a toolset in storage, you ensure every blade or tip is accounted for. This helps keeps your workspace safe and prevent losses. Misplaced blades can easily cause injuries.

Keep the plastic mat covers

Your mat will come with a transparent plastic cover. You will be tempted to discard it. Don't. It helps keep the cutting mat free from dirt and dust when you use it when storing your cutting mat.

Use a Lint cleaner to remove debris

If you use your cutting mat regularly, it is easy for debris to stick to the mat. Continuous accumulation of such makes it difficult for the material to remain stuck to the mat while cutting. Rolling a lint cleaner over the mat helps rove tiny pieces of debris that make it difficult for materials to stick. This works far better than weeding out the dirt pieces individually.

Use spray cleaners to clean your cutting Mat

Several spray cleaners are available that are strong enough to remove the stubborn dirt yet mild enough not to weaken the adhesive nature of the mat. You just have to spray it and scrape off the dirt.

Use old gift cards or credit cards to scrape the mat

Old gift cards are beneficial in scraping off dirt still attached to the mat. When attaching materials to the cutting mat, bubbles may pop up. The old cards are useful in smoothening over the bubbles.

Label your cutting mat

Label your mat so that you don't load it the wrong way. Without marking which side goes in, you will put it in the wrong way several times mistakenly. Keeping it would forestall any errors.

De-tacking your cutting mat

Upon first use of your cutting mat, you'll notice it is very sticky. It is often so moist that it can easily damage your projects. De-tacking is the process of making your cutting mat less sticky by priming it. When you de-tack your cutting mat properly, you can easily detach projects without any damage to them whatsoever. Here is a simple way to de-tack your cutting mat.

- Place a clean, dry fabric over the cutting mat.
- Press it firmly until it sticks.
- Gently pull it off.
- Repeat the process three or four times until it is significantly less sticky.

You can test if the cutting mat is well primed by placing a sheet of paper on it and then gently pulling it off. If the paper comes off without any tears, the cutting mat is well primed. If the paper tears, you will have to repeat the de-tacking process.

Making Your Cutting Mat Sticky Again

Use a lint roller to remove debris and pieces of dirt.

Clean the mat with a spray cleaner and allow it to dry.

Tape the edges of the mat with some painters' tape so that the mat edges do not get sticky and stick to your Cricut Maker rollers.

Get a spray adhesive and spray the cutting mat.

Allow the cutting mat to dry overnight.

Prime the cutting mat if adhesive applied on the mat turns out too strong.

The first step in setting up a Cricut is to determine where the machine will be best located. Ideally, the machine will be placed near a computer or tablet, a power source, and where it has room to work. Even if the machine does not require to be hooked up to a computer, try to keep it within reach to make the process of loading and unloading easier.

Spacing around and above the machine should also be considered. A minimum of 10 inches to the front and back is ideal for the mats to move around as needed. The space in front of the machine should be flat and level with the machine, so the mats lay flat. If the mats are not flat, some materials will not work well. A minimum of 12 inches above the machine is desired, so tools can be inserted under the lid quickly.

The installation of a newer Cricut machine can be done in minimal steps. After completing all the installation steps, you will start with a free trial of Cricut Access, which gives access to additional projects and images. This trial cannot be paused, so make sure you use the time optimally.

To begin:

Turn on the machine after it is connected to the power source.

Use Bluetooth or the USB cable to connect the machine to the computer or your device.

To set up a Cricut on a Mac or Window's computer.

Go to the website for setup: https://design.cricut.com/setup

If you do not have a Cricut.com account, create one to log in, or use your account information to log into Cricut.com

When prompted, the Design Space plug-in should be downloaded and installed on the computer.

Cricut Access will ask for acceptance of the terms of use to activate the free trial.

When the prompt to make the first cut appears to set up is complete.

To set up a Cricut on an iOS device:

Visit the App Store and download the Design Space app.

Create a Cricut.com account or log into your account once the app is launched, and it prompts the login.

Open the menu and tap "Machine Setup and App Overview."

Select "New Machine Setup."

Finish the setup by following the screen prompts.

When the prompt to make the first project appears to set up is complete.

If the machine does not get set up entirely during the first time it is connected, in the Design Space account menu, go to "New Machine Setup" or visit cricut.com/setup after the machine is reconnected the computer or device. Follow the prompts to complete the setup process.

If you have any problems or the instructions are not clear; I advise you to visit the main Cricut website on how to set up your machine:

http://help.cricut.com/help/manuals

Introduction to Cutting

There are many materials a Cricut can cut. Vinyl is one of the most popular items people like to use. There is also a wide range of vinyl types. Cricut claims there are over 100 types of materials the machine can cut. Some of the top materials include:

- Iron-on
- Paper
- Vinyl
- Fabric
- Plastic

Other items include crafting materials, like foam, paper with glitter, washi tape, and thick materials like woods, leather, and magnets. Repurposed materials are another option and are a cheap and environmentally friendly option. Some of the things people have used include aluminum from cans, cardboard from cereal boxes, and chipboard.

When beginning a project, always do a test cut on a scrap of material. Do not use the final material, which is often more expensive, in case there is a problem with the design. Try to choose a scrap material similar in weight and texture to your final material for accuracy.

Many people skip this step but end up regretting it when the material is ruined. Problems can include the cutting pressure is too hard and slices the mat, destroying the cutting mat, or at the very least, an extra cut may be required for success.

This process shouldn't take a long time, but it can save a lot of time and money afterward if a design mistake has been made.

Cutting with Fabrics

Fabric is a challenging medium to cut on for most Cricut machines, mainly because there are so many types of fabric to choose from. This material usually requires a lot of trial and error to discover what works best. Sometimes a material will cut fine while other times, it will snag and drag over the cutting mat.

A tip for working with fabric, particularly thin fabrics, uses a bonding material, so the fabric sticks to the cutting mat. Use a roller or brayer to adhere to the mat.

If bonding is not an option, at least use stiff interfacing to help. Again, test cuts are essential in all projects, but they are especially important when working with fabrics.

Cutting with Vinyl

After preparing and reviewing a project to be cut, when it is sent to the machine for cutting, make sure to adjust the machine's Smart Dial to the appropriate materials, for example, vinyl. Older machines may not have this material listed. It is best to review tutorials online for suggestions on how to modify an older machine to work with this material. If working with iron-on vinyl, turn the "Mirror" switch on to ensure it prints correctly.

Select the mat that the vinyl will be cut on and adhere the vinyl to the mat, placing the paper located on the back of the vinyl facing down on the mat and put it in the machine to be cut.

If there are multiple colors or vinyl to be cut, gently peel the finished, cut vinyl from the mat, and adhere to the next piece. Weeding may be required for the background vinyl before attaching it to the project.

Chapter 4: Design Space

WHAT IS THE DESIGN SPACE?

Design Space is the free design software that comes with each of the Cricut machines. It is very user-friendly and, as such, is easy to use. It is a cloud-based software solution that means that all project files are accessible on any device from anywhere you have Internet access.

Design Space is compatible with Windows, MAC, iOS, and Android, giving a wide range of device options to work on. Most of the newer Cricut machines also have Bluetooth options, making it easy to connect with mobile devices.

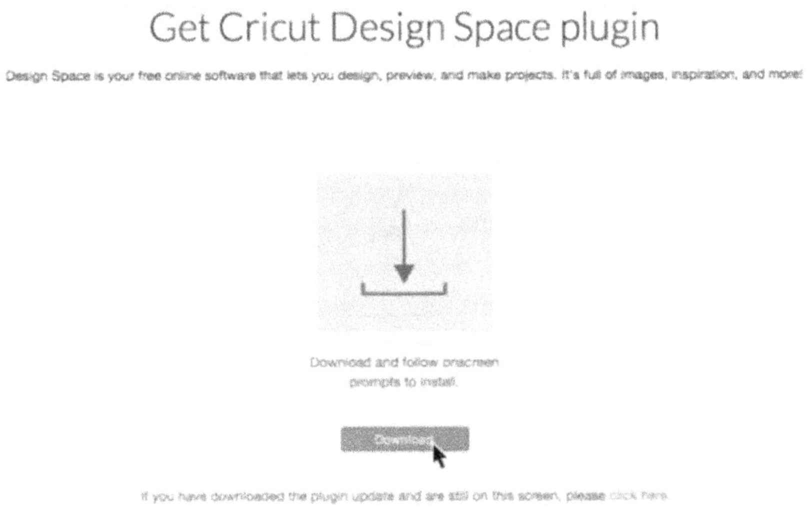

INSTALL THE DESIGN SPACE TO YOUR COMPUTER

To download the Design Space plugin and install it, it is super simple. To know that your setup process is complete is when you are prompted to start your first project.

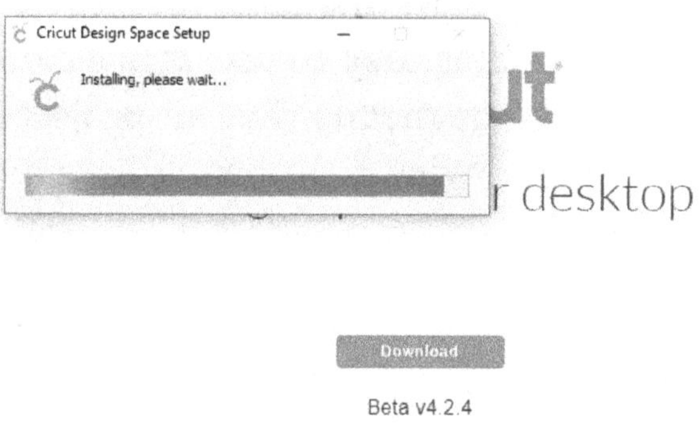

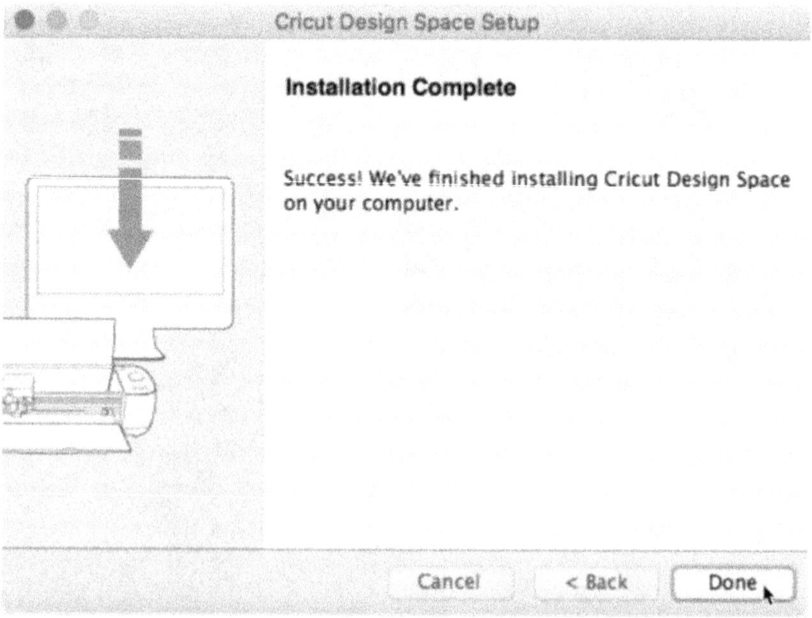

For iOS/Android

Use the power outlet to plug your Cricut machine.

Power ON your Cricut machine

Pair your Cricut machine with your iOS or Android device via Bluetooth

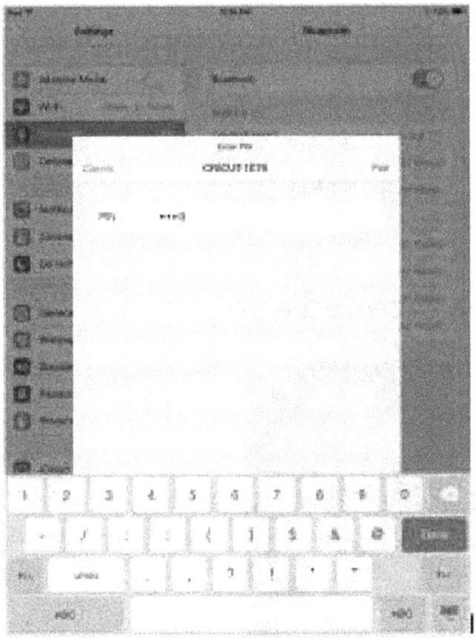

Download the Design Space plugin and install it.

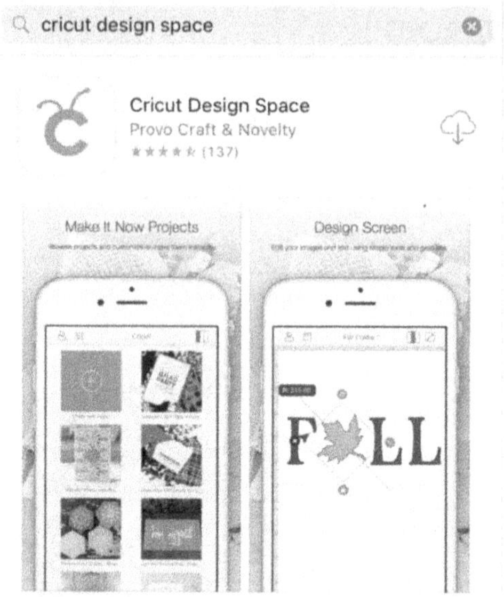

Launch the downloaded app

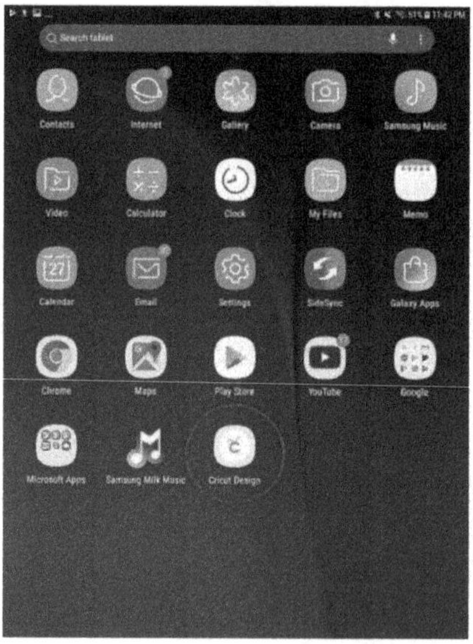
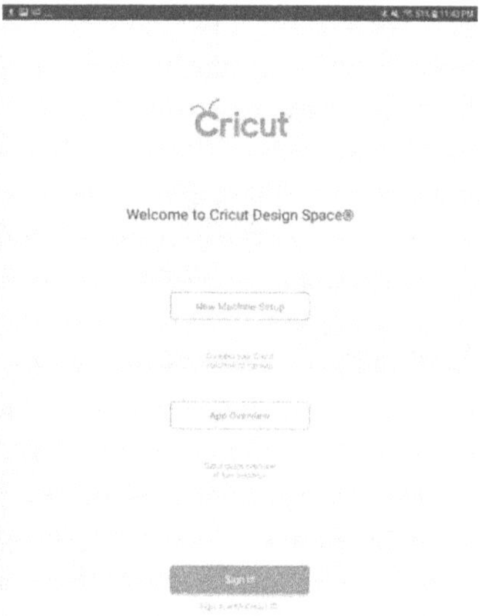

Create a Cricut ID to sign in and if you have one already, use it to sign in

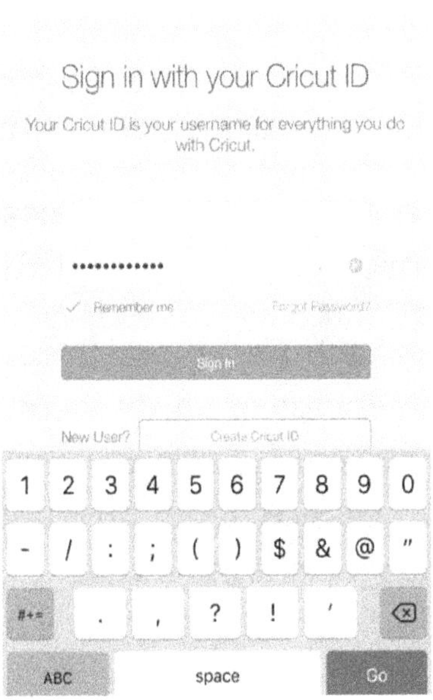

Select the menu and tap Machine Setup & App Overview

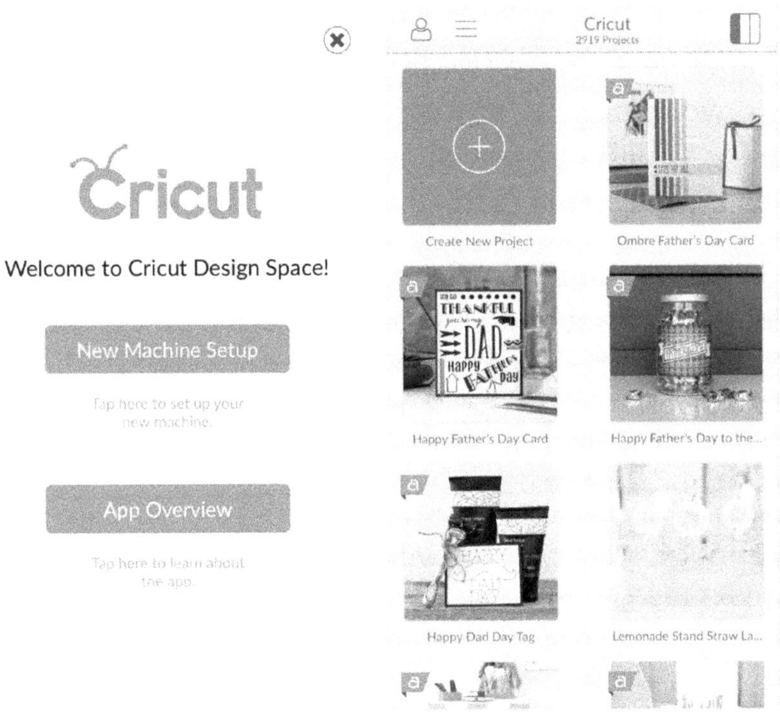

Tap New Machine Setup

Follow the prompts on your screen to finish the setup

Again, to know that your setup process is complete is when you are prompted to start your first project.

Note that your machine is registered automatically during the setup process of your Cricut machine. There is no cause for alarm if, for any reason, you did not complete the process when you first connect your computer to your Cricut machine. Go to step 5 and continue from there using the onscreen instructions.

Workspace/Canvas

The workspace is where you will position images, shapes, text, etc. to create your projects. Cricut refers to the workspace as the canvas, as it is where you will make your works of art. It is the largest part of the workspace and is in the middle of the screen.

The canvas consists of a grid representing inches as the default setting and runs across from 0 to 60, which is the x-axis. The y-axis runs from 0 down to 60.

The workspace has a ruler along the top and down the left-hand side of it.

Although you can do oversized projects and lay them out on the screen, the Cricut machines generally use 12" x 12" cutting mats. This means that any bigger projects than 12" x 12" will need to be cut in stages.

ZOOM CONTROL

Located on the bottom of the canvas, you will find the zoom control. It is not visible until you roll the mouse over it.

This is a convenient tool for larger projects as it allows you to zoom into the project to see the bigger picture.

DESIGN PANEL

The design panel is located to the left of the canvas. It is where you can reset or create new projects, select templates, images, shapes, text, or upload your ideas.

The design panel consists of the following menu options (from top to bottom):

New

The 'New' menu option refreshes the canvas to start a new project. It is like putting a brand-new canvas on an easel to create an new painting.

Templates

The 'Template' option will place an outline on the screen of various items to better visualize the project. For instance, if you were going to design T-Shirt logos, you would choose the 'Template' option and search for a T-Shirt. A template offering the front and back views of a T-Shirt will show on the canvas. You can customize some of these templates' size and shape, depending on the template's characteristics. It is good to note, however, that templates do not cut or print out. They are only for display purposes.

Projects

Cricut has libraries full of ready-to-create projects that you can buy to help you get started. The wonderful thing about these projects is that you can customize them. For Cricut beginners, they are a great way to learn about using various shapes and designs.

Images

Cricut comes loaded with libraries of various images. There are both free images and those that you have to buy. But the price is minimal, and if you do not have the time to create your own, they can be instrumental. You can also buy cartridges that contain different image libraries.

Text

To put text on the screen, choose the 'Text' option. Cricut comes with system fonts, fonts that can be purchased, and some free Cricut fonts.

Shapes

The 'Shapes' option allows you to use shapes on the canvas. There are quite a few standard shapes offered that you could learn to manipulate to create additional ones as you get more familiar with Cricut. The score lines are used to hold marks for folding projects such as cards or gift boxes. They mark the fold lines.

Upload

Upload is where you can upload your projects, designs, and images, or projects that you may have purchased or downloaded from the various websites that offer already-made projects.

HEADER BAR

The header bar is the dark grey bar at the top of the canvas. This bar holds the following options and information:

Three horizontal bars

When clicked, the three bars drop down into a menu of options. These options are for setting up the machine, changing basic software settings, legal notices, managing custom materials, and so on.

Canvas

The Canvas option helps you navigate back to the current canvas from the Home Screen, images, templates, etc.

Page Title

The page title will start as 'Untitled' for new projects until they are saved. If you open a saved project, the name of that project is reflected.

My Projects

The 'My Projects' option is a shortcut to open up previously saved projects.

Save

The 'Save' option is a shortcut to use when you want to save your project. You should keep your projects every few minutes or when you have completed a section of a project.

Make It

The 'Make It' green button is the 'Go' button to send your project to the pre-cut phase. Here, you can check the boards and the way that the project is going to be cut. From this phase, you will send the project to inkjet for a print and cut or to the Cricut to be cut. This is where you will set up custom materials and blade selection, depth, etc. for the machine.

Edit Bar

The edit bar remains grayed out until an image, shape, template, or text is placed on the canvas. It is located directly beneath the header bar, but now on top of the canvas.

The selected object on the canvas determines the options on the edit bar:

Templates

When you use a template, the edit bar will tell you if you can adjust the template. The system predetermines these, and you will need to make your selection based on what the template has been designed with. The edit bar will list the changes you can make; for instance, a T-Shirt template gives the option of 'Type', 'Size', and 'Color.'

Common options

There are some standard options that both text and images used on the edit bar. These are options are:

Undo

This will undo the latest edit, addition, or deletion.

Redo

This will redo something that has recently been undone.

Linetype

This option tells the Cricut to use a blade to 'Cut', 'Draw' with a pen, or use the Scoring stylus or wheel to create a score line. You can 'Deboss' with the debossing tip, 'Engrave' with the engraving tool, and change a line to perforated, which is 'Perf' or wavy 'Wave'. These are add-on tools to use with the Cricut.

Linetype Swatch

This is the little box next to the 'Linetype.' When you click on the box, it will bring up a color swatch. This will change the color of the object selected on the screen.

Fill

The 'Fill' option is used for cutting or printing. This option tells Design Space where to send the project to first. It is used for print and cut projects.

Fill Swatch

This will change the fill of the object selected on the screen.

Select All/Deselect

This is used to select all of the objects on the screen at once. When used, the option will change to 'Deselect'.

Edit

The 'Edit' option is where you will find the editing options such as 'Cut', 'Copy', and 'Paste'.

Align

The 'Align' function helps align objects with the top, bottom, center, left, right, etc. It can also be used to distribute selected objects on the screen evenly.

Arrange

The 'Arrange' function changes how objects appear on the screen when they are layered on top of each other.

There is a stacking order to objects when they are layered on the screen. 'Send to Back' sends the selected object to the bottom of the layer stack. 'Move Backwards' moves the selected object one layer back. 'Send to Front' sends the selected object to the top of the layer. 'Move Forward' sends the selected object one layer forward.

Flip

This option is used to flip the image horizontally or vertically to create a shadow image or mirrored image.

Size

You can change the selected objects' size on the screen by selecting them and dragging them with the mouse. This option allows you to size the chosen item or entire text box more accurately if you need an exact size. You can set the width and height of an unlocked object. Locked objects will set to scale.

Rotate

This option rotates the selected object by the degree you set in the box.

Position

You can move selected objects around the screen by selecting them and dragging them with the mouse. For more accurate positioning, you can set the x-axis and y-axis position in these boxes.

Font

There are different types of fonts to choose from. Some are free, and some can be purchased. The system will also pick up the system fonts you have installed on the device you are working on.

Style

This option allows you to change the style of the font to Bold, Italic, Underline, Bold and Underline Regular or Writing.

Font Size

Set the font to the necessary size.

Letter Space

This option is used to increase or decrease the space between letters in a word.

Layers Panel

The layers panel is located to the right of the canvas. This shows the different layers of an object. It has a few useful tools that you will need when you are creating your projects.

Color Sync Panel

The color sync panel can be found on the right-hand side of the canvas and is the tab next to the layers panel.

This panel is useful when working with multiple colors to cut down on the number of materials the project will call for.

Chapter 5: A Guide To Tools And Accessories For Work With Cricut Maker Machine

TOOLS AND ACCESSORIES OF A CRICUT MAKER

Cricut has much to offer in the way of tools and accessories. There are machines they offer to suit different crafting purposes, which have their accessories and tools.

For the Cricut cutting machines, here is what's available:

Cricut Maker Cutting Blades

In addition to the Explore Cutting blade, the Cricut Maker has additional cutting blades that allow for intricate cutting details on various materials.

The Cricut Maker comes with one additional blade, the revolutionary rotary cutting blade for cutting all sorts of fabrics. Unlike the average rotary cutter, this one lasts far longer because it avoids the nicks that typically come with its line of duty. You can buy additional blades individually, but one blade should last throughout multiple projects.

Cutting Mats

Cricut cutting mats come in a variety of sizes and degrees of stickiness. Depending on what material you are using, you will want less or more stickiness on your mat to hold the material in place while cutting.

The Cricut Weeder

The weeder tool, which looks similar to a dental pick, is used for removing negative space from a vinyl project. This weeder tool is a must when doing any type of project that involves vinyl. Trying to get rid of access vinyl is nearly impossible without a weeder, especially with materials like glitter iron-on. A weeder is a useful tool for any type of project using adhesives. Instead of picking up the adhesive with your fingertips, user the weeder tool, and keep your fingers sticky mess-free!

The Cricut Scraper

The Circuit Scraper tool is essential (and a lifesaver!) when you need to rid your cutting mat of excess negative bits. This tool typically works best with paper, such as cardstock, but other materials can easily be scraped up as well. Use the mat's flexibility to your advantage as you scrap the bits off the mat to ensure you are not scraping up the adhesive on the mat as well. You can also use the Cricut Scraper as a score line holder, which allows you to fold over the scoreline with a nice crisp edge. It can also be used as a burnishing tool for Cricuttransfer tape. It will allow seamless separation of the transfer tape from the backing.

The Cricut Spatula

A spatula is a must-have tool for a crafter who works with a lot of paper. Pulling the paper off of a Cricut cut mat can result in a lot of tearing and paper curling if you are not diligent and mindful when removing it. The spatula is thinly designed to slip right under the paper, allowing you to ease it off the mat carefully. Be sure to clean it often as it is likely to get the adhesive build upon it after multiple uses. It can also be used as a scraper if your scraper tool is not readily available!

Scissors

These sharp tools come in handy more often than you can know with Cricut projects. Having a dedicated pair makes it so much easier to complete your projects.

Craft Tweezers

These reverse-action tweezers have a firm grip, precise points, and alleviate cramping after prolonged use.

Spatula

Sometimes you feel like you need an extra set of hands when you're peeling or laying down a project. This tool gives you that extra support and maneuverability where you need it.

Scoring Stylus

This tool can be loaded into clamp A in your Cricut machine. This will allow the machine to draw deep lines into your project to give it texture or a precise folding point. This same effect can be achieved with other tools on the market, but Cricut makes it simpler and faster with this accessory.

Portable Trimmer

This is a precision cutting tool that allows you to get fast, crisp, straight cuts on your projects 100% of the time. Other versions of this product are available on the market, so keep your eye out for ones with great reviews and a low price point.

Rotary Cutting Kit

This kit includes a gridded cutting mat and a rotary cutting tool. Cuts are fast, sharp, and precise. This is far from the only rotary tool available on the market, and it's great for cutting fabric and scrapbook pieces.

XL Scraper/Burnishing Tool

This provides a level of control that cannot be beaten. It exerts pressure evenly and helps to eliminate uneven layering and air bubbles. This tool comes very highly recommended by the community of users.

Paper Crafting Set

If you're mainly into papercraft, you will find the edge distresser, quilling tool, piercing tool, and craft mat in this set to be entire to your liking. Quilling or paper filigree art is gaining popularity these days. These are some of the best tools available for that craft.

TrueControl Knife

This is a precision blade that is comparable to XACTO in quality and type. For more precise freehand cuts, this knife is beneficial at any crafting station.

Cricut Explore Wireless Bluetooth Adapter

This product is to help your Cricut Explore machine connect with Bluetooth to your computer or device. The Cricut Maker has this capability built-in, but it can be added to your Explore machine as well.

Deep-Point Replacement Blades

These help your Cricut machine to make more precise cuts with thicker materials!

Bonded Fabric Blades

These blades are meant to retain their extremely sharp point, cut after cut into fabric in your machine!

Replacement Blades

Different purposes like debossing, engraving, perforation, and more, can be purchased from Cricut as well. These are specifically for the Cricut Maker model, whereas the replacement blades specified above are for the Cricut Explore models.

The Cricut Easy press

Suppose you begin to venture into iron-on projects and want to upgrade from a traditional iron and ironing board. In that case, the Cricut Easy press is the right way to go. It will make projects so much easier than using a traditional iron. The Cricut Easy Press is known to help keep them adhered for longer, essentially no more peeling of designs after one or two uses and washes. The Easy press also takes all of the guesswork out of the right amount of contact time and temperature. You will not run the risk of burning your transfer paper or fabric!

The Cricut Brightpad

The lightweight and low-profile design of the Cricut Brightpad reduces eyestrain while making crafting easier. It is designed to illuminate fine lines for tracing, cut lines for weeding, and so much more! It is thin and lightweight, which allows for durable transportation. BrightPad makes crafting more enjoyable with its adjustable, evenly lit surface. The bright LED lights can be adjusted depending on the workspace. The only downfall to this accessory is that it must be plugged in while it is used. It does not contain a rechargeable battery.

The Cricut Cuttlebug Machine

The Cricut Cuttlebug is an embossing and dies cutting machine that offers portability and versatility in cutting and embossing a wide variety of materials. This machine gives professional-looking results with clean, crisp, and deep embosses. This machine goes beyond paper, allowing you to emboss tissue paper, foils, thin leather, and more!

Chapter 6:
A Guide To Materials

The capabilities of your Cricut Machine are influenced by the blades you are using (or can use with it). Depending on the blades you are using, you can cut more or fewer materials. Using the Cricut Explore Family machines you can cut plenty of materials, most of them with the Premium Fine-Point Blade. Of course, when cutting the materials, you need to modify the cut pressure. If you have issues cutting that specific material and increasing the pressure doesn't solve the issues, you may need to adjust the blade depth.

The type of materials you will choose for your cut will significantly depend on the kind of projects you want to engage in. Some of these materials work with different blades and can be used with more than one Cricut blade—this makes them be the essential materials associated with Cricut cutting and are the primary materials for your Cricut Explore machine.

To be more organized, we will mention some of them by category. You may be familiar with some of them as a beginner. However, you can pick up new materials from these categories and start trying them out on new projects.

Paper and Cardstock

It seems somewhat necessary to start with this category because they are the most popularly used class material when designing. They have over thirty-five different kinds of materials under them, making them the category with the highest number of resources.

Paper is another primary material you can use for cutting. You can make homemade greeting cards and envelopes from cutting paper with different designs. You can always choose from various types of paper from corrugated cardboard, kraft paper, foil, glitter paper, and many more.

Types of Paper or Cardboard:

- Construction paper
- Cardstock
- Kraft board
- Metallic paper
- Copy paper
- Transfer Tape

This is a clear, medium-strength adhesive tape that comes in sheets. This is an invaluable step in the process. We have some tips for getting the most out of your transfer tape and choosing a transfer tape that will come in the quantity and power that is right for you and your projects.

I will tell you that the Cricut brand transfer tape comes in a single, rolled 12" x 48" sheet. You can cut pieces to your liking and use them multiple times before disposing of them. These sheets from Cricut are currently $8.99 at a local crafting retailer, while other brands offer a 12" roll of six to ten feet for a similar price.

While transfer tape is an integral part of the process of using your Cricut machine, the brand is not nearly as important. Do some shopping around, find a sample size that works for you and your price point, and get started!

Like with any new type of crafting project, it will take some time to get used to the supplies and products and find the things that really work the best.

Now that a lot has been said about different types of materials used on Cricut machines, you should be getting inspired to try out new different projects with these materials. However, only a beginner would stop here. We're not even close to unfolding the fantastic parts of the usage of Cricut machines. You will get to know much later on in this book about Cricut machines' capabilities and what you can do with them on an advanced level. Buckle up!

Vinyl

Professionals use vinyl materials a lot because they find it very useful and outstanding for making graphics, stencils, decals, signs, etc. There are about 11 materials made from vinyl that can be used on Cricut machines.

Iron-On

This is also a vinyl product, but with a different framework. Some people know it as heat transfer vinyl. You can use this type of vinyl to design and decorate tote bags, T-shirts, caps, and other clothing items. There are around nine iron-on materials that are usable on Cricut machines.

Iron-on vinyl is also one of the treasured materials to cut with Cricut Explore Air 2. You can use the iron-on vinyl to design bags, T-shirts, and any other items.

Types of Iron-on:

- Printable iron-on
- Glossy iron-on
- Metallic iron-on
- Foil iron-on

Fabric and Textiles

Fabrics are naturals on Cricut machines; they work seamlessly on almost every Cricut machine model. There are about 17 different materials under this category. However, they, most of the time, need stabilizers to be added before cutting.

Textile or Fabric is not an unusual material for some Cricut users. Still, because the variety of fabric available to choose from is so broad, it needs to be mentioned again because there are some techniques and materials that are a little more unusual. For example, cutting a lace-like pattern into fabrics can immediately add a color-palette of fancy lace to any project. This also makes it possible to have the same lace pattern on a variety of complimentary fabrics or colors.

There is a fabric blade specific to the fabric material; all you need to do is keep the fabric set in place on the settings dial. Cricut has some fabric materials online that you can cut with.

Types of Fabric

- Leather
- Canvas
- Duck cloth
- Silk
- Linen

Infusible Ink

Infusible ink is an exciting material from Cricut, which allows heat transfer on white and light-colored materials. It comes in different colors, patterns, and gradients and is designed to be resistant to peeling, flaking, and washing. It can be used for shirts, totes, coasters, etc.

Other Materials

Apart from all these five categories of materials we have discussed, several other unique materials can also be used on Cricut machines. Ranging from by-products of foils, woods, sheets, board, Bellum, chips, tapes, and too many other natural and artificial resources, at least 30 of them can be worked upon by Cricut machines. There are materials people think are not compatible with Cricut machines. Well, you'd be surprised.

Faux Leather and Leather

Depending on your preference, you can use either material. Despite what you choose, both are suitable materials to cut with the Cricut. Custom jewelry, like necklace pendants or earrings, are simple and stunning projects. These make beautiful and personal gifts or add the right touch to a particular outfit. Leather can also be used for making fashionable bracelets or cuffs.

Having an intricate cut on a lovely piece of leather or faux leather, the bracelet can be attached to an adjustable band. Hair bows or bows to add to clothing or handbags are also possible. For a hair bow, hot glue a hair clip to the back when the bow is finished. Use hot glue or another adhesive to attach the bow to clothing or a purse. Other hair accessories can be made, like flowers and other shapes.

These can be attached to hair clips, like the bows, or attached to hard or stretchy headbands. Leather can also be used as an embellishment to pillows or other fabrics, like chair backs, or made into manly coasters.

Felt

Felt is another multi-functional material that you can use for a host of projects. Because this item is relatively sturdy but has good flexibility, it is perfect for just about anything.

Besides, it comes in all different colors and is relatively inexpensive. Some unique projects that can be made from felt include garlands of multi-layered flowers to hang over a window curtain or above a bed, a textured phrase attached to a pillow, an interactive tree-shaped advent calendar, banners, ornaments, and cupcake or cake toppers.

Chapter 7: The Most Beautiful Workings That Can Be Done With Cricut Maker Machine

Custom Shirts

Custom shirts are incredibly comfortable. I like to use the iron-on vinyl because it's easy to work with. Just take your image and upload it to Design Space. Then, go to the canvas and find the image you want. Once you've selected the image, you click on the whitespace that will be cut – remember to get the insides, too. Ensure that you choose cut image, not print from the cut image, and then place it on the canvas to your liking size. Put the iron-on vinyl shiny side down, turn it on, and select iron-on from the menu. Choose to cut, and make sure you mirror the image. Once done, pull off the extra vinyl to remove the vinyl between the letters. There you go! A simple shirt.

Printable Stickers

Printable stickers are the next project. This is super simple and fun for parents and kids. The Explore Air 2 machine works best.

With this one, you want the print then cut feature, since it makes it much more comfortable. To begin, go to Design Space and download images of ice cream or whatever you want, or upload images of your own. You click on a new project, and on the left side that says images, you can choose the ones you like, and insert more of these on there.

From here, choose the image and flatten it, since this will make it into one piece rather than just a separate file for each. Resize as needed to make sure that they fit where you're putting them.

You can copy/paste each element until you're done. Once ready, press saves, and then chooses this as a print then cut image. Click the big button at the bottom that says make it. Make sure everything is right, then press continues, and from there, you can load the sticker paper into the machine. Make sure to adjust this to the right setting, which for sticker paper is the vinyl set. Put the paper into there and load them in, and when ready, the press goes – it will then cut the stickers as needed.

From there, take them out and decorate. You can use ice cream or whatever sticker image you want!

Personalized Pillows

Personalized pillows are another fun idea and are incredibly easy to make. To begin, you open up Design Space and choose a new project. From here, select the icon at the bottom of the screen itself, choosing your font. Type the words you want, and drag the text as needed to make it bigger.

You can also upload images, too, if you want to create a massive picture on the pillow itself.

From here, you want to press the attach button for each box to work together, and both are figured when centered.

You then press make it – and you want to turn to mirror on, since this will, again, be on iron-on vinyl. From here, you load the iron-on vinyl with the shiny side down, the press continues, follow the prompts, and make sure it's not jammed in, either.

Let the machine work its magic with cutting, and from there, you can press the weeding tool to get the middle areas out.

Set your temperature on the easy press for the right settings, then push it onto the material, ironing it on and letting it sit for 10 to 15 seconds. Let it cool, and then take the transfer sheet off.

There you have it! A simple pillow that works wonders for your crafting needs.

Cards!

To make this, you first want to open up Design Space, and from there, put your design in. If you like images of ice cream, then use that. If you want to make Christmas cards, you can do that, too. You can design whatever you want to on this.

Now, you'll then want to add the text. You can choose the font you want to use, and from there, write out the message on the card, such as "Merry Christmas." At this point, instead of choosing to cut, you want to choose the right option – the make it option. You don't have to mirror this, but check that your design fits appropriately on the cardstock itself. When choosing material for writing, make sure you choose the cardstock.

From there, insert your cardstock into the machine, and then, when ready, you can press go, and the Cricut machine will design your card. This may take a minute, but once it's done, you'll have an excellent card in place. It's super easy to use.

Cricut cards are a great personalized way to express yourself, creating a one-of-a-kind, sentimental piece for you to gift to friends and family.

Cricut Cake Toppers

Cricut cake toppers have a little bit of added difficulty because they require some precise scoring. The Cricut maker is probably the best piece of equipment for the job, and here, we'll tell you how to do it. The scoring tool is your best bet since this will make different shapes even more manageable, as well. You will want to make sure you have cardstock and the cutting mat, along with a fine-point blade for cutting. The tape is also handy for these.

First, go to Design Space and choose the rosettes you want. From there, the press makes it and follows the prompts. The single wheel will make one crease, and the double wheel will make a parallel wheel that will crease – perfect for specialty items. Plus, the double wheel is thicker, so it's easier to fold.

Once you score everything, you remove it and replace the scoring wheel with the fine-point blade.

From here, you simply fold everything and just follow the line. This should make the rosette, and you can then use contrasting centers and create many of these to form a lovely backdrop.

Cricut Gift Bags

Remember to put the foil poster board face-down on the mat itself, to help prevent the material from cracking and showing through to the white backdrop when you fold them together after you score them.

To make these, you want to implement the template you'd like to use in Design Space. From here, I do suggest cutting out the initial design first, and then putting it back in to create scoring lines, following the same steps. After that, you can then take your item and fold along the score lines and then use adhesive or glue to help put it all together. This is a great personalized way to do it but can be complicated to work with at first.

Cricut Fabric Coasters

Fabric coasters with a Cricut maker are great, and they need only a few supplies. These include the maker itself, cotton fabric, fusible fleece, a rotary cutting mat or some scissors, a sewing machine, and an iron.

Cut the fabric to about 12 inches to fit the cutting mat – if it's longer, you can hang it off, just be careful.

From here, go to Design Space, then click shapes and make a heart. You can do this with other shapes, too. Resize it to about 5 inches wide. Press makes it, and you'll want to make sure you create four copies. Press continue, and then choose medium fabrics similar to cotton. You then load the mat and cut, and then you do it again with the fusible fleece on the cutting mat, changing it to 4.75 inches. This time, when choosing the material, go to more, and then select fusible fleece. Cut the fusible fleece, and then attach these to the heart's back with the iron and repeat with the second.

Clip the curves, turn it inside out, and then fold in the edges and stitch it.

There you go – a fusible fleece heart coaster. It's a little bit more complicated, but it's worth trying out.

Giant Vinyl Stencils

Vinyl stencils are a good thing to create, too, but they can be challenging. Big vinyl stencils make for an excellent Cricut project, and you can use them in various places, including bedrooms for kids.

You only need the explore Air 2, the vinyl that works for it, a pallet, sander, and, of course, paint and brushes.

The first step is preparing the pallet for painting, or whatever surface you plan on using this for.

From here, you create the mermaid tail (or any other large image) in Design Space. Now, you'll learn immediately that big pieces are hard to cut and impossible to do all at once in Design Space.

What you do is section of each design accordingly, and removes any middle pieces. You can add square shapes to the image, slicing it into pieces to be cut on a cutting mat that fits.

At this point, you cut out the design by pressing make it, choosing your material, and working in sections.

From here, you put it on the surface that you're using, piecing this together with each line, and you should have one image after piecing it all together. Then, draw out the line on vinyl and then paint the initial design. For the second set of stencils, you can simply trace the first one and then paint the inside of them. At this point, you should have the design finished. When done, remove it very carefully.

And there you have it! More oversized stencils can be a bit of a project since it involves trying to use multiple designs all at once. Still, with the right care and the right designs, you'll be able to create whatever it is you need to in Design Space so you can get the results you're looking for.

Creative Ideas to Do on Your Cricut

Now that you know what a Cricut machine is and how to set it up, it is now time to delve into the best part of the Cricut—making your designs! We will look at the materials you can use, what can be cut, and what crafts can be made. In all honesty—the options are endless as crafters are continually coming up with new ideas and new craft using the Cricut, so each time, you'll find something new.

Cricut Paper Crafts

What do you need? You need some standard weight paper, or you can also use cardstock. Cricut has both these options, which you can purchase. You can use this, or you can use any paper you like. Here is a selection of ideas that you can kick start your Cricut papercrafts. Just click on the links of the specific craft to get more details:

Creating a 3D Paper Bouquet

Cricut is an excellent tool to make beautiful, one-of-a-kind paper bouquets simply because they have plenty of flower patterns you can choose from. You can make these paper bouquets using paper of any kind and in any color. Using different hues from the same color would be ideal because it gives you depth and texture.

No-Sew Paper Garland

See all these fantastic paper garlands during weddings and events? How do people do this in many garlands? Well, they probably used the Cricut. No-sew paper garlands brighten up any space, and you can use different kinds of shapes to create your garlands. Once you cut it out using your Cricut, all you need to do is string thread through these cutouts and hang them up. That's how it's done!

Personalized Napkin Rings

If you do not have a design in mind to make your napkin rings, head over to the Cricut Design Space, type in 'napkin rings,' and you'll find a host of designs that you can tweak and use to your liking. You can make your napkin rings with initials or even images of your own to make your event personalized.

3D Flowers

Cricut flowers, while beautiful, can be a little tedious and tough to assemble. Thankfully, this handy, step-by-step guide provided by Hey Let's Make Stuff is useful for crafters looking to add some floral paper arrangements to their dining table centerpiece, a mantel, or decoration a wedding vase.

Lampshade

This craft requires you to work on an existing lampshade and upgrade it. All you need is a lampshade that has seen better days and thinks about you want to redecorate it. You can paint the lampshade with fabric paint and then print out different motifs, such as butterflies, to paste on the lampshade to give it a beautiful 3D effect.

Paper Marigolds

Take your decoration game to the next level with Cricut. Put on a great show for the Day of the Dead by taking out your Cricut and making beautiful yellow and orange marigold paper flowers. With the Cricut, you can make these paper flowers as realistic as can be and as big and bold as you want it to be. Making paper flowers large, and as many as possible will be quickly done with the Cricut. The hardest part is assembling them according to their sizes.

Notebook Revamp with the Cricut

With some black vinyl and notebooks that you have lying around, you can amp up your notebooks to the next level. How? Use the Cricut on its vinyl settings, place your black vinyl on the grip mat, and get to work. By the end of the day, you can have a bunch of fashionable, black-letter notebooks worthy of being in a bookstore.

Paper Swag

This paper swag can be any motifs you like, but leaf motifs are among the favorites. Find a leaf collage on the Cricut Design Space, cut the motifs out, and use a scoring tool to score a line straight to the middle of the leaf to fold on the lines. You can use floral tape and wire to secure leaves, and use ribbons or any other adornments to make the swag beautiful.

Paper Succulent Centerpieces

Don't like gardening but still like the look of succulents? The Happy Scraps has a fantastic tutorial on how you can create a succulent paper centerpiece. Cricut even has succulent colored cardstock, which you can use to create this look the way Happy Scraps has done precisely. Make these flowers and place them the way a succulent garden would look—in a beautiful container.

Pop-Up Cards

If you love making cards and giving them to your near and dear or even selling them on your Etsy store, then investing in a Cricut is the way to go. You can make pop-up cards of any kind and any cardstock. All you need is a little bit of creativity. Like this pop-up rainbow card, it is so versatile you can make it any motifs such as shades of red hearts for Valentine's Day, snowflakes for Christmas greeting cards, four-leaf clover shapes for St.

Patrick's Day, or even book-shaped motifs where you can add in your favorite short quotes.

Luminaries

Do you ever look at luminaries and think 'How beautiful they are' and wonder how those intricate paper carvings were done? Luminaries are great for the holidays or table centerpieces at a restaurant. They are among the popular decorations for weddings and light up the aisle, as table decorations, and so on. In this tutorial by Jennifer Maker, she uses layers of beautifully cut panels to provide contrast and texture. You need vellum to complete your luminaries. This is paper—do not use candles, but LED candles would be a better and safer option.

Cricut Vinyl Crafts

One of the most common projects plenty crafters choose to work on is with vinyl with the Cricut. Cricut offers a fantastic variety of vinyl to choose from, and they are all of excellent quality. You can get the standard vinyl, more premium ones, glitter pieces of vinyl that are the crowd favorite, printable vinyl, dry erase ones, and chalkboard vinyl. Here is a selection of things you can do with them:

Pantry Labels

This craft idea makes for a fantastic beginner's craft. Labels are one of the most natural things to make with the Cricut and the most straightforward. All you need for this is Vinyl, transfer tape, label designs that you can get from the Cricut Design App, and your machine.

Vinyl Board

You can use any board to create a vinyl of words or images to update your board. Using chalkboard is one of the favorites as it creates beautiful decor for the home. You can cut out words from your vinyl and stick it on to your board. It can say 'Welcome Home,' or 'Grocery List,' or even a motivational quote.

DIY Drink Coasters

Coasters are another kind of beginner's craft to do with your Cricut. You can personalize it any way you want, such as using fonts, images, colors, or glitter vinyl—the options are endless. You need a standard grip mat to work with, the essential Cricut tools, the type of vinyl you want to use, and some transfer tape. Of course, your coasters' choice is also essential for this project, so don't forget this. A clear varnish is also needed to finish the project.

Playroom Accent Wall

This accent wall for your child's playroom makes a colorful statement to brighten up your kid's day. The most tedious part of this project would be measuring and painting the wall. After that, the fun part begins with the Cricut machine to do fun decorations. The primary Cricut Essential Toolset must have in vinyl projects to take out intricate cuts smoothly and efficiently.

Memory Game

This is a fun kid's craft project that uses a vibrant lime vinyl. In this craft, you make tiles featuring animal images. Cricut released its Cricut Vinyl Brights, which includes 12" x 12" sheets of vinyl in vibrant colors from Grape, Sunshine, Caribbean, Lime, Flamingo, and Azure. These colors are fun, which is perfect for summer crafts.

Chalkboard Robot Town

Using Cricut Vinyl for wall decals makes decorating these walls easy if you want to color up and decorate your children's room walls. All you need to do is design or find symbols that you like, resize it to the size you want to fit your walls, cut it, weed it, and stick it. It is always best for projects involving murals to measure your space and create a design on your Design Space App, placing the motifs or symbols or images to where you envision it on the wall, on your canvas in the app.

Once you are happy with what you have, connect it to the Cricut, cut it out, weed it out, and then start sticking.

Personalized Sports Gear

Yes, you can your sports gear scream your name! Have you joined a group workout or sports clubs and brought your gear along only to find it's gone missing because someone mistook your stuff for theirs? Well, suppose you have ever found yourself in a situation like this. In that case, it's best to get your gear emblazoned with your name on it, so nobody mistakenly retakes it. This is a perfect idea for your luggage too. Use the vinyl Cricut settings to create your name with an image of your choice—anything that stands out against the color of the object you want to personalize. Hence, it is visible, and it can be spotted from a distance.

Holographic Phone Case

Suppose you are one of those people who love changing your phone cases. In that case, the Cricut makes it possible for you to have every season or whenever you feel a change coming your way—except with half the cost and exactly the way you want it to look. Holographic cases have become quite popular, and Cricut crafters have many tutorials and SVG files that you can use, like this one from Laura's Crafty Life. To do this project, you would need a clear phone case, of course, that suits your phone size, as well as holographic vinyl. Explore the designs you like to use and use your Cricut to make this happen.

Decorated Vinyl Flower Pots

Suppose you love keeping plants and have a few indoor plants all around your home, time to give them an upgrade by adding some fun motifs to your pots. Some people add intricate designs, some add gold bands to give it some extra class, some put on labels, and some just put on fun motifs. You can use any vinyl that fits your creative ideas and use your Cricut to get this idea to reality.

Cricut Iron-On Crafts

Another must-do and popular craft among the Cricut fraternity is the iron-on. Iron-on is among the most popular after paper or even vinyl crafts simply because you can use it on everything from wood ornaments to T-Shirts, jeans, tote bags, and onesies. You can even make your holiday gifts with the Cricut Iron-On crafts for your family and friends.

Vinyl Decals and Stickers

One of the projects you can carry out with the Cricut Maker is the cutting to vinyl and stickers.

You just have to create your design in Cricut Design Space, instruct the Maker to cut, then weed and transfer the design to whatever surface you choose.

Fabric Cuts

The presence of the Rotary Blade in the Cricut Maker makes it a well-respected machine. The Maker can cut any fabric type, including; chiffon, denim, silk, and even heavy canvas. With this machine, you can cut huge amounts of fabrics without using any backup, and this is because it comes equipped with a fabric cutting mat. Awesome machine!

Sewing Patterns

One significant benefit of owning the Cricut Maker machine is the extensive library of sewing patterns that you'll have access to.

The library has hundreds of patterns, including Riley Blake Designs and Simplicity; all you need to do is select the pattern you want. The machine will do the cutting.

Balsa Wood Cuts

The Knife Blade, coupled with the machine's 4kg force, means that the Cricut Maker can easily cut through thick materials (up to 2.4mm thick). With these features, thick materials that were off-limits for earlier Cricut Machines are now being done.

Thick Leather Cuts

Just like Balsa wood, the Cricut Maker is also used for thick leather cuts.

Homemade Cards

Paper crafters use the Cricut Maker because the machine's power and precision make cutting cards and paper far quicker and more comfortable. With the machine, homemade cards just got better.

Jigsaw Puzzles

With the Cricut Maker, crafters can make jigsaw puzzles because the Knife Blade cuts through much thicker materials than ever before.

Christmas Tree Ornaments

Cricut machine owners can easily make Christmas tree ornaments. All you have to do is go through the sewing library for Christmas patterns, use any fabric of your choice to cut out the pattern and sew them together.

Remember, the Rotary blade cuts through all sorts of fabric.

Quilts

Thanks to the partnership between Cricut and Riley Blake Designs, Cricut Design Space now has several quilting patterns in the sewing pattern gallery.

The Cricut Maker is now used to cut quilting pieces with high precision before they are sewn together.

Felt Dolls and Soft Toys

The "felt doll and clothes" pattern is one of the most straightforward designs in the sewing pattern library. Thus, it is used for homemade dolls and toys.

The process is easy; just select the pattern you want, cut, and then sew.

T-Shirt Transfers

The Cricut Maker is used for cutting out heat transfer vinyl for crafters to transfer their designs to fabric. To achieve this, you have to make your design in Design Space, load the machine with your heat transfer vinyl, cut the material, and iron the transfer onto the t-shirt. Alternatively, you can use the Cricut EasyPress to transfer the vinyl.

Baby Clothes

The Cricut Maker cannot cut adult clothing patterns because the mat size is only 12'x24. However, you can easily make baby clothing patterns with the machine.

Doll Clothes

Just like baby clothes, the Cricut Maker can easily make doll clothing patterns because the mat size is big enough.

Fabric Appliques

The bonded fabric blade doesn't come with the Cricut Maker. Still, if you buy it, you will use your machine to cut intricate fabric designs like appliqué. For the bonded fabric blade to cut effectively, there has to be bonded backing on the material.

Calligraphy Signs

The stand out feature of the Cricut Maker is the Adaptive Tool System. With this feature, the machine will remain relevant in the foreseeable future because it fits with all the blades and tools of the explore series and all future blades and tools made by Cricut.

The Calligraphy pen is one such tool, and it is ideal for the sign and card making.

Jewelry Making

For crafters that like to explore jewelry making, the power of the Cricut Maker means that you can use thicker materials. While you can cut things like diamonds, silver, or gold, you can try to make a beautiful pair of leather earrings.

Wedding Invitations and Save the Dates

Weddings are capital intensive. We all know how the so-called 'little' expenses like STDs and invitation can add to considerable cost. However, if you have the

Cricut Maker machine, you can make your invitation and STDs yourself.

The Maker is capable of making invitations of the highest quality. It cuts out intricate paper designs, and the calligraphy pen is handy too.

Wedding Menus, Place Cards, and Favor Tags

The Cricut Maker is not restricted to the production of pre-wedding Invitations and STDs. With the machine, you can also produce other items such as place cards, wedding menus, favor tags, etc.

To keep the theme front and center, the crafter is advised to use a similar design for all their stationery.

Coloring Book

With the Cricut Maker, you can make 'mindful coloring' books from scratch. To achieve this goal, you need a card, paper, and a beautiful design. Then you command the Cricut Maker to create your personal and unique coloring book with the aid of the Fine-Point Pen tool.

Coasters

In the sewing library, there are some beautiful coaster patterns, and as such, the Maker is used to coasters.

With the Cricut Machine, you can work with materials such as metallic sheets, quilt, leather, and everything in between.

Fabric Keyrings

The Cricut Maker makes fabric keyrings, and the process is simple – It cuts out the pattern and then sews it together. Besides, there are several designs for fabric keyrings in the sewing pattern library.

Headbands and Hair Decorations

The Cricut Maker is known to cut through materials like thick leather. This has inspired the production of intricate headbands and hair decorations. The machine is so inspiring; crafters in the fashion world use it for creative designs and projects.

Cut-Out Christmas Tree

It is a typical tradition for people to buy Christmas trees during the holiday season. However, if you don't have enough space for a big tree in your living room, or maybe you're allergic to pine, then you can create your own Christmas tree.

The production of an interlocking wooden tree is something the Cricut Maker does easily because the blade is capable of cutting through thick materials like wood. With the Cricut Maker, you don't have a laser.

Cake Toppers

When Cricut bought over the Cake cutter machine, the idea was to create shapes made of gum paste, fondant, and others, etc.

The Cricut Maker can't cut as good as the Cake machine; however, it can be used to produce small and intricate paper designs that can be used to decorate cakes.

Fridge Magnets

Cricut machines like the Maker and Explore air are capable of cutting out magnetic materials. Thus, crafters can use the Maker to make those fancy magnetic designs placed on refrigerators.

Window Decals

If you're one of those that love to display inspiring quotes on your window or even `fancy little patterns on your car, then the Maker got you covered.

You just have to load the Maker with window cling and get your design created.

Scrapbooking Embellishments

The Cricut Maker is used for embellishments when scrapbooking. It is public knowledge that Cricut machines are super when it comes to cutting intricate designs. However, the Cricut Maker takes it to a whole new level. The responsive new blades take away all forms of complexity.

Craft Foam Cuts

In the past, Cricut machines found it difficult to cut craft foam (especially the Explore Machines). However, the Cricut Maker, with the 4kg of force, cuts through craft foam very easily.

Boxes and 3D Shapes

The Cricut Machines comes with a Scoring Stylus, and this tool can create items with the sharpest edges imaginable.

We all know that the Cricut Maker can execute all kinds of sewing patterns thrown at it. It can also cut paper crafts, including 3D shapes and boxes.

Stencils

The Maker comes in handy for people that create things that are used to create other items. The machine is incredible for making stencils, bearing in mind that you can utilize thicker materials to create the stencils.

Temporary Tattoos

If you're one of those who want to have tattoos, but don't want them permanent for life, then the Cricut Maker is your go-to machine.

With the Cricut Maker, you can etch your design on a tattoo paper (mostly coated with transfer film) and use it on your skin.

Washi Tape

Crafters that use Washi tape for scrapbooking can testify to how expensive it can be, especially when buying bulk from craft stores. However, those who own the Cricut Machine can use it to cut out Washi sheets – they can print and cut their designs.

Addressed Envelopes

The Cricut Maker is an amazing machine that can save you from spending on certain items. Remember, we talked about making handmade wedding invitations; with the Cricut Machine, you can also make envelopes to go with the cards. Another useful feature about the machine is that it is equipped with a Calligraphy pen and a Fine-point pen, meaning that it can automatically address your envelopes. All you need to do is make sure that the words are clear enough for the postman to read.

Glassware Decals

With a Cricut Maker, you can cut vinyl to make glassware designs. People that host themed parties will love this one, e.g., if you're hosting a summer house party and you're serving mojitos, then you can decorate your drinking glasses with coconuts and palm tree decals. Also, people holding Xmas parties can design and cut themed stickers to use on their cups.

Decorations

There are a couple of other desktop craft machines that are used to create general household decorations. Still, the Cricut Maker is one of the best – If not the very best.

With the Cricut Maker, you'll be empowered to create 3D wall hangings, beautiful cut-outs in the living room, and even things like signage in your closets, etc.

Cushion Transfers

With your Cricut Maker, you can brighten up your cushion and pillows by adding your homemade designs. With the flocked iron-on vinyl, you can create a lovely textured cushion using heat transfer vinyl on the Cricut Machine.

Gift Tags

We all know that gift tags consume some of our money during the holiday season. However, with your Cricut Maker, you don't have to buy them any more; you can just make your own.

Clutch Bags and Purses

The sewing pattern library is fantastic; thus, you can make different types of full-size purses, coin purse, and even clutch bags.

Chapter 8:
Maintenance Precautions

Blade Life

A blade can last up to 1500 single cuts before it can be replaced. The life expectancy for a cutting blade mostly relies on the settings you use and the materials you cut. This is why you need to monitor your cuts' quality, and when the quality of its cut decreases, that's when you have for replacement. To have the best possible results, make sure you only use Cricut Replaceable Cutting Blades that can be found most often in the Cricut Shop, but also at other retailers.

Replacing the Cutting Blade

This is a process you will come across, especially if you are frequently using the Cricut Machine. Never replace the blade when the Cricut Machine is still on. You need to unplug it before replacing the cutting blade. After the machine is unplugged, you will need to take out the cutting blade assembly. You will then need to find the blade in its assembly to push it in for emerging to its assembly. Next, slowly pull out the blade from the magnet that is holding it in place.

For blade installation, release the blade and cautiously insert the blade's shaft in the hole at the bottom of the blade assembly. Then, you will notice how the blade gets "sucked" inside its shaft and installed correctly. Place back the blade machine to Cricut Machine following the reversed procedure of removing the cutting blade.

Cleaning and Greasing Your Cricut Machine

Every product can show signs of usage. A Cricut Machine may collect some paper particles and dust, or you can even see grease from the machine-building up in the carriage track. You need to consider the following tips first:

- Make sure you unplug the power from the machine first before cleaning it
- You can use a glass cleaner sprayed on a soft cloth to clean the machine
- If you notice static electricity build-up leading to the accumulation of paper particles and dust, all you have to do is to wipe it off with a clean, soft cloth
- If you see grease building upon the bar across which the carriage travels, gently remove it using a soft cloth, tissue, or cotton swab

Maintaining the Cricut Cutting Mat

You also have to clean and maintain your Cricut cutting mat because that is where the cutting occurs.

If the cutting mat isn't clean, it can stain the machine. Also, if your cutting mat has stopped sticking, it can spoil your designs and creations.

When your mat is no longer sticky because of debris and grime, cleaning it and making it sticky again will bring it back to life.

I will mention the solutions that are not ideal for the pink cutting mats, only for the green, blue, and purple.

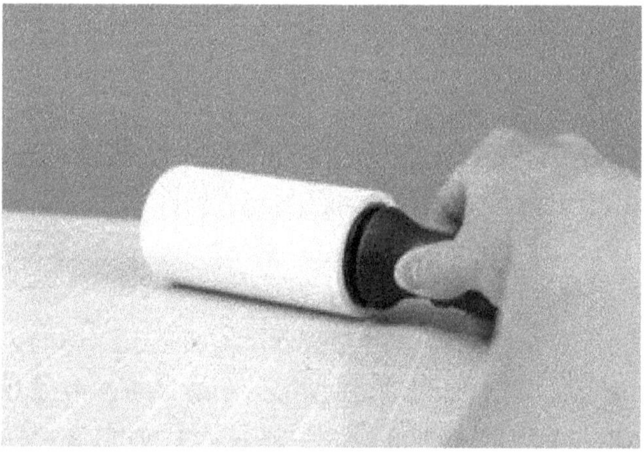

There are many ways to clean your cutting mat.

Using baby wipes:

Make use of alcohol-free, unscented, and bleach-free wet wipes to clean your mat. You should use the plainest baby wipes you can find to add lotions, cornstarch, solvents, or oils to your cutting mat. If not, you could affect the stickiness and adhesive of the mat. Also, after cleaning it, let it dry completely before using it.

Using a Sticky Lint Roller

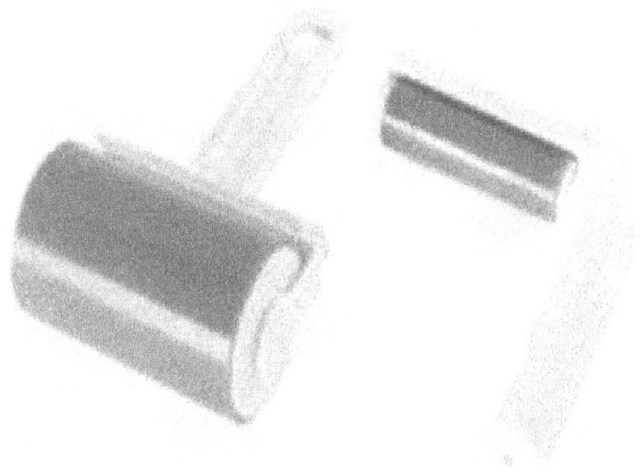

You can also use a roll of masking tape if you don't find a sticky lint roller. Run the roll across the mat to get rid of hairs, fibers, specks of dust, and paper particles.

This cleaning routine can be done daily or between projects to accumulate on the mat. This is a fast way to remove dirt apart from using tweezers or scrapers.

Using warm water with soap

You can also clean the mat with soap and warm water. You should use the plainest soap possible too so that you don't mess with the mat. Use a clean cloth, sponge, soft brush, or a magic eraser. Also, rinse it thoroughly and don't use it until it is scorched.

Using an adhesive remover

In heavy-duty cleaning, you should use a reliable adhesive remover to clean it properly. When using an adhesive remover, read the directions properly before you start.

Then, spray a little amount on the mat and spread it around with a scraper or anything that can act as a makeshift scraper.

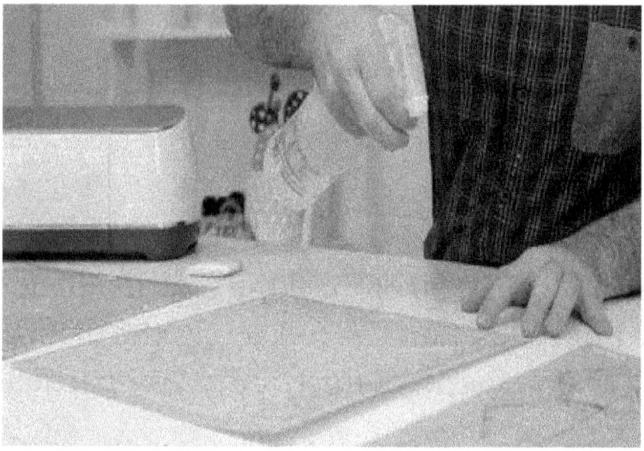

Wait for a few minutes so that the solvent can work on the mat. Then, scrape the dirty adhesive off your mat using a scraper, tissue paper, or cloth.

After this, wash the mat with warm water and soap if there is leftover residue and let it dry properly.

How to Make Your Cutting Mat Sticky Again

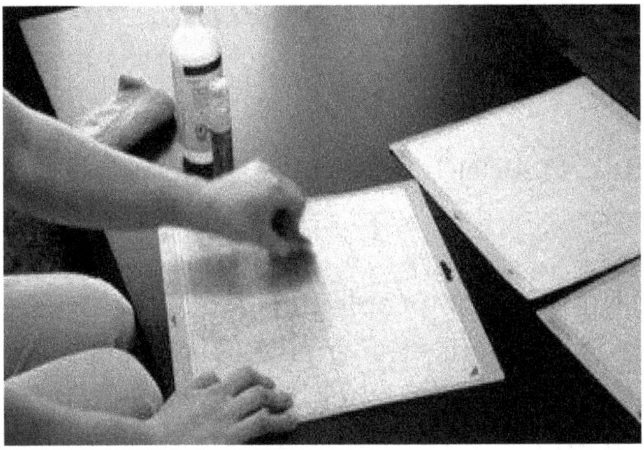

After washing or cleaning your cutting mat, you have to make them sticky again.

The most advisable way to make your mat sticky again is by adding glue to it. Get a solid glue stick like the Zig 2-Way Glue Pen and apply it on the mat's inner portion. Then, stroke the glue around the mat and ensure no glue residue on the edges of the mat.

After about 30 minutes, the glue will turn clear. Suppose the cutting mat turns out to be too sticky after you apply glue. In that case, you can use a piece of fabric to reduce the adhesive by pressing the material on the parts of the mat that are very sticky.

Cover the mat with a clear film cover after a few hours.

You can also use tacky glues or spray adhesives that are ideal for cutting mats.

Chapter 9:
Most Common Problems

Material Tearing or Not Cutting Completely Through

This is the biggest problem with most Cricut users. When this happens, the image is ruined, and you've wasted material. More machines have been returned or boxed up and put away due to this problem than any other.

But don't panic. If your paper is not cutting correctly, you can take several steps to correct the problem.

Most important is this: Anytime you work with the blade, TURN YOUR MACHINE OFF. I know it's easy to forget this because you're frustrated, and you're trying this and that to make it work correctly. But this is a necessary safety precaution that you should remember.

Make simple adjustments at first. Turn the pressure down one. Did it help? If not, turn the blade down one number. Also, make sure the mat is free of debris, so the blade rides smoothly.

Usually, the thicker the material, the higher the pressure number should be cut through the paper. Don't forget to use the *multi-cut function* if you have that option. It may take a little longer to cut 2, 3, or 4 times, but it should cut clean through then.

Those of you using the smaller bugs that do not have that option, here, *make your multi-cut function*. After the image has been cut, don't unload the mat. Just hit load paper, repeat last, and cut. You can repeat this sequence 2, 3, or 4 times to ensure your image is completely cut out.

If you are using thinner paper and it is tearing, try reducing the pressure and slowing down the speed. When cutting intricate designs, you have to give the blade enough time to maneuver through the design. By slowing it down, it will be able to make cleaner cuts.

Clean the blade's edge to be sure no fuzz, glue, or scraps of paper are stuck to it.

Make sure the blade is installed correctly. Take it out and put it back, so it's seated firmly. The blade should be steady while it's making cuts. If it makes a shaky movement, it's either not installed correctly or a problem with the *blade housing*.

Be aware that there is a deep cutting blade for thicker material. You'll want to switch to this blade when you're cutting heavy card stock. This will also save wear and tear on your regular blade. Cutting a lot of thick material will wear your blade out quicker than thinner material and cause you to change it more often.

Power Button Blinking Red

When you notice that the power button is blinking unexpectedly, observe what time and what project you carried out that elicited such abnormality. This issue sometimes happens when you are powering on your Cricut machine or updating firmware. It also happens when cutting a project or when loading a mat. The red light can serve as a warning or a notification that something had gone wrong with a project.

In the case of the power button blinking red when loading a mat, the roller bars may have gathered specks of dust. In this case, power off the machine, move the carriage, and blow away the speck of dust. When cutting a project, the red light could signify that the blade is stuck in a material or the machine is faulty. Contact Cricut support for further assistance.

Machine Freezing

Remember always to turn your machine off when you switch cartridges. When you switch cartridges, leaving the machine on it's called "hot-swapping," it can sometimes cause the machine to freeze. This is more of an issue with the older models and doesn't seem to apply to the Expression 2.

You know how quirky electronic gadgets can be, so give your machine rest for five or ten minutes every hour. If you work for several hours continuously, your machine might overheat and freeze up.

Turn the machine off and take a break. Restart it when you come back, and it should be fine. Then remember not to rush programming the machine and give it an occasional rest.

Don't press a long list of commands quickly. If you give it too much information too quickly, it will get confused in the same way a computer sometimes does and simply freeze up. Instead

of typing in one long phrase, try dividing up your *words into several cuts.*

If you're using *special feature keys,* make sure you press them first before selecting the letters.

Power Problems

If you turn your machine on and nothing happens, the power adapter may be at fault. Jiggle the power cord at the outlet and where it connects to the machine to make sure it's firmly connected. Ideally, you want to test the adapter before buying a new one. Swap cords with a friend and see if that fixed the problem. Replacement adapters can be found on eBay by searching for a Cricut adapter power supply.

The *connection points* inside the machine may also pose a problem; here is how to test that. Hold down the plug where it inserts into the back of the machine and turn it on. If it powers up, then the problem is inside the machine, and the connection points will have to be soldered again.

If the machine powers up but will not cut, then try a hard reset. See the resource section for step-by-step instructions on resetting your machine.

Here are a few tips, especially for Expression 2 users. Have you turned on your machine? You watch it light up and hear it gearing up, but when you try to cut, nothing happens? Or you're stuck on the welcome screen, or the LCD screen is unresponsive.

Well, here are two quick fixes to try. First, try a hard reset, sometimes called the *rainbow screen to reset* to recalibrate your die cutter. If that does not resolve the problem, you're going to have to restore the settings.

To help cut down on errors, try to keep your machine updated. When an update is available, you should receive a message encouraging you to install the latest version.

For those of you using third-party software that is no longer compatible with the Cricut, you probably already know that *updating your machine may disable that software.*

When you cut heavy paper, and your Expression 2 shuts down, try switching to the standard paper setting and use the *multi-cut function.*

Machine Dial Not Working

If you ever come across issues with dialing on your Cricut Machine, you can just follow the troubleshooting steps below

When Explore Smart Set Dial doesn't turn:

- In this case, you will need to look for your proof of purchase and prepare a short video of the issue.
- You will need to contact Customer Care, using one of the options for assistance
- Unfortunately, there is no way to troubleshoot this issue
- When the material is not changing in Design Space:
- Check the connection of the USB cable on both your Cricut machine and your computer.

Unplug the Cricut machine from the computer and then power it off. Next step, reboot or restart your computer. When the computer is back on, turn on the Cricut machine and reconnect it to the computer, then try to see if it's cutting again. If it still doesn't work, make sure you try the following step.

Consider reconnecting your Cricut machine through a different USB port on your computer. If it still doesn't help, move on to the next step.

Check if the issue happens with a different Internet browser. If the issue is happening regardless of the browser you are using, please consider the next step.

Try to see if a different USB cable works to see if the Cricut machine can cut with a different cable. If your machine is in warranty and you don't have another cable, you might want to consider contacting Member Care.

Check for any possible updates (make sure the Firmware is updated) on your Cricut Machine.

If there are no available updates, please get in touch with Member Care for further assistance.

Machine Tearing or Dragging Materials

All these variables can be fixed using some necessary troubleshooting steps. Therefore, if your Cricut machine is dragging or tearing through the material, make sure you check the following: Check if you selected the right material setting in Design Space, or make sure that Smart Set Dial is on the right setting:

- If you are making a Custom setting, you can make sure that you select the right material from the dropdown menu
- Check the intricacy and size of the image. When cutting an image that is small or very intricate, try cutting it larger or simpler.
- If you are using Cricut Maker or Cricut Explore Air 2 in Fast Mode, make sure you disable the Fast Mode and reattempt the cut again.

- Take off the blade housing from the machine, then the blade, and make sure there isn't any debris on the blade or inside the housing.

Decrease pressure settings for that specific material type in the Manage Custom Materials window by increments of 2-4. You can access the Manage Custom Materials screen from the account menu, or by going to the Edit Custom Materials option from the upper right corner of the Mat Preview screen.

It may have to be done 2-3 times to change the cut result.

Try to cut a different material using the right setting for that material. Try to see if the problem is only with the material you are trying to cut, or the issue persists with other materials.

Consider using a new mat and blade. In this case, both of them can cause cut issues.

Suppose you followed all the steps above, but the issues persist. In that case, I encourage you to contact the Member Care for further assistance.

CRICUT MACHINE MAKING A DISTURBING NOISE

The type of noise your Cricut machine will make will determine the best approach to use to resolve the issue. Unusual noise is an indication that your Cricut machine needs help. If you hear a grinding noise, the carriage is faulty, or the configuration/setup is wrong. To troubleshoot the issue of grinding and unusual loud noise.

Check the carriage and report to support on what to do next.

Make sure you are using the power cord and the accessories that came with the machine. A different power cord and accessories may result in the machine producing an unusual grinding noise.

Check the pressure setting for the material type. If it is too high, try adjusting it to a lower level. Do this more than twice to see a change.

If you notice your Design Space is unusually loud, check if fast mode is activated. If it is not, contact support for technical support.

Cricut Machine Having Firmware Updates Issues

Firmware update issues are typical issues that users experience in their Cricut Design Space. If updates are failing to install or not completing, follow the steps below:

First of all, ensure your system meets the minimum requirements for Design Space.

If your system meets the minimum requirements, make sure that the desktop or computer you are attempting to install the update is connected to your Cricut Explore Air 2. USB is faster and better than

Bluetooth. If the update is failing with a USB cable, try another one.

Use the Google Chrome browser as it's more compatible to use.

Cricut 'Print then Cut' Calibration not working

Sometimes, calibrating the Cricut machine to work with the Print then Cut option is difficult. This is because you get to a point in the calibration process and you are stuck. All you have to do is get the correct calibration sheet by downloading it online and loading it into your Cricut machine. This way, you won't have to go through the calibration process. Ensure the sensor marks are showing to enable a good cut.

Carriage Will Not Move

If the carriage assembly does not move, check to see if the *belt has broken or if the car has fallen off the track.* Provo Craft does not sell replacement parts, which is nuts, so try to find a

compatible belt at a vacuum repair shop.

If the wheels have fallen off the track, remove the plastic cover, and look for a tiny screw by the wheel unscrew it. You now should be able to move the wheel back on track.

Unresponsive Keyboard

Suppose you are sure you are pressing the keys firmly. In that case, you have a cartridge inserted correctly and a mat loaded ready to go. However, the keypad is still not accepting your selection. The problem may be internal.

You will have to remove the keyboard and check if the *display cable is connected to the keypad and the motherboard.* If the connections are secure, you have a circuit board problem, and repairs are beyond this book's scope.

An important reminder, please do not attempt any repairs unless your machine is out of warranty.

Weird LCD Screen

The LCD screen is now showing strange symbols or is blank after doing a firmware update. Try rerunning the update making sure your selections are correct.

When the image you choose is more significant than the mat or paper size you selected, the preview screen will look *grayed out* instead of showing the image. So, increase the paper and mat size or decrease the size of your image.

Also, watch out for the gray box effect when using the *center point feature.* Move the start position down until you see the image appear. The same thing may happen when using the fit to length feature. Try changing to landscape mode and shorten the length size until the image appears.

Occasionally using the *undo button* will cause the preview screen to turn black; unfortunately, the only thing to do is turn the machine off. Your work will be lost, and you have to start again.

Cartridge Errors

Sometimes dust or debris accumulates in the cartridge port gently blow out any paper fiber that may have collected in the opening. Make sure the contact points are clean and that nothing is preventing the cartridge from being read correctly.

With any electrical machine, overheating can be a problem. If you get a cartridge error after using your machine for a while, turn it off and let it cool down for about fifteen minutes.

Suppose this is the first time you're using the cartridge and you get an error. In that case, I'm sure you know the trick about turning the cartridge around and inserting it backward.

If you thought you could use your Imagine cartridges with your Expression 2, think again. You will get an error message because you can only use the *art cartridges* to cut with the colors and patterns of cartridge prints.

Even brand-new items fresh out of the box can be defective. Suppose you see a cartridge error 1, 2, 3, 4, 5, 6, 9 or 99 call customer service and tell them the name. In that case, serial number and error message number, and they may replace the cartridge.

Trouble Connecting to Your Computer

All Cricut machines come with a USB cord that lets you connect to your computer and use the other products like the Cricut Design Studio software, Cricut Craft Room, or the Cricut Gypsy with your machines.

Double-check your USB connection and try another port.

Check to see if you may have a firewall or antivirus software that is blocking the connection.

See if you're running the latest firmware. You may need to update. Older machines update via firmware (Personal Cutter, Expression, Create, and Cake). The newer (Expression 2, Imagine, and Gypsy) use the Sync program to update.

Conclusion

I am much obliged to you for pursuing it until the end. I am too certain that this book will address your fundamental concerns if you attempt to make sense of which Cricut you ought to get. Or on the other hand, regardless of whether you need one in any case.

The Cricut machine was made for many reasons. Nowadays, many people can imagine that this gadget is only used to create albums, but not. With the Cricut machine, you can spoil more than just stack. If you notice that he turns off the Cricut machine and drives his creative mind crazy, you can think of many unusual Cricut thoughts that can give him life or make him happy.

Cricut machines are awesome gadgets to own because they do not only boost creativity and productivity; they can also be used to create crafts for business. With Design Space, crafters can create almost anything and even customize their products to bear their imprints.

All over the world, people use these machines to make gift items, t-shirts, interior décor, and many other crafts, to beautify their homes, share with friends and family during holidays, and even sell, *etc.*

As a crafter, without proper knowledge of Design Space, you're not only going to cut out inferior products, you will also make little or no in-road in your quest to find success.

Understanding Design Space is important because it empowers crafters with enormous tools and materials to create generalized and custom products. It is a potent tool that just cannot be overlooked by anyone that intends to follow this path.

Thus, the understanding of Design Space is a MUST for people that intend to do business out of Cricut machines or even utilize it as a hobby. With the software, crafters can create their designs from scratch or use already-made designs on the Cricut platform. Those who have an active subscription to Cricut Access have access to thousands of images, projects, and fonts. They can cut out their products using these images or projects, and they can also edit them to suit their style and taste before cutting.

Cricut Design Space comes with some exciting tools and features that can make crafting easy and straightforward. These tools are not so hard to use. Thus, to get conversant with them, you need to research and consistently apply the knowledge you gain from your research and reading. Expert crafters know all about the critical tools in Cricut Design Space and their role in the design of projects. Some of these tools include; the slice tool, weld tool, contour tool, attach tool and flatten tool, *etc.*

Cricut machines do not function separately -when you purchase them, they come with accessories and tools required for them to function. Minus the tools and accessories that come in the pack, others can be purchased separately to boost the machine's functionality and output. We have the essential accessories and tools needed for crafters to use and their machines for optimum functionality and ease of design and production.

In terms of the Cricut Design Space software and app, some tips and tricks aid project design and production. The software is easy and straightforward to learn and design on. However, like every other application and software, it still has some related issues and problems.

Everything on earth needs maintenance, including Cricut machines. These machines are continually cutting out materials of different textures, shapes, and quantity, *etc.* Thus, they need routine maintenance to boost their productivity levels and increase their life span.

The routine maintenance of these machines does not require a lot. The hardware needs cleaning after cutting out materials. Thus, non-alcoholic baby wipes are highly recommended for cleaning material residue on the machines. The cutting mat is another item that needs maintenance from time to time because excessive usage without proper care reduces its stickiness.

In terms of projects, there are so many items that can be designed and cut out from Cricut machines.

Cricut Vocabulary And Terms

You will repeatedly hear various words and expressions when you start interacting with Cricut owners (and even Silhouette owners) or checking them when you surf the web looking for help and instructional exercises.

Clingy Mat

This is the cutting mat that you will use to hold the material you need to cut. The material shouldn't be allowed to move while the machine is attempting to slice, score, or draw on it. The clingy tangle holds it in place. There are various degrees of "clingy" depending on the material you are working with.

Tools

This typically refers to a pack of tools used along with a Cricut machine group or that you buy independently as an accessory. These typically include a sort of spatula for pulling your design off the clingy tangle, tweezers for lifting and pulling, a pick that resembles a dental instrument for "weeding," and scissors.

Weeding

This term is quite confusing lol. It refers to pulling or removing the "undesirable" pieces out of your design, within the "e" or within a shape that you need to be vacant.

Load and Unload

generally simple. It's the process of stacking and unloading your clingy tangle into the Cricut machine.

Pressure

you will have an option to automate your machine that alters the pressure on the sharp edge, pen, or turning edge. You change this depending on your material's thickness and the speed that you choose to cut your design at.

Speed

The speed to which you set the machine to cut out the design. Often you can use quicker speeds for more simple designs. The more complicated the design, the slower you need your machine to process and cut.

Cricut Design Space

This is the application on software that you will use to change, set up, and eventually send the cut instructions to your machine to cut the materials as indicated by you your design.

Materials

These are a set of things you add to the clingy tangle to be cut. This can include paper, fake calfskin, copper sheeting, fabric, sticker paper, vinyl, slender wood, chipboard, froth center, and the sky is the limit from there!

CRICUT DESIGN SPACE:

The practical step by step guide to follow to find out what design space can do. The tricks and new design ideas inside, will take your cricut to another level.

KAYLA ARORA

Table of Contents

Introduction

This book will help you get started with Design Space so that you can create awesome projects and get the most out of your Cricut machine.

The Cricut design studio program enables you to view before you cut, a substantial newspaper saver.

Design Space allows you to do whatever your imagination can conceive. It is very user-friendly and ideal for novice users. If you're an experienced user of other design software and tools, you'll find that it's a breeze. Moreover, it is intended to work exclusively with the Cricut machine. So, if you use other design programs, you'll still have to import those images into Design Space.

As you can see, Design Space is very easy to use, especially if you have experience with other design software. Nevertheless, even a novice designer will have no trouble getting the hang of making great creations. A good rule of thumb is always to test out your cut before cutting the real material you wish to use. In doing so, you can avoid frustration if your design doesn't come out exactly as you had intended to. Also, you can experiment with the various ways in which you can make interesting and innovative designs.

If there are different advances, your Cricut will convey guidelines to show on your PC or gadget screen. It can let you know whether and when you have to do other project steps. For instance, it will guide you to stack your next piece of paper (or other material) or swap various shades of pens.

Chapter 1:
Start with design space

HOW TO DOWNLOAD CRICUT DESIGN SPACE

Visit **design.cricut.com,** and you will be required to log in or create a username and password. Register your details on the website, and make sure you write down your login details if you log out in the future. Once you have taken care of that, click on a new project on the screen's top right. This action will alert you to download the Design Space plugin. When the download process is complete, you will have to open the file, depending on your computer or browser.

If you are using a Chrome browser, it will be located at the bottom of your download bar. Click to open and click run or next, as prompted.

Follow all the download prompts. You will have to accept the terms and conditions and click install. The procedure is straightforward, and the prompts will walk you through everything. Finally, Design Space is downloaded, and it's time to explore.

Before your machine can cut out projects, you will have to create your designs inside Design Space (also called Design Space canvas).

On the canvas, you will use the menu on the left side to kick off your designs.

You will click upload to upload SVG files or images that you intend to cut. SVG is abbreviated for Scalable Vector Graphic. It is the most used file for cutting designs because it is explicit. SVG files can be found anywhere; you can find them on blogs, Etsy, and other places.

The next menu on the left is Shapes. You can make use of stars, squares, circles, and other shapes to make your design. If you intend to scorecards or do other paper projects, you'll find score lines here.

The third item on the left menu is text. You can do many things with text, including; curving texts, making monograms, and using your fonts.

The fourth item on the menu is Images. If you click the images icon, you will be redirected to the designs you can use to subscribe to Cricut Access or the designs you can buy from Cricut if you have no subscription.

Fifth on the left menu is Projects. If you click on projects, you will see a display of projects that are up for sale. However, there is another dropdown menu that you can use to select your projects. Your saved projects are also located in that area.

Sixth on the left menu is Templates. Some crafters do not use this feature, but you can use them to ascertain the size of the design you intend to cut and how it is meant to look on a shirt or apron. Mind you. It is used as a guide; thus, the actual template won't be cut out.

Seventh on the left menu is the New+ button. If you want to start a new project, this is the menu to click.

Always save your current project if you intend to keep it before starting a new one. The save button is located at the top right corner.

To access the Design Space software for a computer or mobile device, you will need an active internet connection.

Downloading and Installing Design Space for Windows

The download is run from *https://design-beta2.cricut.com/#/launcher*.

Choose Download to start the Design Space for Desktop download.

When the system is downloading, the screen will prompt "Downloading Design Space for Windows." This can take a few minutes, depending on the connection and your device.

Once the download is complete, go to the Downloads folder on the PC and double click on the file — Cricut Design Space Install v4.2.4.exe (the version number may differ depending on the updated version).

There may be a pop-up window asking for permission to trust the application — select to trust the application or not install it.

Follow any on-screen prompts, selecting the default settings until the software starts to install.

There will be a pop-up box with an installation progress bar during the installation to show how far the installation has progressed.

Once the installation is complete, you will be asked to "Sign in with your Cricut ID."

First-time users of the software will need to create a Cricut ID by clicking on the button below the sign-in sheet on the screen.

The Cricut desktop icon automatically gets added to the Windows desktop or found under the 'All Programs' taskbar where you find your installed programs.

To access Cricut Design Space, click on either the desktop icon or the program under the All Programs taskbar.

Downloading and Installing Design Space for MAC

The download is run from https://design-beta2.cricut.com/#/launcher.

Choose the option to Download.

When the system is downloading, the screen will prompt "Downloading Design Space® for MAC". This can take a few minutes, depending on the connection and your device.

Once the download is complete, go to the Downloads folder on the MAC and double click on the file — Cricut Design Space Install v4.1.6 (the version number may differ depending on the updated version).

When the Cricut icon appears, drag it into the applications folder, and the installation will begin.

Once the installation is complete, you can drag the application icon to the dock to create a shortcut or access the program from the application folder.

The first time you use Cricut on a MAC, you may get a warning, "Cricut Design Space is an app downloaded from the internet. Are you sure you want to open it?" — Click on the Open button to continue to Design Space.

On the first Design Space screen that appears, you will be asked to "Sign in with your Cricut ID".

First-time users of the software will need to create a Cricut ID by clicking on the button below the sign-in sheet on the screen.

To access Cricut Design Space, click on either the desktop icon or the program under the Applications folder.

Downloading and Installing Design Space for iOS

On an iOS compatible device, you will need to go to the App Store.

In the Search option, find the Cricut Design Space app.

To download and install the app, select Get. You may have to verify the download, depending on your iTunes setup.

When the app has finished downloading and installing, you will be directed to the "New Machine Setup" page. If you do not wish to go through the setup right away, you can either go to the app overview screen or click on the X in the top right-hand corner to exit.

You can access the Cricut app by clicking on the application icon on your iOS mobile device.

Downloading and Installing Design Space for Android

On an Android device, you will have to access the Google Play Store to get the Design Space app.

In the Search box, find the Cricut Design Space app.

To download and install the app, select Install, and the application will start to download.

When the app has finished downloading and installing, you will be directed to the "New Machine Setup" page. If you do not wish to go through the setup right away, you can either go to the app overview screen or click on the X in the top right-hand corner to exit.

You can access the Cricut app by clicking on the application icon on your Android mobile device.

How does Cricut Design Space Work?

What a Cricut machine is and how Cricut Design Space works is just like your project recipe. In Design Space, what you do only tells your computer where to cut, rate, or compose.

When your system is connected to your computer or another device, it can only complete a full design if only one move is taken.

Your Cricut can communicate instructions on display on your monitor or tablet screen if there are several steps. It can tell you if and when other project steps are required. You will be told to load your next sheet of paper or swap different colors of styles for starters.

Choose A Font

Press to open the file and save it.

Tip: Set up a folder for all your fonts, and there will be no end once you start collecting!

Your Cricut font will most likely be downloaded as a zip file. You can right-click the file and click to extract everything.

Open the Cricut Font File

Find the file on your computer and open the TrueType font file (double-click). It opens up to a font view. Depending on your source, you can only obtain a TrueType file and have no other choices.

Install the Font

To install the font on your computer, click the Install button.

Cricut Font Problems

Now that the font has been mounted on your screen, it's all there! You can now scan and use the new font in Cricut Design Space.

I sometimes go into the Design Space, and after creating a text box, I find my font, but it doesn't appear properly. Don't your downloaded fonts appear in Cricut?

You have to do this to get your font to show up in Design Space: first, try to refresh the page and see if it brings the genuine font. If not, sign in and outside the Design Space and check to see if that does the job.

Cricut Design Space Canvas Area

Before you cut up your projects, the Canvas area is where all the designing and arts happen. Here, you can organize your project, upload images or fonts.

The Cricut Design Space is similar to the other design programs that most of us are useful, like Adobe Creative Cloud, Photoshop, or Illustrator. And so, if you have any experience with these programs, then it won't be difficult for you to understand the Design Space.

There is also the choice of getting a Cricut Access membership, which will be explained later. With this, you can create your designs and let your creativity flow.

The Canvas Area comprises the Right Panel, Left Panel, Top Panel, and Canvas Area.

Right Panel

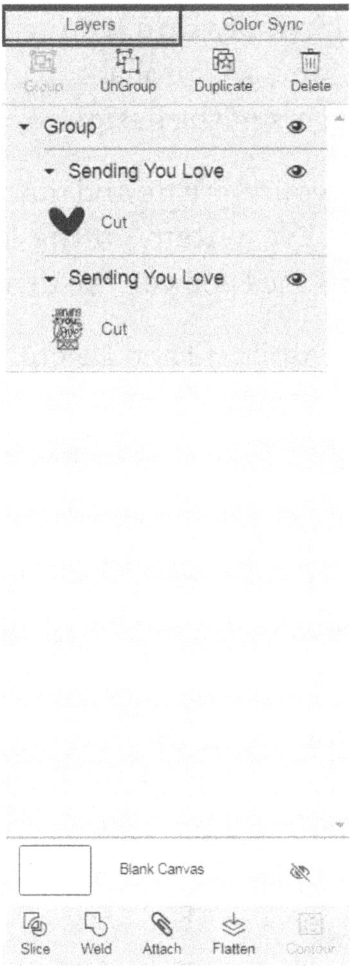

Photo credit: help.cricut.com

The Right Panel deals with layers, and so it can also be called the Layers Panel. Layers signify the designs that are on the canvas area. The number of layers you use depends on your design's complexity or the project you're working on.

When making a birthday card, you will have texts and different decorations, and probably a picture or two. All of these are the layers of the design.

This panel allows you to create and manage layers when making a design. Every item on the layers panel will display the Fill or Line type you are using.

Group, Ungroup, Duplicate and Delete.

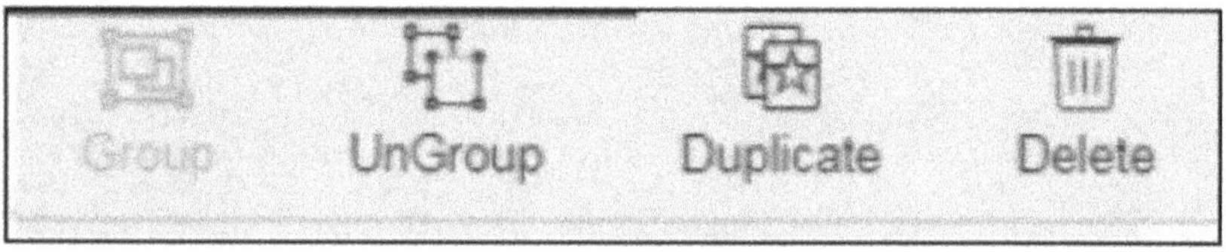

These settings allow you to move different designs around the canvas area.

- Group: This allows you to group layers. When you have different layers that come together to make a complicated design, you use this option to bring them together. For example, if you're making a house, there will be different parts of that house. A standard home will have a roof, door, walls, and windows. 'Group' allows you to arrange all the layers and ensure that they stay together when you're making a design.

- Ungroup: You can also separate the design of different layers by clicking on this button. This is pretty much the opposite of 'Group'.

- Duplicate: As the name implies, this option will duplicate the layers that you select on the canvas.

- Delete: This option will delete any layer that you select and remove it from the canvas.

Blanck Canvas

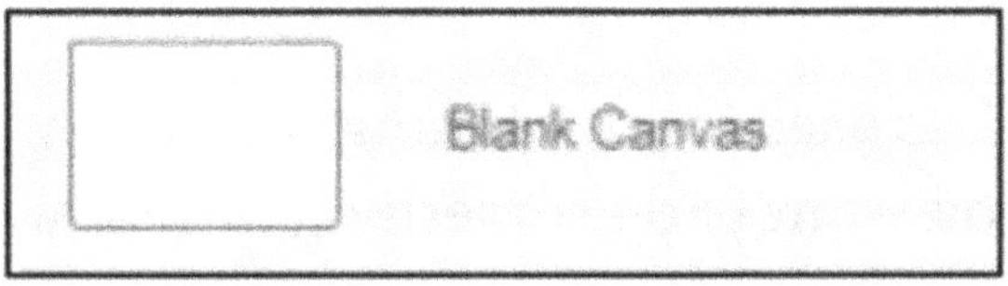

This is also a layer in the Right panel that gives you the option of changing the canvas's color. If you’re experimenting with your design, you can use this option to place it against various backgrounds.

Layer Visibility

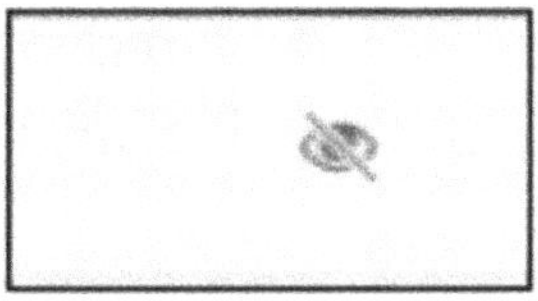

This is represented by a little eye that is on every layer on the panel. It signifies the visibility of that layer or design. During designing, if you see that a particular segment or element doesn't look right, you can click on the eye to hide it. That way, you don't end up deleting it permanently if you decide to put it back. The hidden item can be identified with a cross mark.

Slice, Weld, Attach, Flatten and Contour

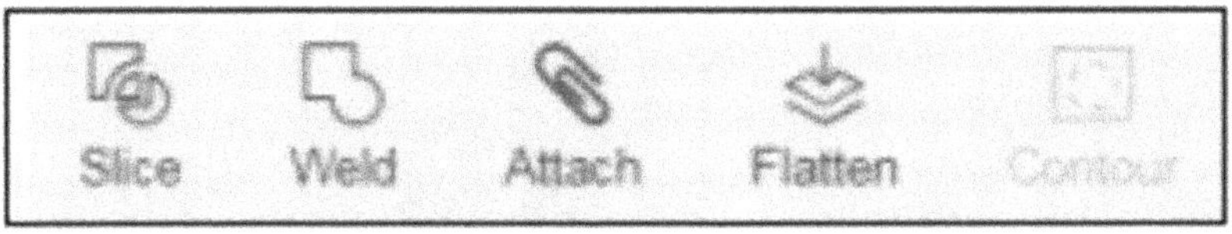

It’s important to learn how to use these five tools. No matter what you're designing, they will come in handy.

- Slice: This tool is meant for cutting out texts, shapes, and other elements from a whole design.

- Weld: This is used for combining shapes to make a new shape. If you want to do something different with your designs, you can join two or more shapes together.

- Attach: This is like a more powerful version of the Group option. It connects shapes and changes the color to match whatever background color that you're using. This will remain even after cutting.

- Flatten: This tool is useful when you’re about to print two or more shapes. To do this, you should pick the layers that you want to print and select the Flatten option.

Contour- If you want to hide a layer of design or just a small part, you can use this option to do so. Although, you can only do this when your design has layers that can be taken apart.

Color Sync

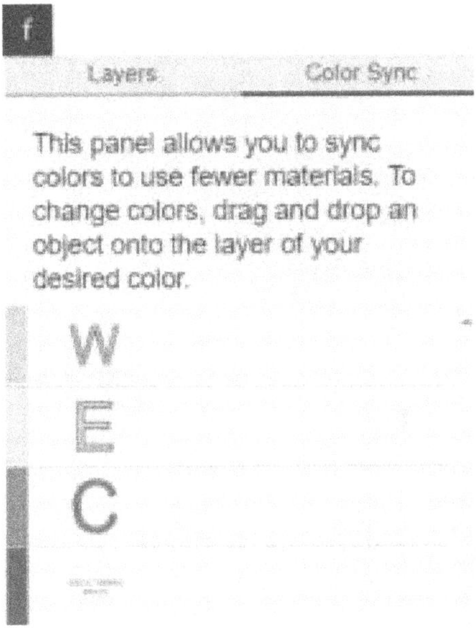

This option is meant for an evening out the colors of your design and even background. You can use this to change different shades of a color to just one color. It synchronizes the colors, as the name implies.

Left Panel

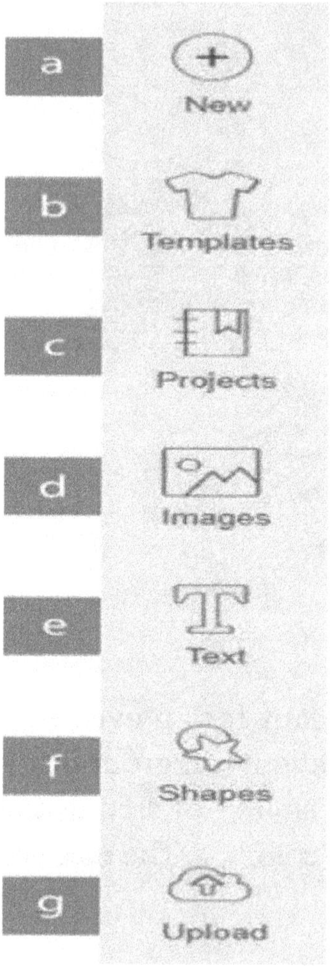

The left panel includes all the options you need for inserting. You can add shapes, texts, images, even ready-to-cut projects.

With this panel, you can add everything that you plan on cutting. The panel has seven options, and we will explore them all.

New

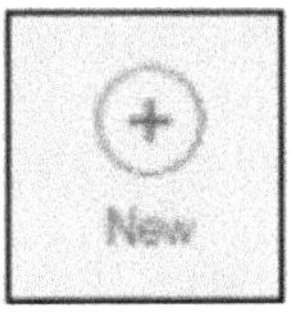

You select this option when you want to create a new page apart from the design you're using.

It's advisable to save your designs before moving to the new page just if you need it at another time. If not, you can lose your designs.

Templates

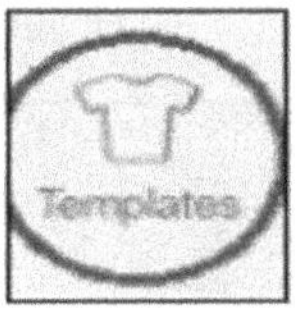

A template is used to give you a feel of what your design will look like when you cut it out on a particular type of fabric like a t-shirt or a bag. If you're making an iron-on design on a bag, it will show you a picture of the bag, and you can place the design on the template so you can plan how it will look in real life.

Templates are great because they give you an idea of what your design looks like when cut out. It won't cut out an actual backpack for you.

Projects

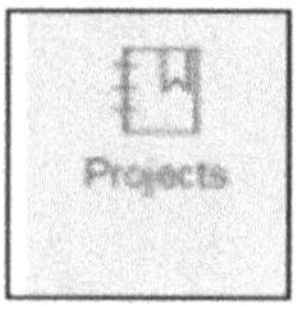

If you're ready to cut, then you should go to projects. You will pick your project, edit it, tailor it to your tastes, and click on the 'Make It' option.

A large number of the available projects are available to Cricut Access members, or some are available for purchase. Apart from these, a few are free.

Images

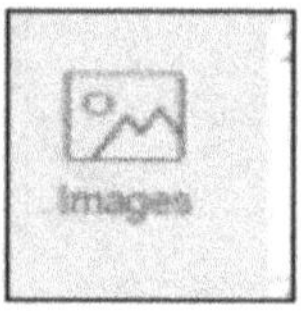

Images allow you to add a personal touch to your designs. With this option, you can insert pictures provided for you on Cricut Design Space.

Cricut even provides free images every week, although some come with Cricut Access.

Text

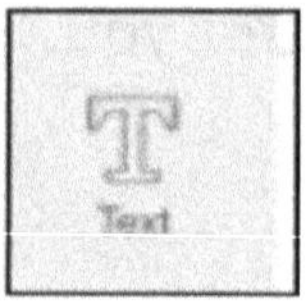

The text option allows you to add a text to your design or just on the canvas area. It opens a small window telling you to add text, and so you can do that and customize the font and color.

Shapes

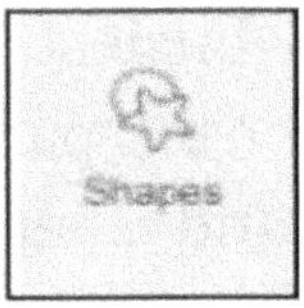

You use this option when you want to add shapes to your canvas area. Cricut Design Space offers some shapes, namely triangle, square, pentagon, hexagon, octagon, star, and heart.

There is also the Score Line tool under the Shapes option. You can use this option to fold the shapes into different shapes, especially when making cards.

Upload

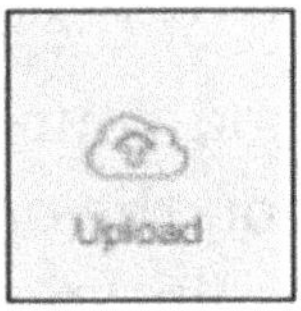

The last tool in the Left panel is the Upload tool, which allows you to upload your files and images apart from those Cricut provides for you.

With this, you can upload images or patterns.

Top Panel

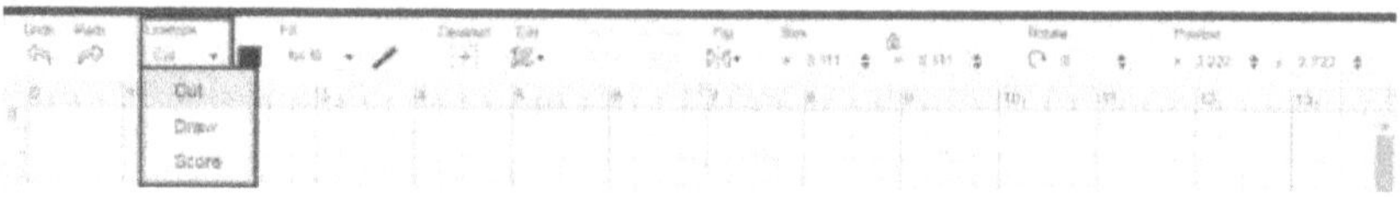

Photo credit: help.cricut.com

The top panel is the busiest. It has two different subpanels. Generally, the top panel is used to generalize and organize elements and layers of design.

First Subpanel

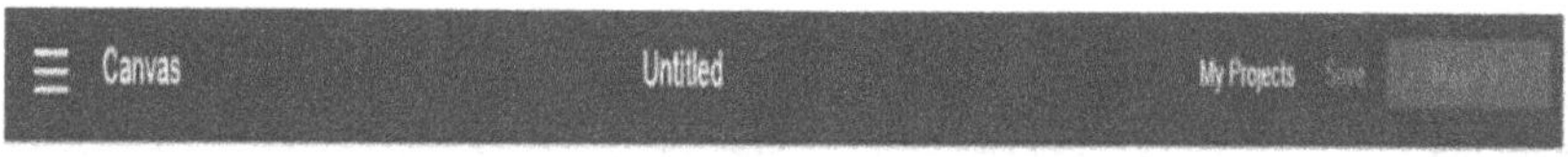

Photo credit: help.cricut.com

This allows you to name your project, save it, and eventually cut it. Here, you can navigate to saving, naming, and sending your project to the Cricut machine for cutting.

- Toggle Menu: This part of the subpanel allows you to manage your account and your account subscriptions. This menu also gives you the option of updating your Cricut Design Space, calibrating your machine, and others.

- Project Name: You can use this to name your project. Your project will be automatically called 'Untitled' until you give it a name that you can use to identify it.

- My Projects: This is a library of all your projects saved on the Cricut Design Space, and so you can always refer to old projects.

- Save: This option saves your project into the library. As you work, you should save in case your browser crashes.

- Cricut Maker / Cricut Explore: When you're using Cricut Design Space for the first time, it asks you if you're using a Cricut Explore machine from the series or a Cricut Maker. As the Cricut Maker is a more advanced machine, it provides more benefits on Design Space than the machines in the Explore series.

- Make It: After uploading your files, you click on Make It so that it can cut. The software will categorize your projects depending on their colors. If you're planning to cut more than one project, you can use this to increase the projects you want to cut.

<u>Second Subpanel</u>

This subpanel is the editing menu. It allows you to edit, organize, and arrange images and fonts on the Canvas Area.

- Undo & Redo:

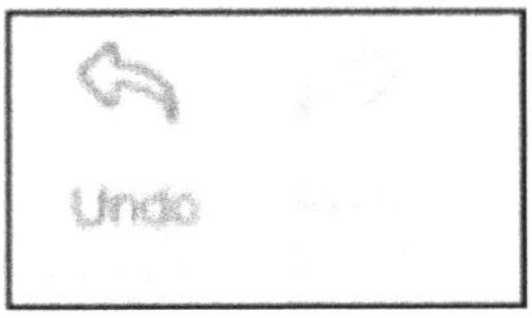

You can click undo when you make a mistake or create something that you don't want. And, you can click on redo if you mistakenly delete something that you need.

- Cut under (Line type): All your layers on the canvas area have this line type. After selecting the Make It option, the Cricut machine cuts the designs on your canvas area. Cut under allows you to change the colors of the layers and the fill too.

- Draw (Line type):

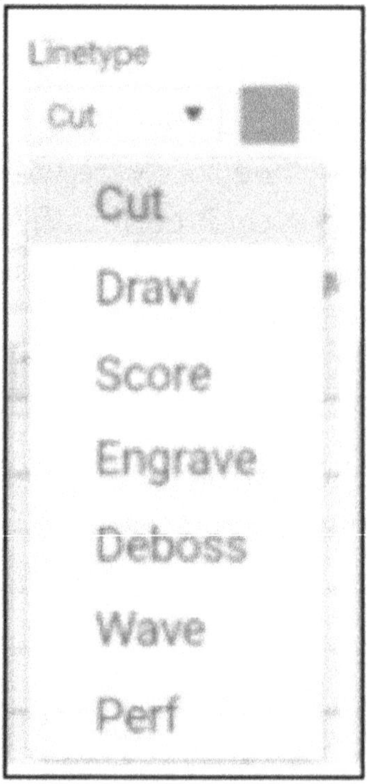

Cricut also allows you to write and draw on your designs. When you select this line type, you're given different Cricut pens, so you can use these to draw on the canvas area.

Here, when you click on Make It, your Cricut machine will draw or write instead of cutting.

- Score (Line type): This is an advanced version of the Scoring Line in the left panel. When you select this option for a layer, the layer will look scored. And so, when you click on Make It, the Cricut machine will score the materials instead of cutting it.

When you want to score, you will require a scoring stylus or scoring wheel. The scoring wheel can only work with the Cricut Maker.

- Engrave, Wave, Deboss, and Perf (Line type): These four tools are brand new! They were released by Cricut recently, and Cricut Maker users can only use them. Also, that user has to have the latest version of the Design Space application. These tools allow you to have significant effects on a lot of materials.

- Fill: This is mainly used for patterns and printing. You can only use this option when Cut is selected as a line type.

- Print:

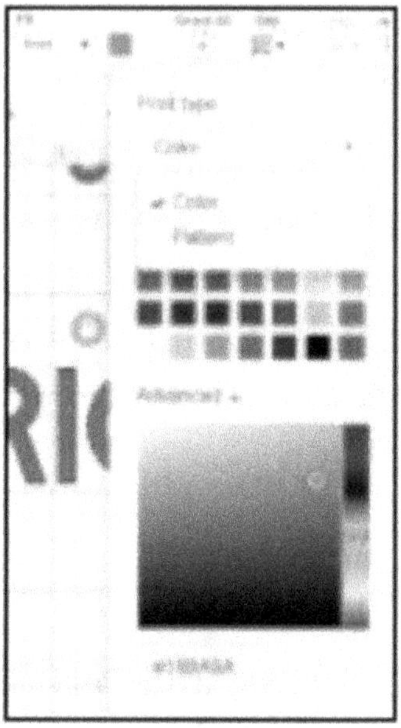

Photo credit: daydreamintoreality.com

Any Cricut user likes this option. This allows you first print out your design and then cut them out. To use the print option, when the fill option is active, you first click on Make It. You then send the files to your printer at home before feeding it into the Cricut for cutting.

- Edit:

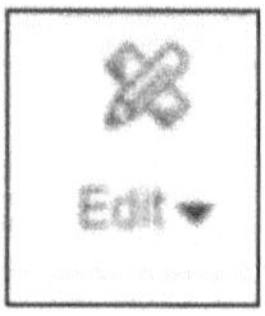

This icon contains three options on the dropdown menu. The cut option allows you to remove an element from the canvas, the copy option that copies the same component without removing it, and then the paste option, which inserts the cut or copied element.

- Select All: You can use this to highlight everything on your canvas area.

- Align: There are different options under this, and you must master all of them. They are:

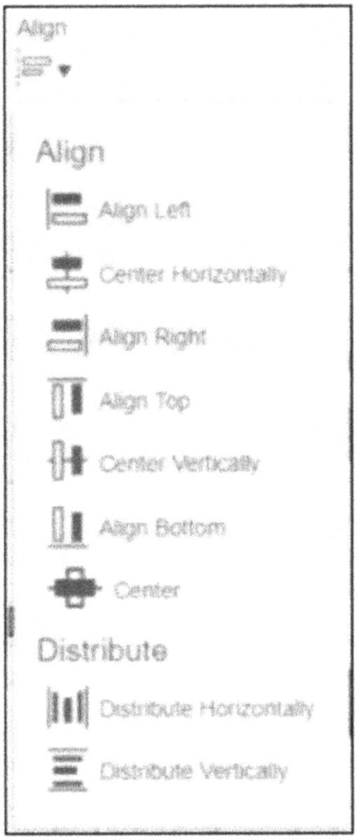

Photo credit: daydreamintoreality.com

Align Left: This option ensures that all the elements are aligned to the left. The detail at the end of the left side will determine how the other details move.

Center Horizontally: This will align all the elements horizontally.

Align Right: This will align the elements to the right. As with align left, the item at the end of the left side will determine how the other items move.

Align Top: This will align the elements you select to the top of the canvas page.

Center Vertically: This will align all the design elements vertically.

Align Bottom: This does the opposite of the Align Top option by aligning the layers or elements to the bottom.

Center: This aligns both the horizontally aligned and vertically aligned elements to the center.

- Distribute: This allows you to create the same spacing between elements or layers.

Distribute Horizontally

Distribute Vertically

- Flip:

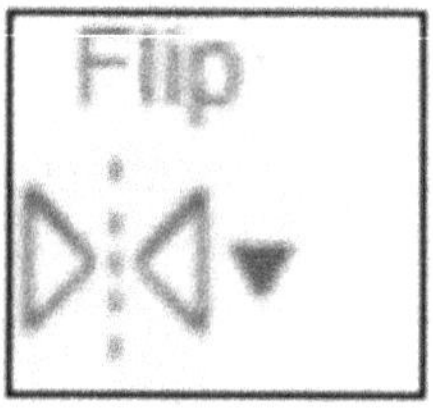

If you want to reflect on your designs as though they are looking at a mirror, you can use this option. It provides two options.

Flip Horizontal

Flip Vertical

- Arrange:

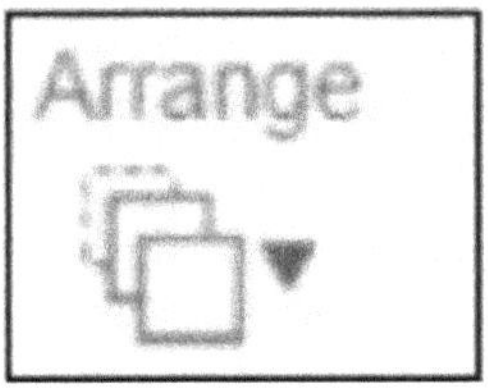

The arrange options allow you to move elements like images, texts, or designs to others' front or back. It provides four options.

Send to Back: This will displace the selected designs or elements and take them to the back.

Move Backward: If you select an element and click on this, the elements move back once. If you have three parts, you can move one to the middle of the other two.

Move Forward: this is the opposite, and it moves the element forward once.

Send to Front: This will displace the selected element and take it to the front.

- Size:

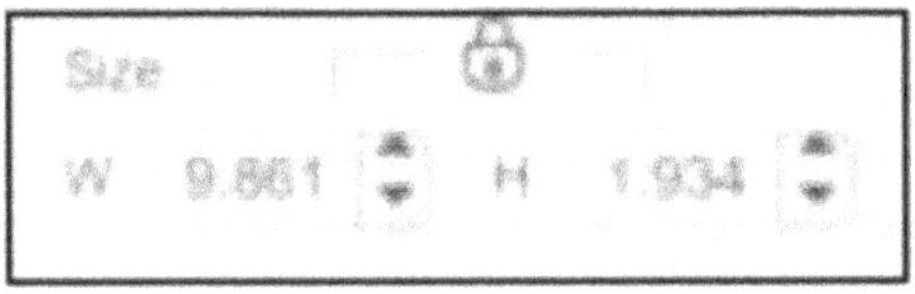

This provides you with the options to adjust, increase, or decrease the elements' size or total design. Everything that you create has a scale, and you use this to modify the size. This is especially if you have a specific format that you're following.

- Rotate:

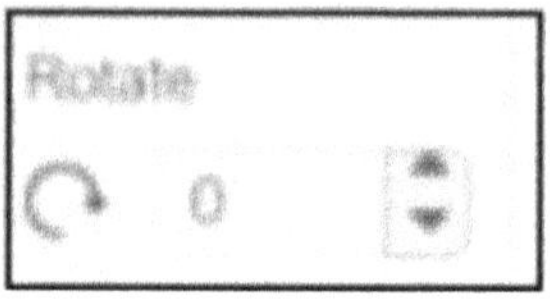

The Cricut Design Space allows you to rotate the element or layer to any angle that you choose.

- Position:

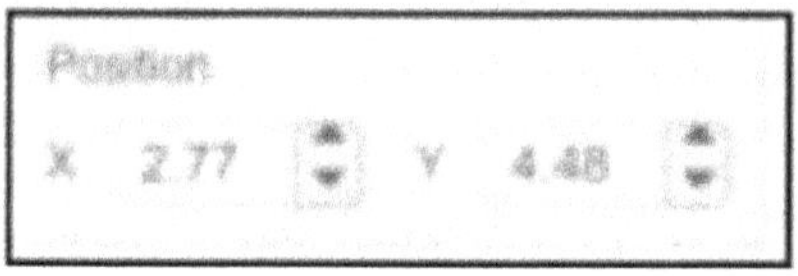

As the canvas area has grid lines, you can use these options to pick a particular position for the X and Y-axis element.

- Font:

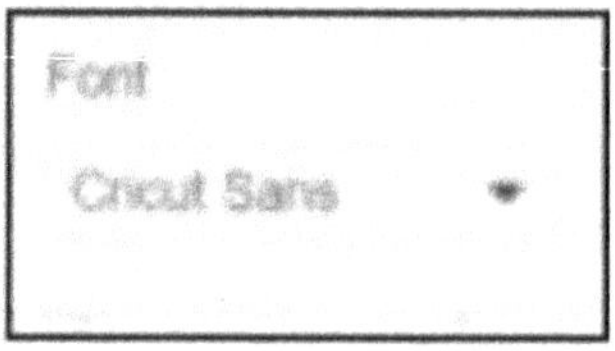

For your projects, Cricut provides you with different fonts if you're using Cricut Access. If not, you can use your system's font or use the Cricut fonts for a price.

- Font Size: This allows you to increase or decrease the size of your font.

- Line Space: This is especially useful when you want to ensure that your texts on your design are evenly spaced or spaced according to your preference.

- Letter Space: This allows you to arrange the spaces between the letters.

- Style:

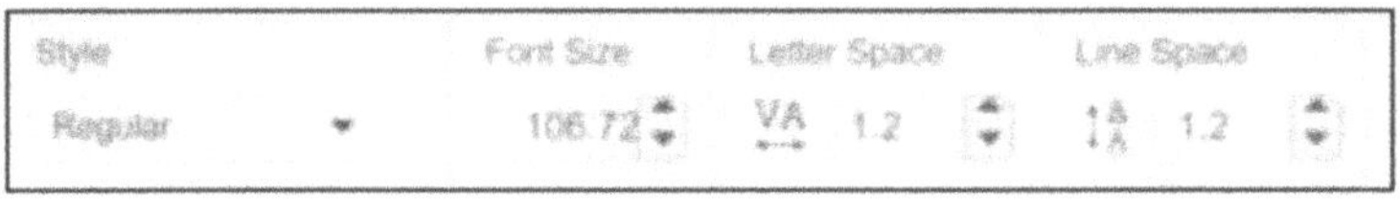

This includes Regular, which is the default setting. Bold, which makes the font thick. Italic, which tilts the font sideways. Bold Italic which combines both the Bold and Italic function.

- Curve:

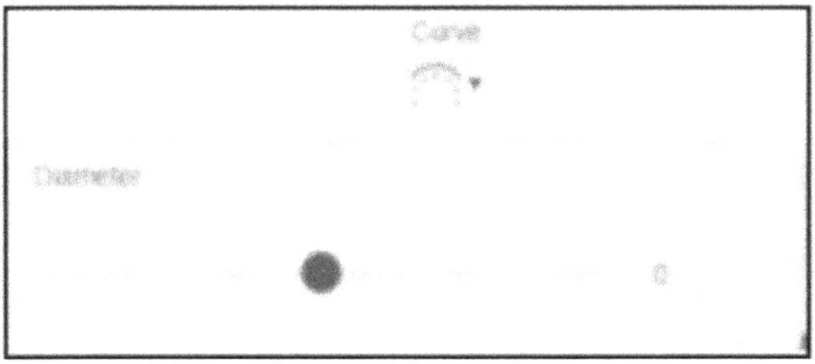

Photo credit: daydreamintoreality.com

You can also design your texts by using the curve setting. You can curve your text upwards or inwards. You can also curve your texts into a circle.

- Advanced:

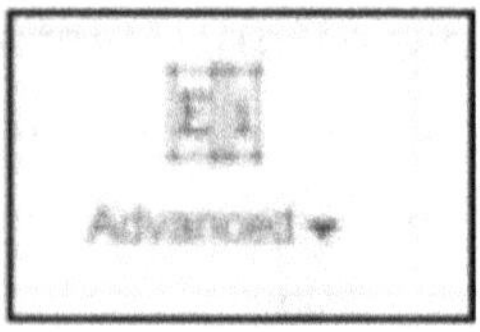

On the top editing panel, this is the last option.

Ungroup to Letters: This allows you to disconnect each letter into single layers each.

Ungroup to Lines: This allows you to disconnect a paragraph on different lines.

Ungroup to Layers: This is a very tricky option. It's only available on Cricut Access or if you purchase it.

Chapter 2:
Project Design

When you're ready to start a new Cricut project, you'll begin by logging into Design Space using the username and password you registered with Cricut. Once you're logged in, you'll see the Design Space homepage. This page includes video tutorials, featured Cricut Access projects, and projects using new materials and tools. It also features a slider showcasing your most recently opened projects, making it easy to review what you've been working on and pick up where you left off.

You have two options at the top right-hand side of your screen: a green New Project button and a My Projects button. To continue editing a project you've already started, click My Projects (you can also select a specific project using the slider as mentioned earlier further down on the homepage). To start a brand-new project, click the green New Project button. This will open a blank canvas, which is a screen with gridlines to help you properly measure and scale your project as you create. At the top of the canvas is your toolbar, which you will use to edit your design.

Creating and Editing Your Project

Once you begin a new project, on the left-hand side of your canvas, you will see a menu with several options: New, Templates, Projects, Images, Text, Shapes, and

Upload. The New tab allows you to begin a new project; when you click this option, you'll be prompted to save whatever you're working on.

The Templates tab brings up a wide range of templates, such as mugs or tea towels, to insert onto your blank canvas. These templates can help you better visualize your design and how to properly size and space images and text. The templates are for reference only and will not be cut as part of your design.

The Projects tab houses Cricut's Ready to do projects. With these designs, you can just open a project and begin cutting – no need for any editing on your part. You can search these projects by category using the drop-down menu. Categories include specific types of projects, such as accessories and home decor, and collections of free projects. Some of these ready-made designs allow you to customize features, such as changing the text to personalize your project. Once you are ready to cut your selected project, simply click the Make It button on the lower right-hand corner of your screen; this will bring up a new mat preview screen where you can select the size of material you want to use and the number of copies you want to make. Design Space will even tell you which type of machine mat to use for the project.

The Images tab brings up the Cricut Image Library, which contains hundreds of graphics you can purchase to use in your design. You can search these images by category, or if you are looking for a very specific type of image, you can type it into the search bar if you see a small green "a" in the top left-hand corner of an image that means that the image is included in your Cricut Access. There is also a Free This Week category. You can also use the Cartridges button to look through the image sets on various cartridges; these sets are then available to purchase to add to your Design Space library.

The Text tab opens up a text box on your canvas. You can type in your personalized text and then use the toolbar above the canvas to customize your font type, style, size, spacing, and alignment. You can also use this toolbar to curve your lettering and create shadowing effects. The Font drop-down box on the left-hand side of your toolbar allows you to select fonts included on your computer, as well as special Cricut fonts that are either included in your Cricut Access subscription or available for purchase. The Filter option in this menu allows you to search for fonts of a specific style, such as writing fonts or multi-layer fonts. To create a handwritten look, select a font that is a "writing" style; when you cut a project using this font, your Cricut will use pens to write your text as if it were done by hand. Cursive fonts fall under the writing style category. On the other hand, files that are not writing styles will appear on your final project as just the outline of the text, meaning the letters will not be filled in.

The Shapes tab brings up basic shapes, like circles or stars, to use in your design. You can edit these shapes, including their size and color, using the toolbar at the top of the canvas.

The Upload tab lets you select image files from your computer or device to use in your design. You can upload a range of file types, including .jpg, .gif, .png, .bmp, .svg, or .dxf. You can also upload an image or pattern to use as a fill or background for your project.

On the right-hand side of your canvas, you will see another menu with a tab for Layers and a tab for Color Sync. If your canvas is blank, this menu will be grayed out, meaning you will not be able to click on any of the options. However, once you have inserted an image, graphic, text box, or shape onto your blank canvas, you will be able to click through this menu as well. Each item on your canvas – each image, text box, graphic, or shape – sits in its layer and is editable independently of all the other design items. The Layer menu includes options in the lower right-hand corner to customize each layer. The Slice option allows you to split overlapping layers into separate pieces.

In contrast, the Weld option lets you merge two or more layers. Use the Attach option to hold a layer in place to make your cut or to add a text box to a shape or image layer; if you do not use this button, the Cricut machine may move the design on that layer when it cuts to maximize the use of your material. The Flatten option merges all of your layers into a "flat" printable image. In contrast, the Contour option lets you see or hide lines on a particular layer.

When you click on a particular layer, you will see a pop-up menu called Layer Attributes. This is where you can assign a color to your layer (for example, making a star shape yellow) and select whether that particular layer will be cut, written, or scored by your Cricut machine.

The Layer menu also includes a Color Sync option, which helps you match colors between layers. This is useful when you are using multiple colors in a single project; the Color Sync feature ensures that your Cricut machine cuts all layers that are the same color simultaneously, removing the need for you to switch materials back and forth multiple times.

Cutting Your Project

When you are happy with your design, click the green Make It button on your screen's top right-hand side. This will bring up your mat preview screen. On this screen, you can select the number of copies you want to cut and the design's size. You can also rotate your designs and move them to sit exactly where you want on your mat. For example, suppose your project includes five small star shapes. In that case, you can arrange them in a single line at the top of your mat rather than scattered around the mat; in this way, you can maximize the space on your material and cut down on material waste.

When your designs are arranged to your liking, make sure that your Cricut machine is connected to your computer or device, either through the USB cable or wirelessly via Bluetooth. Click the green Continue button in the lower right-hand side of your screen, and your machine will begin your cut.

Practice, Practice, Practice

Suppose you owned a legacy Cricut model that functions using physical cartridges. In that case, the Design Space software may seem a bit intimidating at first. However, the freedom the software gives you in creating unique, truly customized projects is well worth the effort it takes to learn the program. The best way to become more comfortable with the software is simply to spend some time clicking through and exploring all of its capabilities and experimenting with new designs. As with anything else, practice makes perfect!

CRICUT ACCESS SUBSCRIPTION

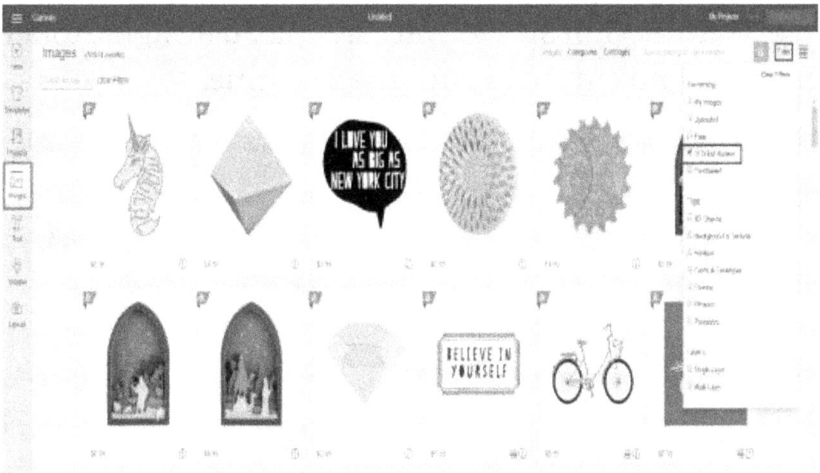

Photo credit: help.cricut.com

In this guide, you might have heard about the Cricut Access Subscription a few times and all the benefits that the members enjoy. You might also wonder if the subscription is worth it.

Cricut Access can be referred to as a paid membership for Cricut members. It gives its members instant and unlimited access to an incredible library to help them design and create projects. The library has over 90,000 images, over a hundred fonts, and many ready-to-cut projects.

You should only use Cricut Access if you're planning on going in-depth with your designs on Cricut Design Space. It's a cool deal because you get a lot of fonts, images, and projects.

There is a simple contrast between Cricut Access and Cricut Design Space. Firstly, Design Space is completely free. With Design Space, you can upload designs, touch them up, and cut them with the machine.

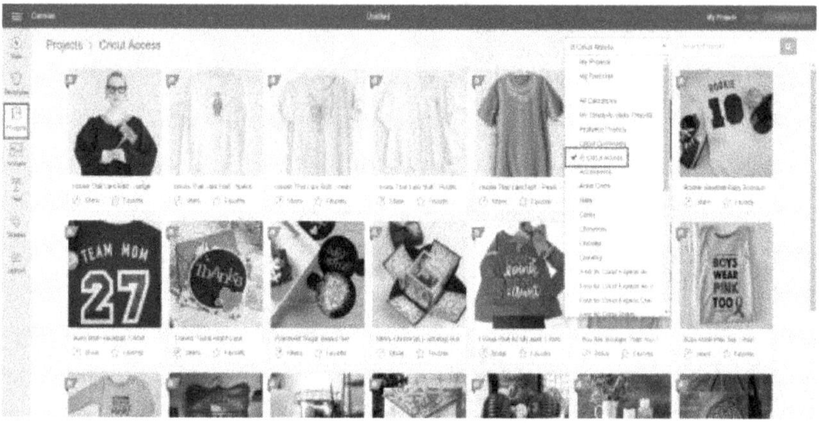

Photo credit: help.cricut.com

On the other hand, Cricut Access is not free, but you have to pay to use it by choosing one of their plans. The designs, fonts, photos, and projects are given to you once you've paid, and you then use them in the Design Space application.

Suppose you're not a Cricut Access member. In that case, that doesn't mean that you will not be able to see the fonts, designs, or photos that are seemingly exclusive to Cricut Access. You can still use them, but you will have to pay for it before cutting it out.

Cricut Access Plans

Generally, all Cricut Access plans to provide the following:

Over 400 fonts for your unlimited use.

Unlimited use of over 50,000 images, ready-to-cut projects, and graphics.

10% savings on cartridges, images, and ready-to-cut projects and fonts from known brands like Hello Kitty, Disney, and others.

10% savings on any of the physical products and merchandise that you purchase on their website.

You also get Priority Member Care Line, which means that you get half the wait time that others get.

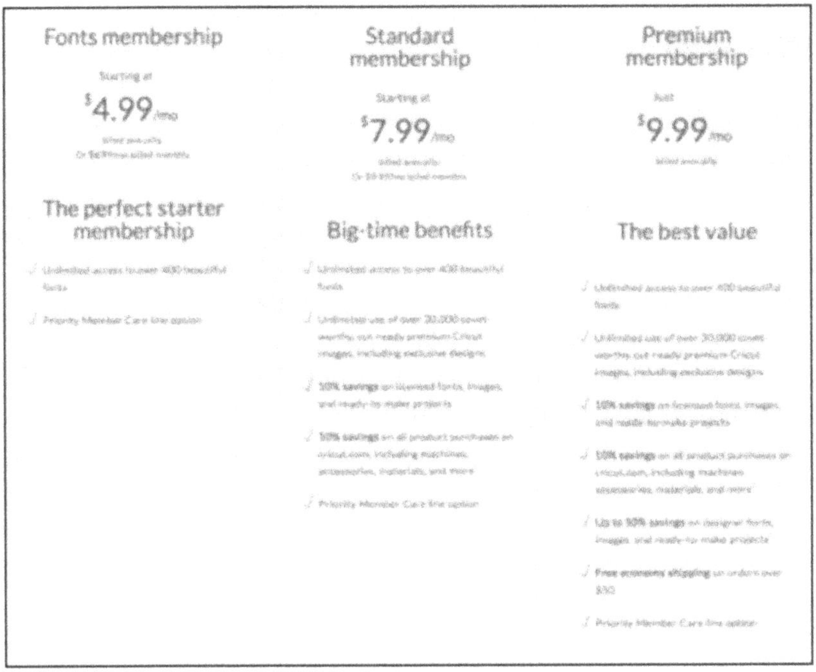

Cricut has three plans which are highly convenient and provide you with a lot of benefits.

Perfect Starter Plan

If you're not sure about using Cricut Access, this is the best plan to test it and see if it's something you need. It provides you with all the benefits mentioned above, and it costs about $10 monthly.

Annual Plan

The Perfect Starter plan and the Annual plan are almost the same. The difference between them both is that, while Perfect Starter is a monthly subscription, this is annual. Here, you make a one-year commitment, and you pay $95.88 yearly. This is $7.99 monthly.

Premium Plan

Apart from the benefits I mentioned above, you also get many more discounts with the Premium plan. You get 50% off on licensed graphics, fonts, and ready-to-cut projects. You also get free economy shipping when you purchase goods worth more than $50.

This is also an annual plan which costs $119.88 yearly. This translates to $9.99 monthly.

Chapter 3:
Images in Design Space: Project to Process

How to Upload Image with a Cricut Machine

The capacity to upload your images into Design Space can be a lifeline, particularly if you can't discover anything remotely like what you're attempting to make. You can upload anything going from a PNG to a multilayered vector document, and Cricut will naturally process it. You will have the option to print, cut, or draw them any way you wish!

After you pick a basic image to upload, you will have the option to see the see and select the image to utilize.

Basic images are fundamental and little documents that contrast hues with a strong foundation.

Respectably perplexing images have more detail and shading, which you can see by look over them in Design Space.

Complex Images are definite and mix hues, so it is hard to tell the foundation from the closer view. Fluctuating degrees of concealing and mixing are remembered for this option. You will doubtlessly need to choose this version to do the most nitty-gritty crafting project.

SVG

The Scalable Vector Graphics is the best when utilizing your Cricut machine. They take into consideration more exact cuts than a PNG or JPG record.

If you download an SVG document from the web, ensure you extra the SVG record on the off chance that it is downloaded as a ZIP record (.ZIP documents can't be uploaded into Design Space).

Bonus Tip

Google, the realistic you are looking for? SVG + allowed us to see the entirety of the openly accessible designs you can bring into Cricut Design Space. Download the SVG record and upload it into Design Space if you can't discover what you're searching for on Cricut's foundation.

Browse the records you have on your PC or distributed storage and discover the image you might want to upload.

Fundamental Image Upload

Upload the record you might want to import to Cricut Design Space. This will probably be a.JPG or.PNG record type. Next, open the document selector or drag the record into the upload section of Design Space.

You will, at that point, can choose Simple, Moderately mind-boggling, or Complex design types. Select the most pertinent and precise sort at that point; click "Continue."

Identify the cutting lines of the uploaded image. Make certain to utilize the Tools on the left high quality of Canvas, for example, Select, Erase, and Crop. If you see a checkerboard design behind your image, that implies the zone has been evacuated successfully.

Click on Preview on to see the cut lines of the uploaded image. If you have to change the outcome, click Hide Preview to return to alter (from the past advance). Click Continue once you are prepared to proceed onward.

Name and label your image so you can discover it in your uploaded documents later. Either select "Print Then Cut" or "Cut image" to show what kind of action you might want your Cricut Machine to take. This will decide how the record is spared and ready to be utilized.

Finally, save the image. You will presently have the option to access and utilize your uploaded image.

Vector Image Upload:

1. Select the.SVG document you might want to import to Cricut Design Space. Either intuitive or physically select and import the image from your PC documents.

2. Name the image appropriately so you can think that it's later.

3. The new image document will appear in the Uploaded Images Library at the base of the screen.

4. Vectors will appear on Canvas as an assembled image. You can ungroup them on the right-hand side of the canvas if necessary.

How To Use Images In Cricut Design Space?

The Cricut library has more than 50,000 images, and these images are updated from time to time. The Cricut Design space permits you to use some of these images for free to determine if these images fit into your desired project before buying them. You can also upload your personally designed image unto the canvas. Here are simple steps on how to use the image(s) in your project:

Sign in to your Design Space and create a new project

Tap on the Image button in the bottom left corner of your screen if you are using an iOS/Android device or click on Images at the left-hand side of your screen if you are using Windows/Mac computer.

Browse the images to choose the ones you wish to use in your project. Use any of the options below:

All Images

use this to search for a particular image in your Library or view featured images.

Categories

use this to browse images by selecting the image categories.

Cartridges

use this to search through the alphabetical list of more than 400 Cricut cartridges or even search for a specific one.

4. Insert your desired image(s) into your project and start editing them.

IMAGES AND HOW TO BROWSE FOR CARTRIDGES.

Designs are made of elements hold on cartridges. Every cartridge comes with a keyboard overlay and instruction brochure. The plastic keyboard overlay indicates key alternatives for that cartridge solely. But recently, urban center Craft has free a "Universal Overlay" that's compatible with all cartridges released when Lammas Day, 2013. The universal overlay aims to modify the cutting method by solely having to be told one keyboard overlay rather than having to learn the overlay for every individual cartridge. Styles will be cut out on a laptop with the Cricut style Studio software system, on a USB connected Traveler machine, or directly entered on the Cricut machine using the keyboard connection.

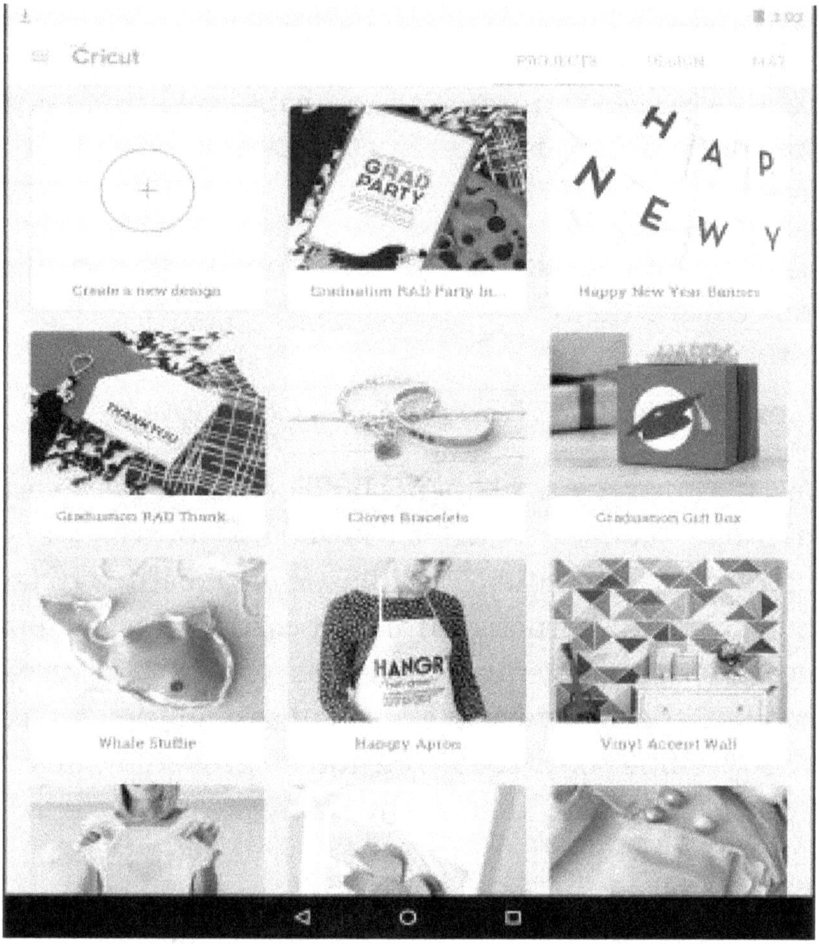

There are two varieties of cartridges form and font. Every cartridge incorporates creative options that may give many different cuts from only one cartridge. There are presently many cartridges on the market, containing fonts and shapes, with new ones added monthly. In contrast, some cartridges are basic in content.

The Cricut line incorporates various costs; however, the cartridges are interchangeable, though not all choices on a cartridge could also be on the market with the smaller machines. All cartridges work solely with the Cricut software system. They should be registered to one user to be used and can't be sold or given away. A casing learned for an out of the print machine is perhaps going to become useless when the machine is finished. Cricut stashes the correct to discontinue support for a few versions of their software system at any time, which may create some cartridges now obsolete.

Editing Images in Cricut Design Space Using The Slice Tool

To assist me in editing pictures in the Cricut Design Space, I used the Slice device. I'm likely still going to use that method for photos I've already uploaded to Cricut Design Space. Let me explain how to edit images using the Slice tool.

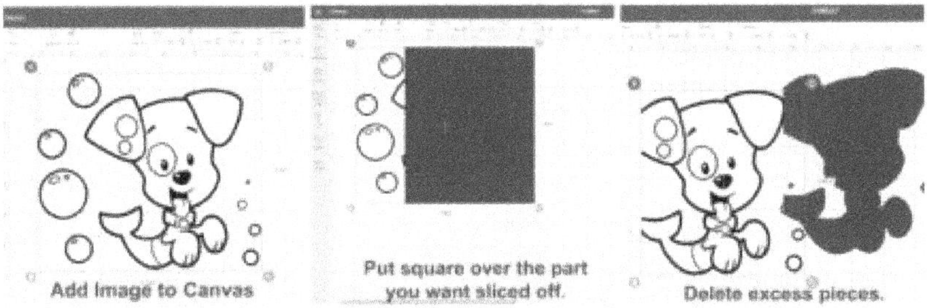

1. Click on the picture and then click Insert Images to add your attached picture to your Cricut Design Space canvas. You can add more than one image to your canvas at a time.

2. Make your picture a lot larger so you can work on it by pressing and pulling it down a little bit on the right upper corner. Just far enough to be able to see it better.

3. I want to get rid of the dog in the image I've uploaded. I don't see any canvas wiping alternative, so I'm trying to use the Slice tool to cut the dog out. In the left-hand toolbox, press Shapes, then press the circle.

4. Unlock the table by pressing below the square on the left upper panel. Do you see the icon of the lock? Click on that. Now, using the right top corner, you can transfer the square in any form you want. I placed the circle over the portion that I was about to wipe out, the dog.

5. Clicking or highlighting the circle, click and hold the change key on your keyboard. Click the picture of the bubble with your mouse, well, bubble for me. This emphasizes both of them.

6. Click the Slice device at the right upper corner with both the circle and the picture outlined.

7. Start taking back your slice's parts. There ought to be three parts. They can be deleted.

8. Continue this method until the manner you want your picture to be printed.

EDITING IMAGES IN THE DESIGN SPACE OF CRICUT WHEN UPLOADING IMAGES

1. For this method to operate, you will need to upload a picture from your desktop. Click complicated once you

upload it, and the next window is where the magic takes place.

2. At the left corner of the top. Look at the wand? Click on it and press on the hair. Click on the continuation button and name the picture. Click the save button.

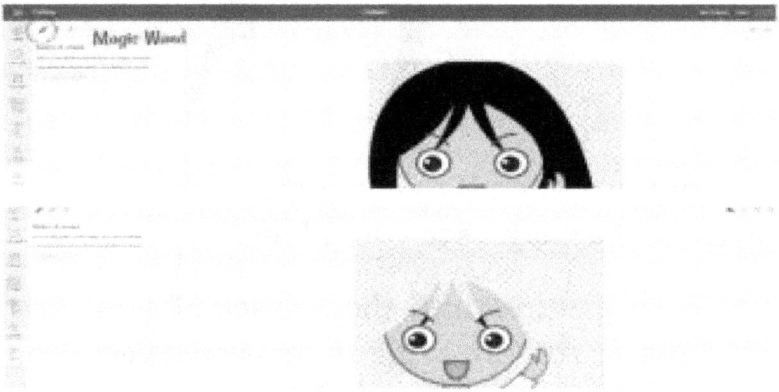

It's gone, and it's been so simple. Now, let's look after her flesh.

3. I have to upload her again. I'm going to operate on erasing the corpse this moment. First, press back on the magic wand to remove the face, arms, body, and any hard-to-reach pieces. Once you've finished that, take the eraser to wash the remainder of your flesh until it's gone.

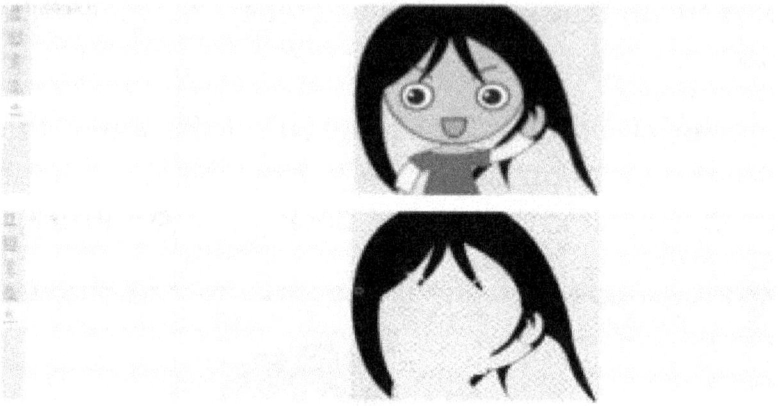

Click Continue, identify your picture, and then press Save when the image is to your liking.

Insert both pictures into the surface of your Cricut Design Space. You can bring them back together once you've got them there. I'm excited about this process because sometimes, I want to change things like hair color. I couldn't change the hair color if I left the picture like it was. But I can do that now.

Would you like to know how to edit images in Cricut Design Space as thrilled as I am? I pray so.

Now, go out and do some crafting!

HOW TO PURCHASE IMAGES AND UPLOAD THEM

There are more than 50,000 images in the Cricut Library. With the Design space, you have permission to try these images for free to confirm its suitability in your desired project or projects. Then after that, you can purchase it.

You can also upload personal images unto the Canvas.

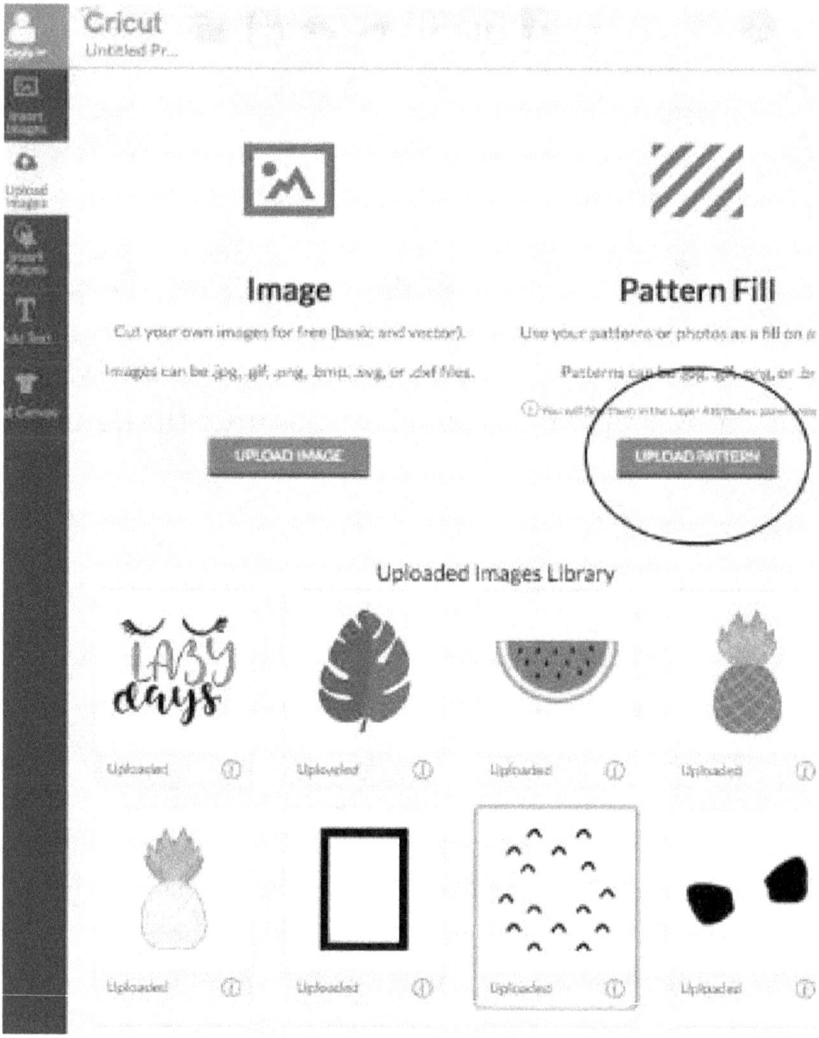

So, how do you use images in Cricut Design Space? Here are simple steps on how to use images in your project:

Chapter 4: Text Guide in Design Space

Working with Fonts in Design Space

One of the unique features of the Cricut Maker machine is the ability to personalize your project. This creative ability, innate in us, gives us maximum satisfaction and a great sense of accomplishment.

Working with texts and fonts shows the individual freedom that this machine's user has, the ability to show the power of creativity. As stated earlier, you can use the Cricut fonts or the one installed on your computer or device. So, how can you add text, select font, install/uninstall font in Windows/Mac? Let us take it one by one.

Add Text to Design Space

Choose the font you intend to use and then type in your text. Note that you can type the text before selecting the font on a Windows/Mac computer.

Select any area outside the text box to close it

To edit the text, double-tap or double-click on the text. You can choose the action you want from the options available, including font style, font size, change the font, letter spacing, and line spacing.

Writing with Fonts

Cricut Design Space offers several Cricut fonts that are specifically designed to be drawn using a pen. To write any font using Cricut pens with the Maker or Explore machine, change your text's line type from "Cut" to "Write." You can choose the font and a "Writing style" after you select a font you intend to use.

The Writing style fonts are similar to text written by hand, but most fonts will trace the letters' outside.

System Fonts

System fonts refer to fonts installed on your computer or mobile device. Every time you sign in, the Cricut Design Space will automatically access your system fonts and allow you to use them for free in the Design Space projects.

Note that the system fonts may vary between devices because system fonts are installed on a particular device.

Some system fonts also have design components that are not compatible with Cricut Design space because Cricut did not design them. Therefore, do not surprise when you have problems importing them into the Design Space or behave unusually when using them in the Design Space.

Use the instructions on the font site or app when downloading fonts to your device or computer. This is to ensure that the installation is done successfully on your device or computer. The instructions are different, depending on your platform. The instructions for Windows/Mac, iOS AND Android are given below: For Windows/Mac

Select 'Text' in the design panel, which is at the left-hand side of the canvas

Form the Text Edit bar that will appear, input the text or even select the font before inputting it.

Click the Font drop-down menu to select the "System" index, displaying only the font installed on the computer.

SELECT THE FONT YOU DESIRE.

For Android:

Go to the bottom of the screen and select 'Text'.

From the displayed font list, search or scroll through the list to find your desired System font from the available fonts. Note that System fonts will have the label 'System'.

Select your desired font and then type in your text.

For iOS:

Go to the bottom of the Canvass screen and select 'Text'.

Select the "System" index from the font list that displays only the installed fonts on your device.

Select your desired font and type in your text.

Step by Step Guide to Write, Score, Cut, and Print with Cricut Maker

Before going into the step by step guide, let us define some important terminologies for a better understanding:

Cut-refers to cutting layer from your material.

Draw-refers to drawing on the layer using a Cricut pen.

Score-refers to scoring the layer using a Scoring Stylus or Scoring Wheel.

Print-refers to printing the layer using your home printer.

Linetype - refers to cutting, drawing, and scoring.

How to Perform Linetype from Windows/Mac

Place your text or images onto the design screen

From the Edit bar, select the Linetype drop-down. Note that the current Linetype is highlighted. Of course, you can change at once the Linetype of multiple layers by selecting the layers to be changed and then choose the desired Linetype from the drop-down. The image of the canvas will change to reflect your selection once this is done.

You can use the Print Then Cut feature by selecting the Fill drop-down. From there, select Print. To add color or pattern fill to the layer, select 'Color' or 'Pattern' from the Fill swatch drop-down.

How to Perform Linetype from Android/iOS

Place your text or images onto the design screen

At the bottom of the screen, tap on the "Layers" to access the Layers panel.

Click on the arrow that is next to the layer to obtain the Layer Attributes Panel. The current Linetype will always be highlighted.

Tap on the desired Linetype, which will change to reflect your selection.

If you are done with your selection, tap on the 'Layers' to close it.

How To Add Text To Cricut Design Space?

For users of Windows, navigate to the left-hand side of the Canvas and select the Text tool. For iOS or Android user, the Text tool is at the bottom-left of the screen.

Select the font size and the font type you wish to use and then type your text in the text box. Do not freak out when you did not choose the font parameters before typing the text. You can type the text with Cricut Design

Space before selecting the font on Windows/Mac computer.

Click or tap on any space outside the text box to close it.

How to Edit Text in Cricut Design Space?

To edit the text is super simple. Double click on the text to show available options. Select the action you wish from the list of the options displayed, including font style, type, size, letter, and line spacing.

Select the text you wish to edit on the Canvas, or you can insert text from the design panel, or select a text layer from the Layers Panel.

When the Text Edit Bar pops up, you can start changing the font using the available options. These options include Font, Font DropDown, Font Filter, Style, Font Size, Line Space, Alignment, and more.

How to Write Using Fonts

A simple way to write font using Cricut pen with Cricut Explore Air machine is to change your text's line type from 'Cut' to 'Write'. Next is to choose the font type you wish to use and select the "Writing style" of your choice. Note that the fonts used in the Writing style are similar to the text written by hand, but the Cricut machine will write it as if it is tracing the outside of the letters. I believe you know how to use fonts now and what the fonts' final form will look like. Now, I want to discuss the different types of fonts.

System Fonts

System fonts refer to fonts installed on your computer or mobile device. Every time you sign in, the Cricut Design Space will automatically access your system fonts and allow you to use them for free in the Design Space projects.

Some system fonts have design components that are not compatible with Cricut Design space because Cricut did not design them. Do not be surprised when you encounter failure to import them into the Design Space or behave unusually while using them in the Design Space. Use the instructions on the font site or app when downloading fonts to your device or computer.

Chapter 5:
Color Guide in Design Space

ADDING COLOR TO AN UPLOADED IMAGE, AND HOW TO MAKE MULTIPLE-LAYER VINYL

Select it and resize it to whatever size you need for your venture once the layout is put on the canvas. Once you have the volume, you need to go to the board of parts and choose' ungroup.' Ungrouping enables us to transfer each layer in place of the entire layout independently.

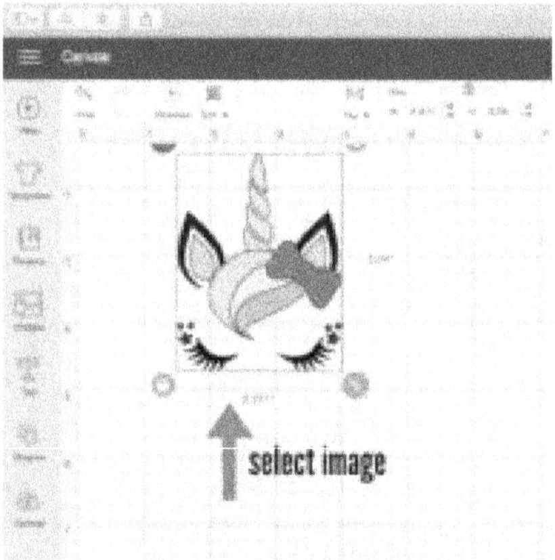

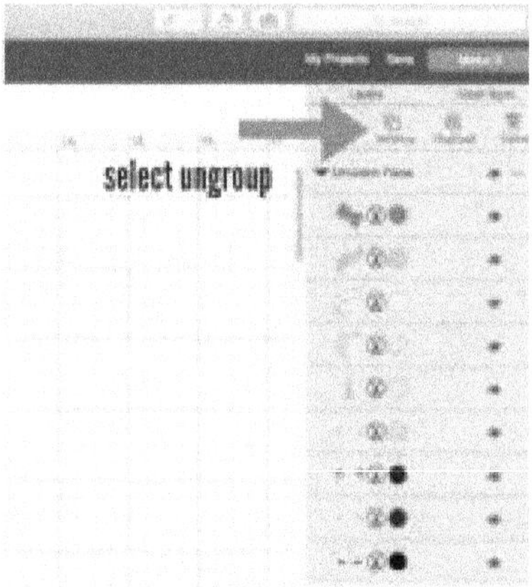

Next, put a shape in it. I used a square, but with stars and triangles, I also saw it. Insert the square and click on the 'unlock' button to manipulate the image in a rectangle. Duplicate it once you have the box size you want it to be.

Line up each rectangle below the original image. These are your registration marks to keep the design aligned on every layer.

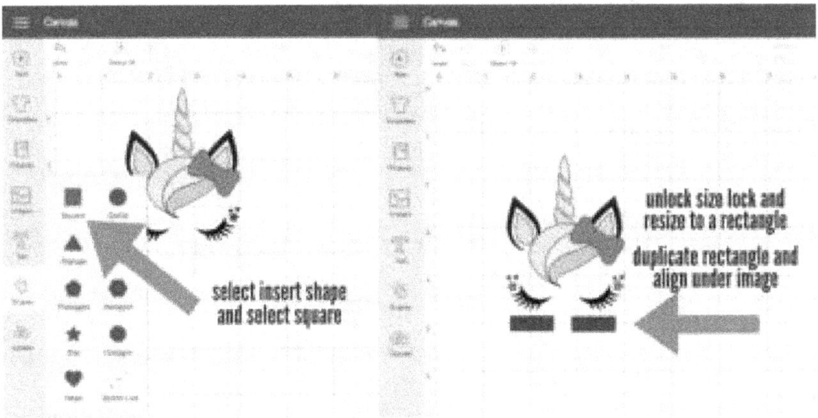

Duplicate Original Image and Registration Marks

Select everything and duplicate it after the original image has the registration marks under it. You're going to do this for every color you have. If you have six colors, you're going to double six times.

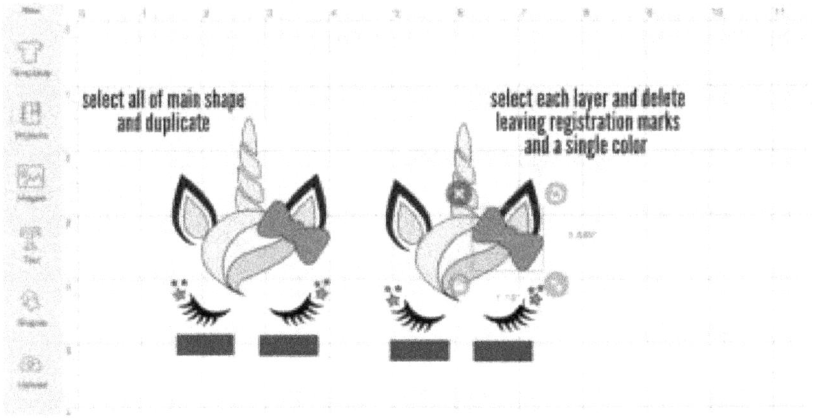

Delete Layers Leaving A Single Color Delete each layer at the moment, leaving only one color for each picture you duplicated. I didn't have light purple for the inner ears, so I chose not to trim that portion.

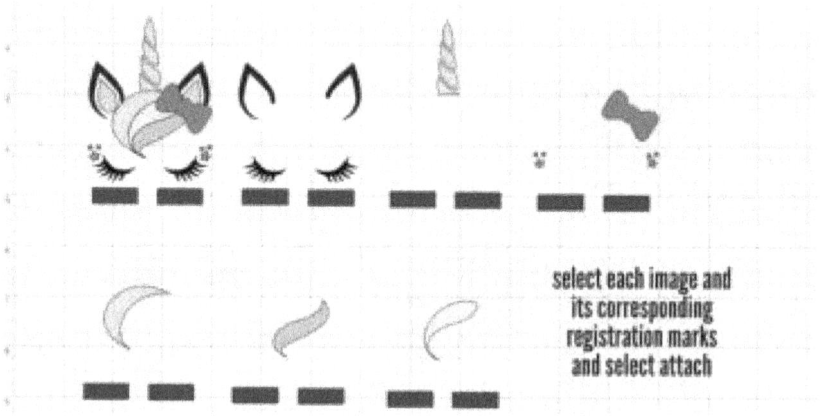

Attach each Set of Images

Choose each layer picture and its respective registration marks (not the primary picture) and then pick' add.' When you go to trim, this will hold the image and the registration marks in position. Otherwise, by putting them as near as feasible, Design Space will attempt to save your equipment. It's not going to assist us!

You will realize that the registration marks shift to your layer's color if you pick' add.'

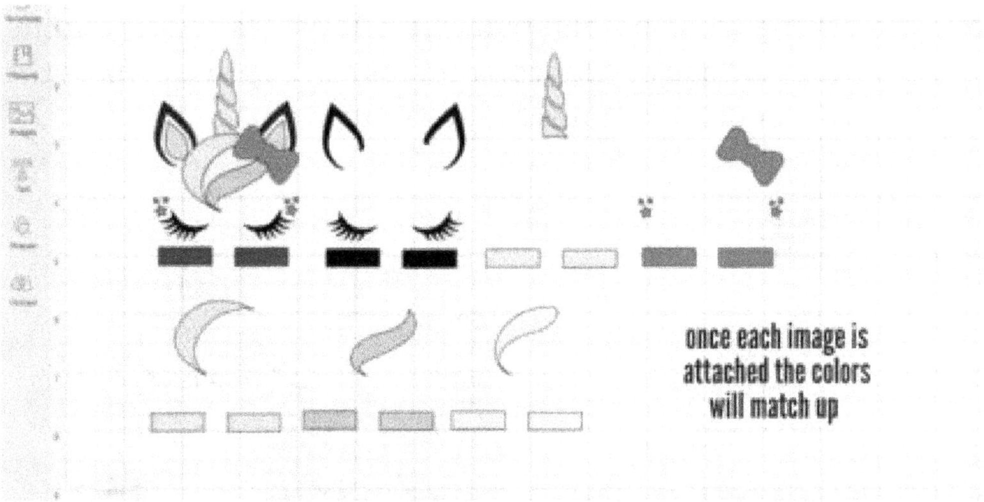

HOW TO LAYER VINYL WITH REGISTRATION MARKS

Hide and hide the main image!

We need to conceal the primary picture before the plates are effectively sliced. If not, it will also attempt to split each of its parts. Select the registry marks and the primary image. Select' band' and then press the little eyeball in the layer's cabinet. It is supposed to hide that primary picture, and it will not be trimmed.

To send the project to the mat, select' Make it.' Every color is going to be on its mat. Cut every color, then weed the picture.

SIDE NOTE*: If you prefer to use scraps instead of charging and reloading each color, pick all pictures and grab' add' after hiding the primary image. They're all going to change gray, so you're going to have to remember the color you wished for each chip. It's all going to be on one mat when it comes to the folding board. Each of your color scraps can be placed where the paper demonstrates they are cutting.

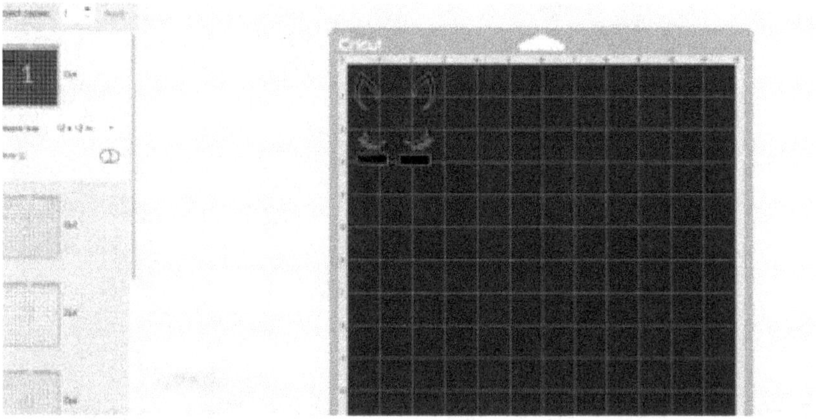

Weed Vinyl Pieces and Apply Transfer Tape

Weed leaving only the design and register marks on each layer.

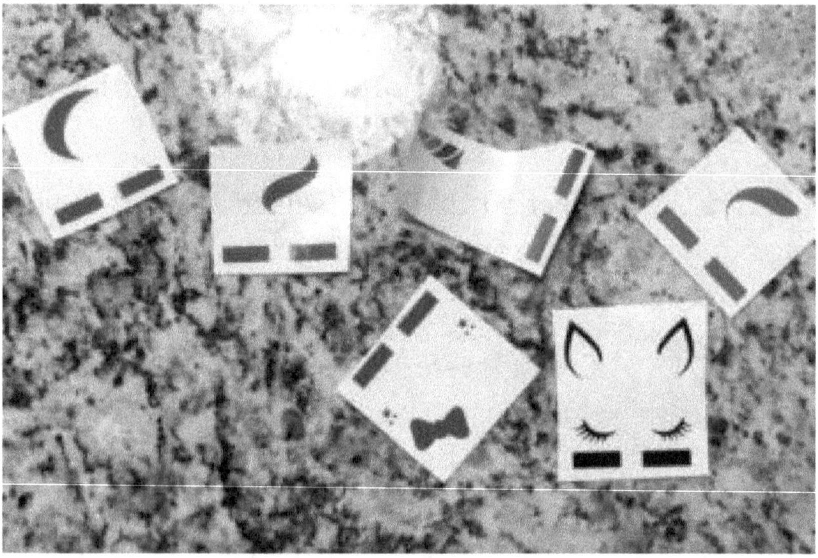

How to layer vinyl with registration marks/ Weed each layer

Add each layer to the Top Layer Down Transfer Tape

The only thing you need to care about is the rectangles as you operate through the layers. Everything else will be as soon as they're lined up. I want to say it's so easy, but it wasn't really for me. It helped tremendously, but knowing that you may not line up every rectangle perfectly. It's all right. Adjust and stay tuned!

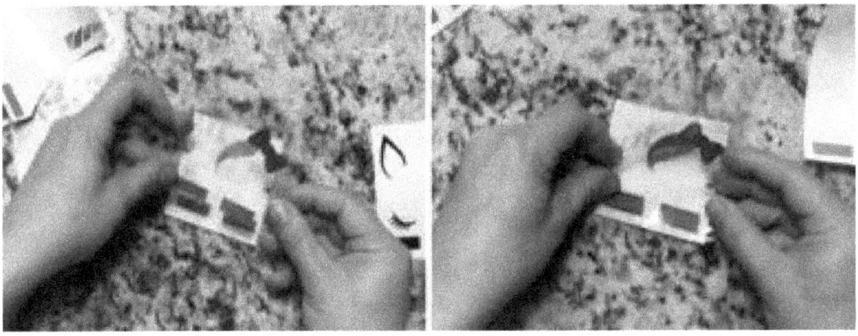

How to layer vinyl with registration marks

I just folded back the paper support where only the rectangles appear, instead of separating the whole paper base of the vinyl and then layering. This can assist you more correctly line up the rectangles. It's okay whatever direction it operates for you. There is no way to' correct' or' false.'

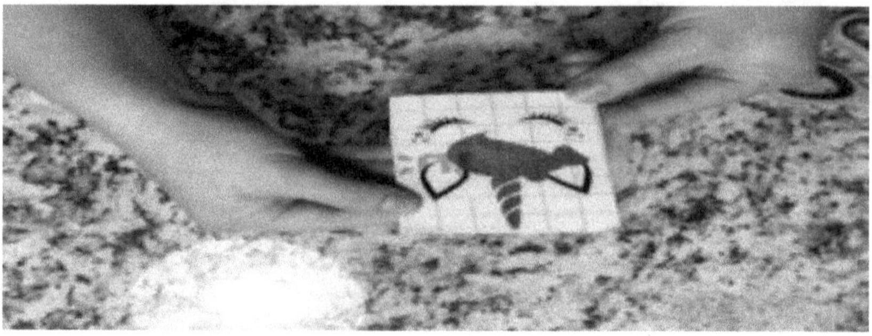

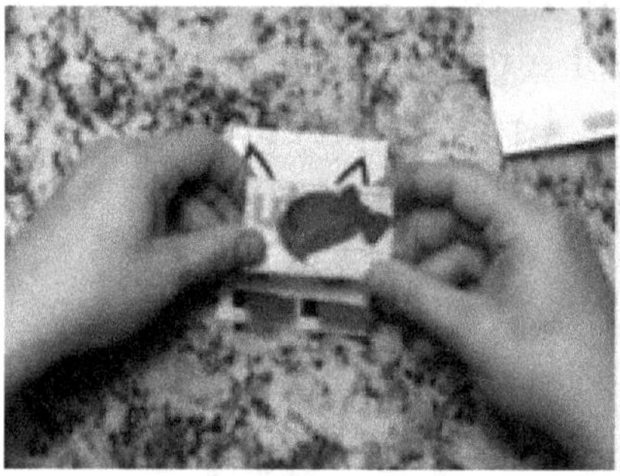

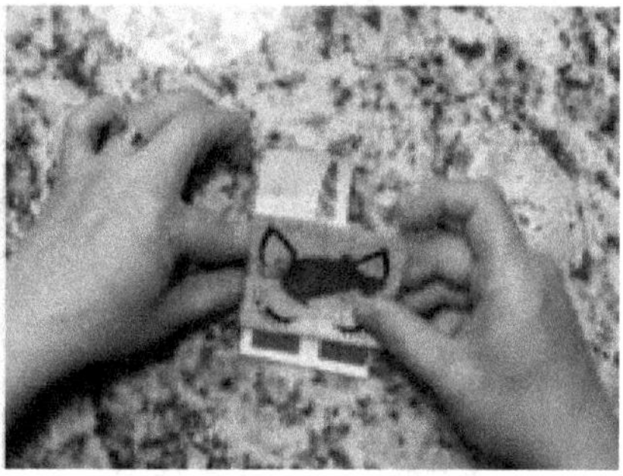

HOW TO DO SPLIT LETTERING WITH A DÉCOR

Use this monogram split-level tutorial on vinyl, heat transfer vinyl, and more in Cricut Design Space! The monogram on the split level is likely my favorite right now. I don't just like the look, but I believe it's less used than other traditional kinds of a monogram. Did you understand that in Cricut Design Space, you can create a split-level monogram? It's easy, but a few steps and the use of the slice tool are required. Open the design space for Cricut, and let's create one!

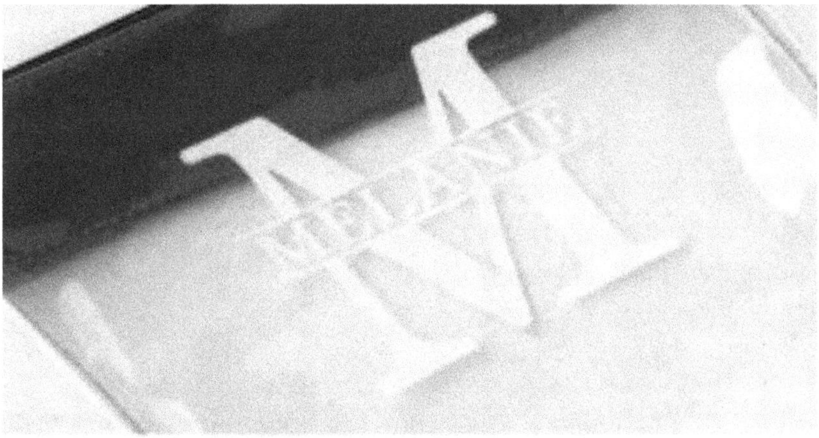

To start with, type the letter you want to split (or letters). Change it to the font you'd like. At the very end, for your project, you can resize it to the size, so do not worry about it right now. I use the font below for Cake Basics.

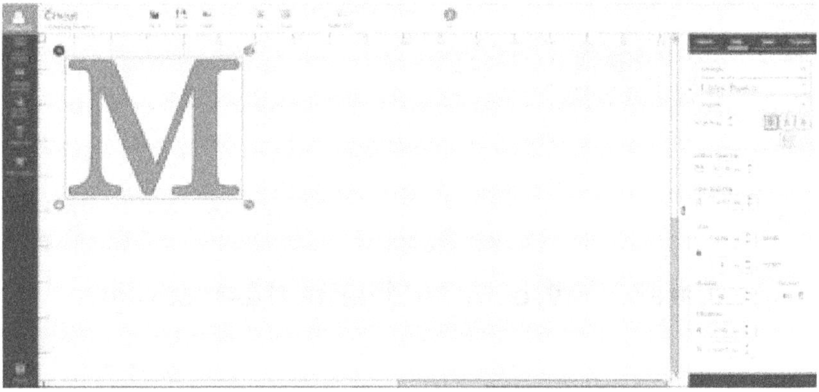

On the left-hand menu, select "insert shapes" and add a square. Click the lock icon on the square's lower left hand, so it turns to unlock.

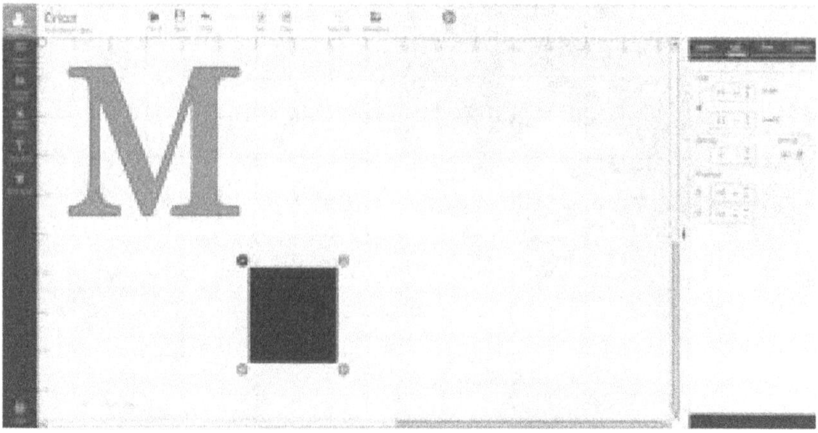

To make a rectangle, pull the circle. This rectangle will be the divided row (see the completed illustration-the row about the complete title and below).

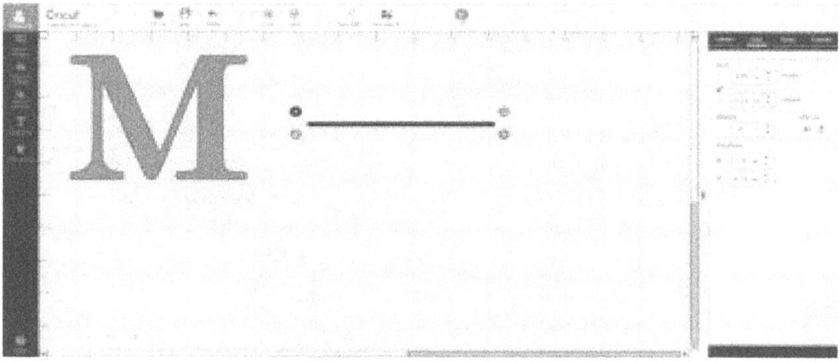

To generate a copy, copy, and paste this rectangle.

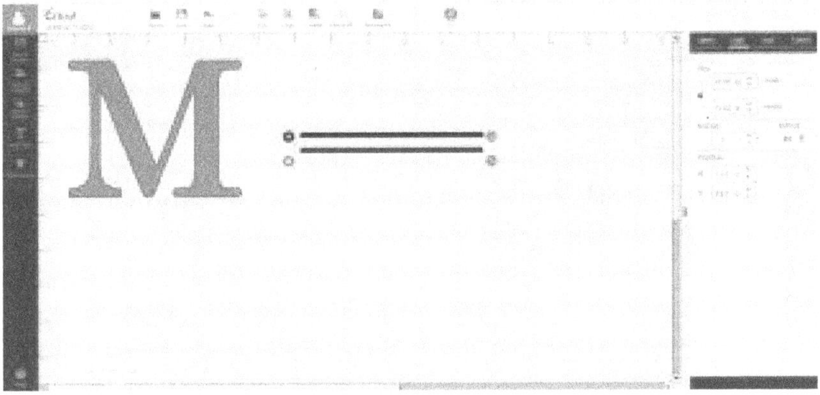

Pullover the large letter one rectangle. Keep in mind that the bottom part of the divided column is determined wherever you position the row. Select the rectangle and the large letter once the rectangle is placed and then press "Weld" on the board of the correct side parts.

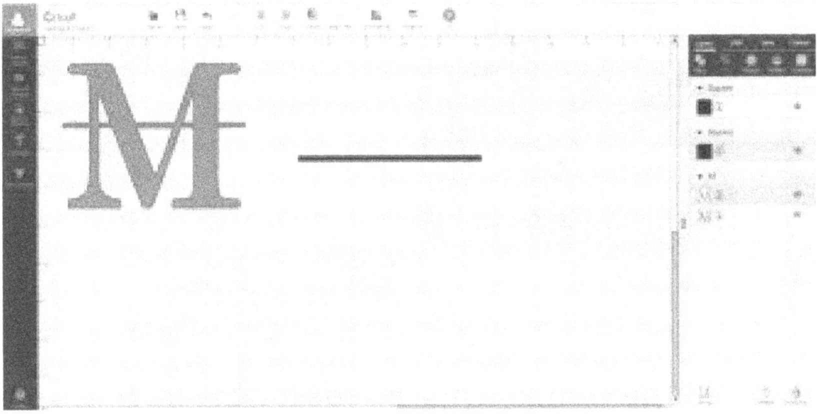

Pull the second rectangle over and SPLIT the FIRST RECTANGLE.

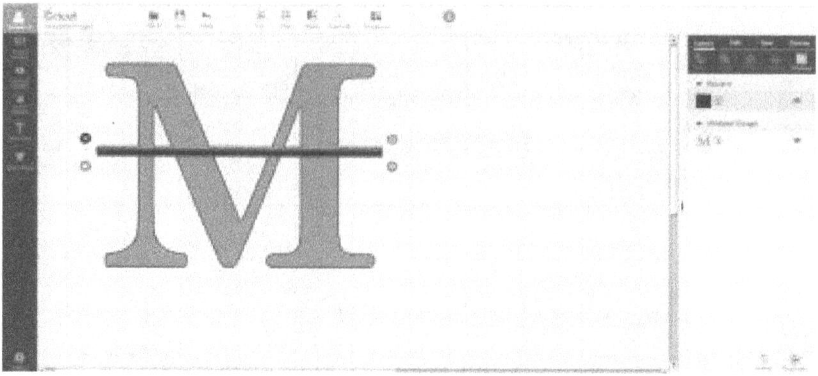

Check to open the lock button and then draw down the SECOND rectangle to cover the text's upper part. Select the second rectangle and the letter that has been welded. Click the "slice" button.

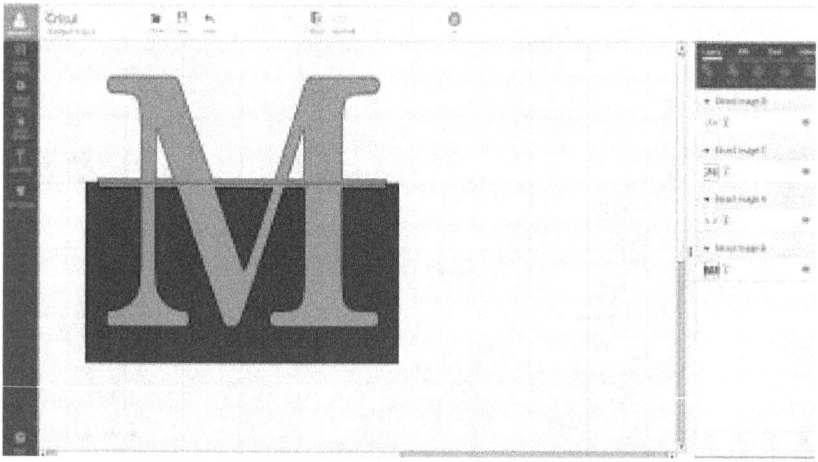

Delete all the components except for the large letter's bottom and the upper quarter.

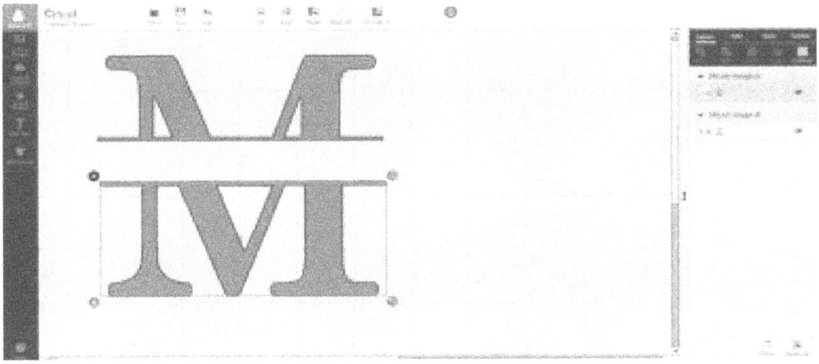

ADD THE WORD/NAME TO THE CENTER.

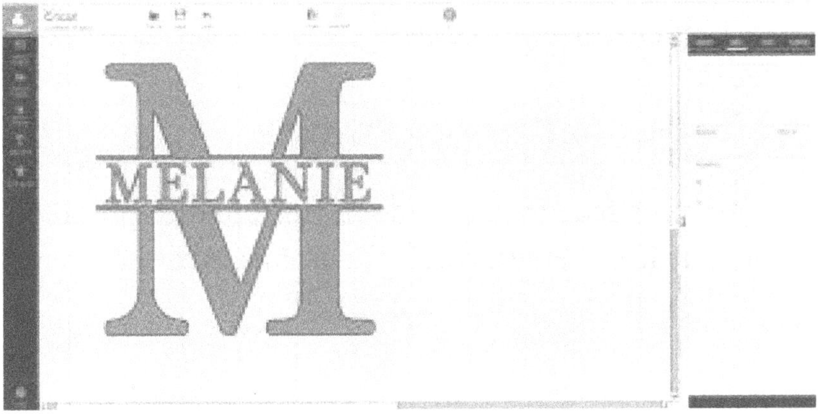

Make sure all layers are aligned and centered as you want. Select all of them, then press "Attach" on the board of correct layers.

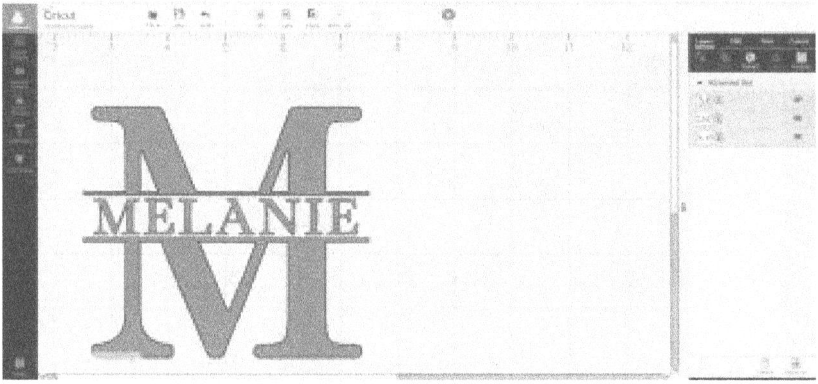

You can resize the whole item to suit your design once the parts are connected. Then submit it for cutting. All performed! All accomplished!

How to use the Contour Feature

Contour: this feature can hide or unhide individual cut or contour lines. However, if the image is multilayered, you will need to ungroup it first.

Chapter 6:
Advanced function

How to Slice

The slice tool is a feature in Cricut Design Space that cuts one design element out of another. You can use it to cut text from a shape, cut one shape from another shape, or cut overlapping shapes from each other. Below is an example, and we will cut text out from a heart shape;

Choose a font

Use any font you prefer, but decrease your letter spacing from to 0.9 so that your letters will link together.

Weld the text

When you're done with the spacing, you have to transform your letters into a single image using the weld tool. When you weld your letters, it permanently connects all the design elements into one image.

Choose an SVG

You can find a heart SVG from Lovesvg.com. You just need to ungroup everything and simply delete the unwanted elements.

Set the size of your design

You need to resize the image. Depending on the size you want, simply type the intended size on the width box. For this example, we'll stick to 5.5 inches.

Arrange the design

You need to arrange the text and heart by clicking 'arrange'.

Use the slice tool

When you have arranged your design perfectly, select your text, hold down the 'ctrl' key, select the heart, and click 'slice'. Now, you can remove the text from the heart and delete it.

Once your design is done, it is time to cut vinyl.

How to Flatten

The flatten tool is a feature used to turn multilayered images into a single-layered image.

Flatten is a tool that turns multilayered images into a single-layered image. The tool is used in the making of decals, labels, stickers, and much more. You can flatten multiple layers of SVG cut files into single-layered images before printing and cutting.

With the flatten tool, you can achieve the following;

Remove cut lines from an image

Transform multilayered images into a single-layered image

Used to transfer regular images into printable images for print-and-cut

Used to maintain distinct colors of multilayered images

Using the flatten tool;

To select the layers, you intend to flatten together, lick 'select all' or hold down 'ctrl' and select the layers

After selecting, click flatten at the bottom right corner

When you do that, the image is now flattened.

HOW TO ATTACH

There are two distinct reasons for using the attach tool;

To keep scoring/writing lines in the right place

To keep shapes in the correct place on the mat as on the canvas

Using the Attach tool to maintain the same arrangement

If you want all the pieces of your project to remain in the exact location during cutting, as it is on your CDS canvas, you have to;

Select all the items of each color

Click 'attach' at the lower right corner

Repeat each color layer process until they are all nested under a label that says "attach."

With the attached tool, you will be able to cut out your projects exactly the way you arranged them on your Cricut canvas.

Basic Object Editing

The canvas comes equipped with an editing toolbar that allows you to make corrections.

If you make a mistake, you can easily fix it. You can use the "undo" and "redo" buttons by clicking them the required number of times.

The undo icon will let you get rid of something you don't like. It acts as an eraser, and each click will undo the previous action.

If you accidentally delete something, you can use the redo button. This will restore your work.

Another editing tool is the Linetype dropdown that will let you change to a cut, draw, or score object. It communicates with your machine, so it knows what tools you're going to be using.

How to center your designs to cut in Cricut Design Space

Sign in to the Cricut Design section. Click on the new project.

Click Download.

Click Upload Picture.

Click Browse.

Save your picture

Select the saved image and insert an image.

Select the picture. Click on it.

As you can see, the picture is automatically moved to the upper left corner.

To prevent this, you can fool the software by placing the image in the center of your design area and the mat. This is useful if you want to create openings in the middle of a page.

Click on the shape tool.

Create a shape of 11.5 x 11.5 inches.

Select the square and change the setting to cut it in the drawing.

The square now appears as an outline.

Click Align and Center with the selected pattern and square.

Click the arrow of your square's size and resize it without moving the top left corner to reduce the size of the square.

Select the square and pattern, then click Attach. Click on it.

As you can see now, the design is centered.

How to convert a PDF to PNG format

After downloading the PDF document to your computer, open your browser and go to png2pdf.com.

Click on the upload files

The "Open File" dialog box starts. Locate the PDF file to

convert (probably in the Downloads folder), click the PDF file and click The file is uploaded. You should see a progress bar. Once the file has been uploaded and converted, a Download button appears below the uploaded file's small image.

Click on the download The file is downloaded as a ZIP file and appears in the status bar at the bottom of the screen. Just click on the filename to open the ZIP file.

The Open File dialog opens, and the downloaded file should be displayed. Since the file is still in ZIP format, you must first unzip or unzip it. Just click Extract All Files.

The Open File dialog opens, and your newly converted PDF file should be displayed in the PNG file. You can open the file with a double-click if you only want to see what the file looks like. Close the window now by clicking on the red X.

After you have converted your PDF file to PNG format, you must upload the PNG file to Cricut® Design Space so that you can use the Print and Cut functions.

Working with Edit Bar in Cricut Design Space

Here are important terminologies to help our understanding of the Design Space Edit Bar will have to be defined. A word of caution, though, is that some of the terms used here are common tools for everyday use on the computer, so it shouldn't be difficult to understand. Still, our computer literacy level is not the same. Therefore, pardon me if you already know many of them. This has been done for the sake of those who do not know. The terms are as follows:

Undo/Redo- refers to undoing any change made to the layer or redo any previously undone action.

Linetype-refers to how the machine will interact with the material on the mat, including cutting, drawing, and scoring, as described below.

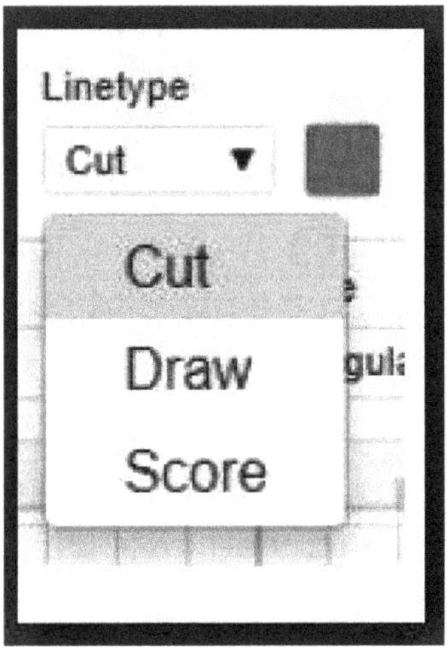

Cut-refers to cutting layer with the aid of a blade from your material.

Draw-refers to drawing the layer with the aid of a Cricut pen.

Score-refers to scoring the layer using a Scoring Stylus or Scoring Wheel.

Linetype Swatch-refers to choosing additional attributes that your layer will use. You can select different options based on the selected Linetype (cut, draw, and score).

Sketching on The Design Space

One of the coolest facts about using the Cricut Explore model is that users can't only upload images. Still, they can also upload images they've drawn themselves! There are two techniques of doing this, one is by making use of Illustrator, and the other is by making use of the Design Space. And since we're discussing the Design Space, I'll only mention how to do so on the latter. The following are the processes:

You first need to have the intended image on your computer by importing it. So, suppose you've hand-drawn what you want on a piece of paper or your tablet. In that case, the next step is to scan it to your computer, snap it with your mobile device and send it to your computer, or save and send it to the computer through your tablet. Whichever way you want to do it, ensure you save it as a PNG or JPEG file.

Convert the sketch using the Design Space by first uploading the image, using the "Upload" tab by the left side.

You will be requested to choose the image type; you should select the option that fits your image background. Proceed by clicking “Continue” and let your image be saved as a Cut image, and then click “Save.” You will notice that your image is now a Cut file.

And that's how you upload and work with your sketch on the Design Space. With this function, you can let your creativity run wild! There are so many things you can do with your hands! Since the Design Space platform does not limit you, don't ever let your imagination be limited!

How to Make Multiple Layer Vinyl

You can layer vinyl by uploading a multi-colored image to your Design Space. When it’s uploaded, you will need to select an image type. There are options available that allow you to choose one that’s closest to your image.

An image with a lot of detail and color can become distorted, or the colors can change, so it’s important to select the image type closest to your image.

The next step is layering. You want to layer from the bottom to the top. Look closely at your image and visualize the finished product. Is the look of the image exactly as you want it? If so, you can keep your image as is without tweaking and rearranging the layers.

You will have the option of a "Print and Cut" image or a "Cut" image. For vinyl, you'll want to choose the "cut" option. You can name your image if you'd like. It can be beneficial to do so. You can name it with the colors of vinyl you'll use or with the first letter or few letters of each color. For example, you can name it R, Blu, Gre, O, P for red, blue, green, orange, and purple. You'll want them in the order that you will be cutting your vinyl.

If you want to separate your colors, you want to use the magic wand tool. This will allow you to separate your colors.

When your vinyl is sorted by color, weed to remove all the excess vinyl. Start with the bottom later and place your image. Next, you will add the second layer. This can be tricky, and clear vinyl transfer tape can help you see what you're doing. Place the second layer on top of the first layer. Repeat the process, being careful as you layer.

Once you've added your layers and haven't made any errors, you're done! You have a beautiful layered vinyl project.

The more you do this, the easier it will become. For vinyl layering, you need a good eye or magnifier and a steady hand.

Using the Contour Feature

Before getting into more complex areas, I'd like to give a quick overview of the contour feature.

This feature allows you to hide part of an image layer by removing unwanted cut lines.

Start by making sure you ungroup your image if it has multiple layers. This is an important step.

On Windows and Mac, you'll select the image and click the ungroup icon at the layers panel's top. If you're using iOS/Android, you'll select the image and click the ungroup icon in the action's menu.

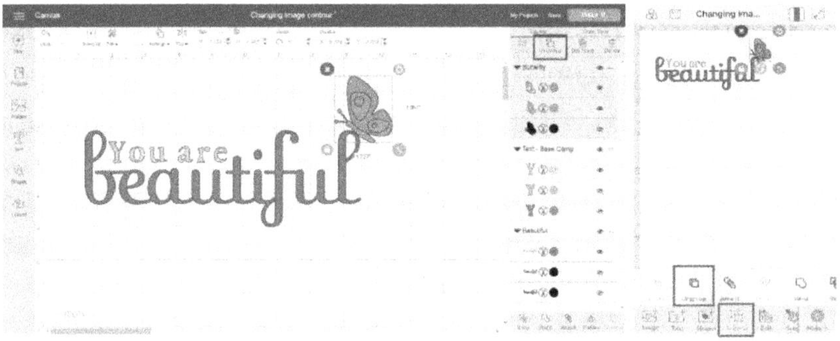

You next want to select the layer you want to remove the cut lines from, and on Windows or Mac, click the contour icon in the layers panel. On iOS/Android, you'll do the same under the action menu.

So far, it's easy. You just need to be sure you follow the instructions for the device you're using.

For Windows and Mac, you'll notice that the image lines are the individual cut lines. You want to click on the cut line you want to hide or select the contour to be hidden. You will find that to the right of your window.

When the hidden contour changes to a lighter shade, that part of the image will not show, and it won't cut.

You need to repeat this process with each cut line you want to hide.

If you're using an iOS/Android, you'll see dark gray lines representing the cut lines. As with Windows or Mac, the line will lighten to let you know the part of the image you selected will not show. Hence, it will not cut.

You need to repeat these steps to continue hiding the cut lines you desire.

When you're finished hiding all the cut lines you choose, click the "X" in the right-hand corner or click outside the window. The hidden cut lines will no longer appear.

This is an easy method to hide the cut lines you no longer want. Following these steps will give you an error-free cut.

How to Add Shadows to Letters

Decorative shadows can add such beauty to a product. Have you ever wondered how it's done?

For those using programs such as Photoshop, it can be simple, but not everyone has an illustration program.

Fortunately, it can be done with Cricut Design Space and a smartphone app called Phonto, available on the Apple Store.

Phonto is a free, easy-to-use app with over 400 fonts and interchangeable text sizes. You can also add your fonts if you'd like.

Don't let the "free" part scare you into thinking there won't be much you can do with it. On the contrary, it has amazing features and so much you can do with it that it's worth the small amount of space it will take up on your device.

There's a video tutorial available, and it's worth watching. It will walk you through all the features.

To begin, open Phonto and click the camera at the bottom of the screen. You'll see options, and you'll want to select "plain image."

You will see a white square in the top right-hand corner. It's next to a black square, and it can be hard to see. Select the white square and click the "upload icon" in the top right-hand corner of your screen. Next, you want to select "use." You will now see a white square in the middle of your screen.

You need to tap on the white square, then tap "add text."

Write your text and click done once you've added what you want it to say. The next step is to click on "style." Three options will appear text, stroke, and background.

A gray highlighted area will appear, and this is where you'll start.

The next part might make you nervous because you will change the text color to white in the color box. Your text will turn white, and you might not be able to see it. Don't panic! It's still there.

Now it's time to add the shadow. To do so, you need to select the "stroke" box. It should be highlighted in gray. You want to change the stroke to black.

Scroll to the bottom of the screen until you see the "width" slider and slide it upward until you get your desired shadow. Select the shadow you want and click "done." Next, click the "upload icon" in the bottom right corner and save the image.

Your shadow is saved, so now it's time to save the text inside of the shadow.

After you remove the shadow, select "text" again and turn your text back to black, select "done," and then select the "upload icon" to save your image.

You now have two images, and you need to transfer them from your phone to your computer or transfer to the Cricut app.

Open Cricut Design Space and upload your images to a new project.

Cricut advises the following: "Make sure you're only deleting the white background around the shadow and not the inner white part. For the word, you'll delete the white background and all the inner parts of the letters just like normal." This is important, as you don't want to delete the inner white part. If you do it by accident, you should restore it.

With your new project started, you'll want to make any adjustments, such as resizing or rearranging. You can select your colors, and you're ready to cut. Your letters should be shadowed as you selected, and your finished project should be awesome.

The Phonto app makes shadowing very simple to do on your phone. You shouldn't have any instability when transferring to your computer or the Cricut app.

You can now make beautiful shadowed letters, just like the Cricut pros make!

Mirroring Images for Iron-on

You'll want to avoid the mistake of having your mirrored image be wrong when you go to iron it on, so I'll explain how to prevent this.

Iron-on material is fun to work with, and you can do so many projects with it. Nothing is more frustrating than ironing a design onto fabric and having it reversed. For some designs, you might think, "Hey, this doesn't look so bad" because the image does look good either way, but for letters, there's only one way to go!

So, let's begin to design our iron-on images. You'll design it the way you design your other images. When finished, double-check the direction of the image and click the "Make It" icon in the design screen's top-right.

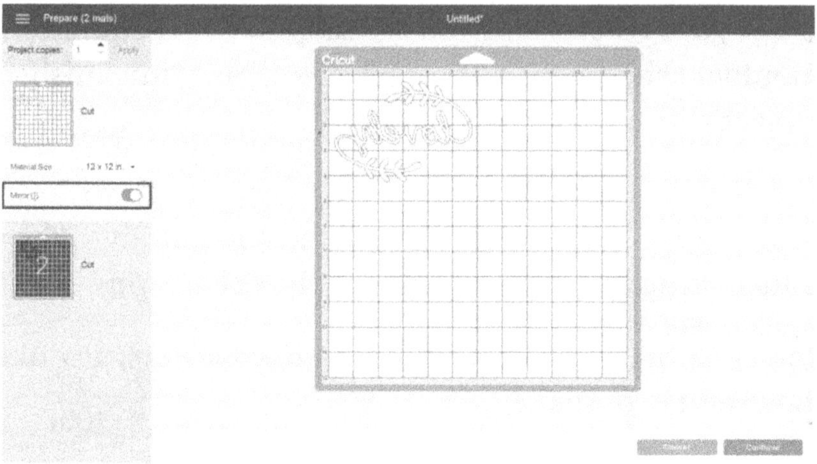

Next, select the mat you will use, check the "Mirror Image" box, and make certain it's for iron-on. You'll need to repeat these steps for each mat that will be used with iron-on material.

Once you select the mirror option, the images will reflect the change on the "Mat Preview." If you set the Smart Set dial to iron-on but didn't mirror your images on the Mat Preview, you will get an alert on the cut screen. If you want to mirror the images, go back to the Mat Preview pane, and check "Mirror." You can now continue, and your image will reproduce correctly.

Working with Templates

This section will be the concluding part of this chapter. Using Templates in Design Space can be quite confusing for a beginner. However, it doesn't look as hard as it seems. You just need to know which template to use and how to use it. Templates are very useful for visualizing projects. You can only use templates on Windows or

Mac computers. It is not available for iOS or Android devices for now.

Let’s go through the procedures of working with the Design Space templates:

Pick the “Templates" tool located on the left-hand side of the Design panel.

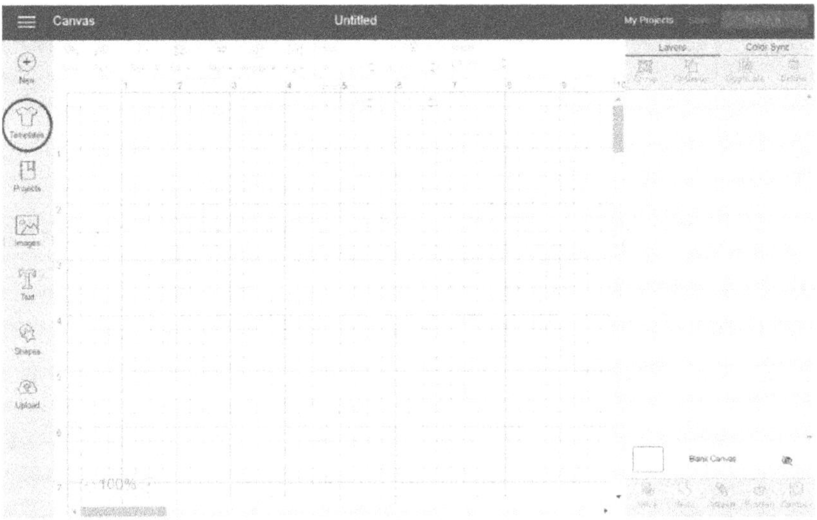

Photo credit: help.cricut.com

To pick a template of your choice, browse through the template gallery, click on the one you want, choose a template category to narrow down the options, or make use of the search function to find a particular kind of template.

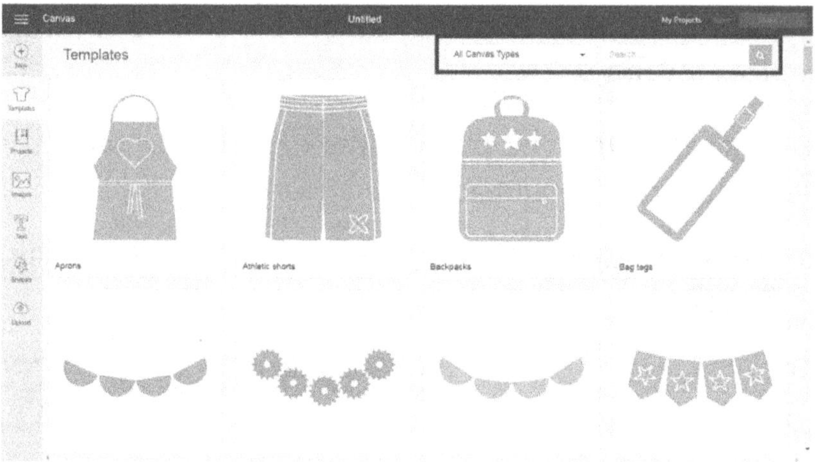

Photo credit: help.cricut.com

Once you've selected a template, it'll be opened on your Canvas screen. You'll see an alert that states, ***"Templates are intended for reference only and will not be saved with your project."***

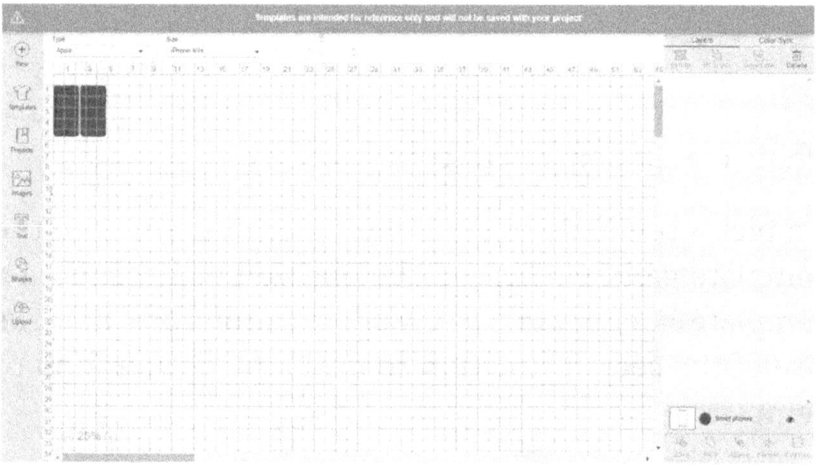

Photo credit: help.cricut.com

Consider putting information regarding the template you're using, the type, color, and the size inside a text box. Then proceed to save the project with the template. Doing this will enable you to swiftly add the used template to another design later when you need it on that project.

The Design Space Canvas zooms out automatically so that a user can see the entire template. Also, the template edit bar will be displayed. You can make use of the "Type" and "Size" options on the template edit bar to choose a template version that is nearest to the element or item you'll be using. Some templates have a Custom option in the "Size" panel that enables you to input the size manually. You can likewise zoom in as needed on the canvas area as you design with the selected template.

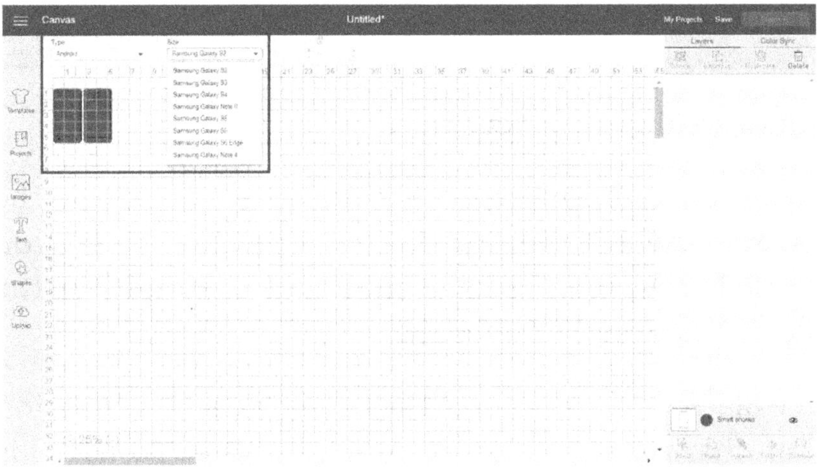

Photo credit: help.cricut.com

If you desire to change your template color, click on the template's color swatch where it displays close to the Layers panel bottom. After clicking on the color swatch, a panel will appear with color options. You may now choose a color from the current project, the basic color palette, input the desired color's Hex code, or use the slider for choosing a color within the Custom color picker. Once a color has been chosen, your template automatically changes to reflect the selected color on the Canvas.

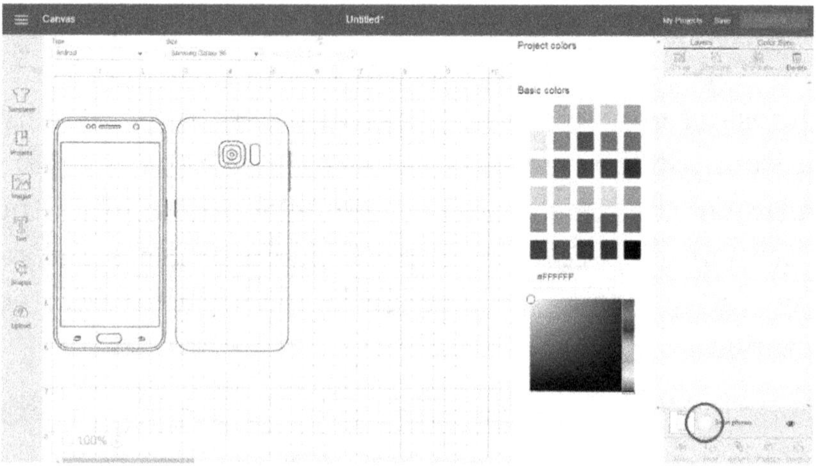

Photo credit: help.cricut.com

To discard any template, click on the template from the Layers panel bottom, and then click on the "Delete" icon located at the upper part of the panel, or simply tap the "delete" key on the keyboard.

The Blank Canvas Layer at the Layers panel is a function that changes the color of your template. To use this function, do the following;

The color swatch that is next to the "Blank Canvas" should be selected. After clicking on the color swatch, a panel will appear with color options. You may now decide to choose the color you desire from the basic color palette, inputting the desired color's Hex code, or using the slider for choosing a color within the Custom color picker. Once a color has been chosen, your template automatically changes to reflect the selected color on the Canvas.

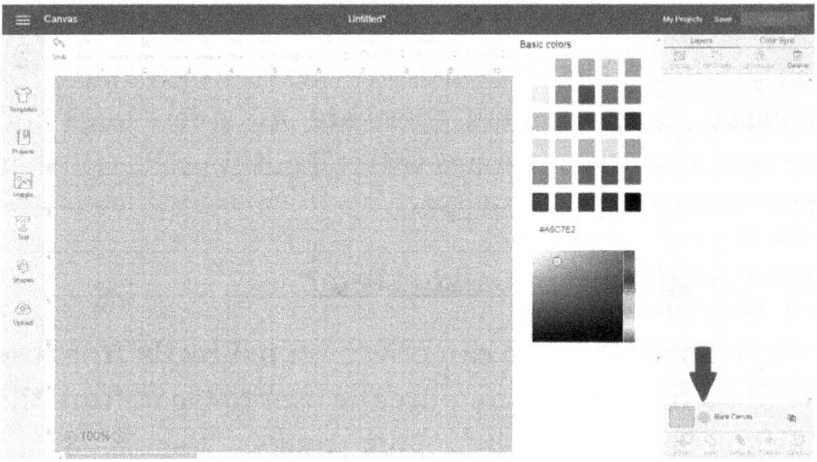

Photo credit: help.cricut.com

If you wish to get rid of the color of the Canvas, then select "Blank Canvas" located close to the Layers panel bottom, and then click on the "Delete" icon located at the upper part of the panel, or simply tap the "delete" key on the keyboard.

Chapter 7:
Latest new features of design space

New Features in Design Space

Design Space has launched the new Design Space for Desktop. As this is new, there are still a few bugs and updates that Design Space will roll out shortly, which is why it's called Desktop Beta.

What Is Different in Desktop Beta?

Design Space Desktop can now be run directly from the Desktop and does not require the user to log in from the Design Space website. This makes Design Space available in offline mode without an internet connection.

The Desktop Design Space application gives the user the ability to save their projects on their PC and keep them in the cloud. This makes working with your favorite projects easy, both offline and online.

Images can now be downloaded for offline use as can projects and fonts.

Downloading Design Space Desktop Beta

Downloading Design Space Desktop Beta requires an active internet connection.

Minimum System Requirements for Design Space

Design Space is compatible with Windows, MAC, iOS, and Android operating systems. To run the software on these systems, devices must meet the following minimum system requirements:

Downloading Design Space Desktop Beta

Downloading Design Space Desktop Beta requires an active internet connection.

Minimum System Requirements for Design Space

Design Space is compatible with Windows, MAC, iOS, and Android operating systems. To run the software on these systems, devices must meet the following minimum system requirements:

Windows Operating Systems

- Microsoft Windows version 8 or higher
- The device must have Bluetooth or USB support
- The CPU should be either Intel Dual-Core or AMD processor of equivalent specifications
- The device must have at least 4GB RAM
- The device must have at least 2GB free disk space
- The screen display should be able to support a resolution of at least 1024px x 768px

MAC Operating Systems

- MAC OS 10.12 or higher
- The device must have Bluetooth or USB support
- The CPU should be at least 1.83 GHz
- The device must have at least 4GB RAM

- The device must have at least 2GB free disk space
- The screen display should be able to support a resolution of at least 1024px x 768px

iOS

- iOS 11 or higher
- iPhones from the iPhone 5s and newer models
- iPad mini 2 and newer models
- iPad Air and newer models
- iPad Pro 12.9" and new models
- iPad 5th generation
- iPod touch 6th generation

Android

- Android 6.0 or higher
- Mobile devices
- Tablets
- Chromebooks are not compatible

Chapter 8: Realize the Project and Sell It

Making Money with Cricut

It is a well-known fact in the world of business that to make money, you first need to invest money. If you are debating if it's worth the investment, then read on. As mentioned earlier, "Cricut" has a range of cutting machines with distinctive capabilities offered at a varying price range. The "Cricut Explore Air 2" is priced at $249.99, and the "Cricut Maker" is priced at $399.99 (the older "Cricut Explore Air" model may be available for sale on Amazon at a lower price). Now, if you were to buy any of these machines during a holiday sale with a bundle deal that comes with a variety of tools, accessories, and materials for a practice project as well as free trial membership to "Cricut Access", you would already be saving enough to justify the purchase for your usage. The cherry on top would be if you can use this investment to make more money. You can always get additional supplies in a bundle deal or from your local stores at a much lower price. All in all, those upfront costs can easily be justified with the expenses you budget for school projects that require you to cut letters and shapes, creating personalized gifts for your loved ones or decorating your home with customized decals, and of course, your jewelry creations. These are only a handful of the reasons to buy a "Cricut" machine for your personal use.

Tips for Making Money Using Cricut

Before you start trying to make money from your Cricut, take some time to think about whether or not it is what you want to do. When I bought Cricut, I thought about starting a personalization and stationery business. However, everything in life is trial and error; I am still in the testing phase.

Here are some things to think about before "launching":

Are you doing it just because your friends say your creations are amazing?

Do you want to support your family financially?

Are you doing it for some extra money?

Are you willing to deal with HARD customers? (there are always difficult clients)

Do you want to turn your hobby into a job?

Can you learn more about marketing on and off the network?

Do you have enough time and space to start a small business?

Do you like to make crafts with your Cricut? So much to do over and over again?

I definitely don't want to discourage you from starting to make money from your Cricut, but you have to put your feet on the ground, and I also want you to ***be smart about it***. Your answers to these questions do not necessarily determine your decision whether to launch or not. Still, they will help you realize what it will be like to start a small business with your Cricut.

ALL ABOUT COPYRIGHT

Since you decided to get into this business, we should talk about licenses and copyrights. This is the area where you can get into trouble the fastest. And the question why? People created all the images, cut files that you download, or even copies from the Internet. The simple fact of finding them on Google does not give you the right to reproduce it or, worse, sell it on the Internet.

Different policies protect images; below, I describe the most common.

Cricut angel policy

Within the same Cricut Design Space system, there is a library of Cricut images to create with the machine. You can create and sell with such designs but under the "Cricut Angel" Policy. Please read this policy carefully. You will find many things there, some things it mentions:

Most Cricut Access images are included in this policy.

Create up to 10,000 items to sell using Cricut images.

Don't just sell individual images.

You must include a copyright notice with your projects.

Do not include licensed content, such as images from Disney or Marvel.

Personal use vs. Commercial use

If you prefer to use very specific images, you can buy them in online stores. Don't just download them from Google images and put them in your projects... It is very likely that if you do, you are violating copyrights.

When purchasing images online, be sure to read the file's terms of use. Most of these images only include a personal use license; that is, you cannot create products to sell with these types of files. There may also be the option to buy the same image but with a commercial license. Just remember to read the terms.

There are images of licensed characters that normally belong to Disney and Marvel, such as (and this will surprise you as much as I do): Elsa from Frozen or Iron Man from Marvel. Using these images is breaking copyright, and you may have trouble using it as a way to make money. My advice would be to stay away from using these images. It can bring you an ugly problem and even a lawsuit or fine.

Starting a Cricut craft business

Now that we are clear on the Legal topic, let's talk about earning money and getting the best out of your Cricut.

Define Your Niche

One of the worst things you can do is do whatever people ask you to do. A glass here, a personalization over there, a cake topper from today to tomorrow. You'll end up with lower margins than the market, perhaps wasted product and a confused audience.

Buy Materials in Large Quantities

Having decided on your niche, you can buy your supplies and materials, what I call "wholesale". This is nothing more than buying large quantities, say 10-foot vinyl rolls, boxes of 10 glasses or cups at lower prices than if you buy them per unit. Cricut also sells wholesale materials.

Quality Matters

One of the fastest ways to destroy your business is to produce a low-quality product. Word of mouth travels faster than we think, and the worst part is that you can't change the ratings you get if you're selling your product in an online store.

How to set the price

It bothers me to see people selling their beautiful super elaborate creations at SO low prices. Those people are not even valuing their own time. They are not taking into account your talent, materials, or other important things when setting prices.

Monetizing your art

You have practiced, perfected, and established a style of that art that you like to do so much. You have decorated cards, personalized objects, created pictures with motivational phrases. With pride, you have shared your work on social networks.

Own studio or on-site?

What will be your minimum charge for small jobs?

Your Time + Energy

This is where the wellness factor comes in, where you need to think about how much your time is worth to you. It's worth a lot more than buying the cheapest combo at McDonald's, but there the questions come... Karissa, how much exactly? How do I find out? It is difficult to answer the frank, but there are certain guidelines that I can tell you that can help you.

The typical answer is that you put yourself a monthly salary with which you feel comfortable. I will speak in an imaginary way based on some local statistics of the Dominican Republic to speak with numbers and understand. Let's say (I made it up) that, on average, a monthly salary in my country is 15,000 Dominican pesos, and this is the number with which you value your time and energy.

This number will be divided by 4.3. This number is established as the average of weeks in the year since months have 30 days, another 31, and February with 28. Are you already starting to see the difference? Now try to use that math to calculate your hourly rate.

Start with the monthly salary you feel comfortable with: ____________

Divide that number by 4.3 and put it here: ____________

Now divide this other number by 44 (remember that this number may vary). So this result is your hourly rate that you will put here: ____________

Cost of Materials

Are you using cheap store markers or artist quality paints? Do you use expensive papers and prepared inks? Are the special items you need? Do you have to order online specific to some part of the world or available near you?

The value increases with the quality of your tools and materials, as well as your knowledge of them. If you answer "What kind of paint do you have/do you use?" With an "I don't know ... I've had it for a long time and the label it has is no longer visible" or "a friend gave it to me, and I don't know where it got it. "Your work will not be as valuable as that of someone whose answer is" I use Winsor and Newton's lightweight, water-resistant watercolors. "

Artist-quality materials cost more, so you must know your materials' cost in case they run out.

Project Size

This is probably one of the first factors to value your project. How big is it? Creating something, for example, a lettering composition is an 8 ½ x 11-inch sheet with ten words that will take much less time and fewer materials than those same ten words on an 8x10 feet board. You can have a price for measurements, let's say square inches, or better use your hourly rate that we work above.

Delivery / Shipping

You must indicate in your budget if the delivery is included or is an extraordinary payment. That means you need to know where the piece is going. You may have to purchase parcel shipping quotes outside of your city based on the weight size and service you need. I recommend that you investigate the rates of the shipping companies and thus have a standard shipping cost.

Original or continuous use?

Will your client use your art once (like a wedding card), continuously (like a business card or blog), or multiple times (like a T-shirt to resell)? It is always a good idea to ask this question in advance. The answer will help you determine how valuable your artwork is to the customer if it will be used continuously to promote or generate direct income for your client; the value increases.

Deliverables

What should you deliver to your customer as a finished product? An original art? Or is it digital? Both of them? What file formats? JPG, PNG, TIF, EPS, AI? Do you have experience digitizing, and do you have the best tools to do it?

Spending time digitizing and preparing multiple files takes time and experience, and therefore should be priced accordingly. There are also those printed from digital art. Will you mail the file? In a memory? Digital start, and then you delivered it printed? All this must be taken into account, considering the time and effort it took to do it. NOTE: a digital job is even more expensive since it can be reproduced. Using specialized programs requires previous experience and learning, which I suppose also cost you to acquire it.

Location (In or Out Of Your Studio)

Your hourly rate will also largely depend on where you will be doing the work.

When you have the luxury of your own space, you can perform several tasks simultaneously. That is, you can be working on two projects at the same time. This makes it easy to access all of your supplies and materials. The most convenient way for you to work in your place, at your own pace with everything you need at hand, you should not worry about traffic.

If the job requires you to be somewhere outside your study (let's say a restaurant, for example), the value of your time will increase significantly. You will have to travel to and from the place (which needs to be included in your work time), carry all your materials with you, and only commit to that work during the assigned hours. That also means that you will be in an uncontrolled environment. This includes distractions, noise, and curious people. It can be a lot of fun working on site, and it can be a real headache.

Sometimes a combination of time in your studio and on-site works best. You can carry out all the designs and preparatory work in the studio so that you are ready to carry out your duties once you arrive on site. This would be shown as two different hourly rates in the quote, breaking down your activities, so your client knows how they invest their money in you.

Project Term

Only you know what time is most comfortable for you to work. If not, I recommend measuring the time you take doing your work to estimate and space if something unforeseen occurs. If a client comes out of nowhere with a crazy panic because they are the most important in the world, ALWAYS add a fee for speed, clarifying the time it takes you in normal time for similar works, and that you will make an exception for him/her. Normally these prices vary between 50% or 100% of the labor price.

It is best to avoid these types of jobs because you start to get used to the client and only accept these cases if necessary.

THE BUSINESS SIDE OF THINGS AND IDEAS TO EARN

Your designs' creativity and the skill you will develop can allow you to create and start your own business if you wish. For enthusiastic novices, many questions would be faced, such as:

Where do I start?

Like any startup business, initial questions need to be addressed to overcome possible difficulties. For example, addressing issues like defining my clientele, the products that might be of interest, where to find them, and how to make a profit margin of my sales are important to tackle from the start. In other words, you will need a good and well-defined business strategy to start with.

Choosing my client

You can target two avenues to sell your products: either by looking at how you can approach the market locally or online. It is advisable to concentrate efforts on one approach to start with as your target is to generate profits as soon as possible. Never forget that your goal is to grow benefits and reinvest it so that your business expands. The quicker you increase your sales, the more likely you will reinvest in new tools or new products, making, in turn, a stronger financial turnover.

Understanding your marketing strategy is key to your success.

Approaching local markets

You can explore selling your products from 'business to business'. In this configuration, the volume of sales is important as the larger the production, the lower the production cost per item is. This is the most challenging balance to reach for a new Cricut based business. The advantage of obtaining contractual work means you can negotiate to buy a large quantity from vendors.

Selling Online

Suppose you are an adept of higher technical knowledge. In that case, you can generate great benefits by providing either quality custom work, bulk offering, or information network. It is advisable to concentrate your efforts on one approach to start with. Suppose you choose, for example, a custom work approach. In that case, you increase the chances to find potential customers looking for your products as they turn to a search engine like Google to find what they are looking for. Websites like Amazon Handmade or Etsy provide a good platform to allow selling custom design services. Equally efficient is the launch of your site. This strategy is worth looking at. Selling online presents advantages such as low startup costs and access to the global market with access to millions of potential customers.

Furthermore, online custom prices tend to be lower than those on the local market. However, access to the global market means that competition is stiff, pushing products competitively. Selling online requires certain knowledge in logistics as far as shipping and packing your products are concerned, a cost factor that needs to be considered in your pricing.

eBay and Amazon have become the largest platforms. On the other hand, if an online retail business approach is more what you may be inclined to do, this approach will allow you to determine the demand for the designs you offer and plan the production accordingly. But selling online means challenging the existing competition!

Finally, suppose you prefer to sell your products online through an information network. In that case, you become an authority in the field, creating the opportunity to generate profit with your Cricut designs. By offering blogs on technical know-how or inspiration work, you become selective on the posts you want to take on.

Starting a new business requires foremost a business strategy, the foundation for your future success. Asking yourself who your potential customers would be, what kind of products you can sell them, and how are the first steps of a future startup business.

In terms of making money from the comfort of your home, you easily achieve that with a Cricut machine. However, you have to bear in mind that there are several competitors out there; thus, you have to put in extra effort to stand a chance to succeed.

TIPS FOR SUCCESS

For you to become successful in the Cricut world of crafts, you have to keep the following in mind;

Dare to be different

You have to be yourself, unleash your quirkiness and creativity.

Those that have been in the Cricut crafts world for some time know all about the knockout name tiles. They became a hit, and in no time, everyone was producing and selling them.

In the crafting world, that is the norm. Thus, you could be among the earliest people to jump on a trend to ride the wave until the next hot seller surfaces. Mind you, that strategy of selling Cricut crafts can become costly and tiresome if you are not careful.

The basic idea here is to add your flair and personal style and not completely reinvent it. For example, let's say you come across two name tiles on Etsy, one looks exactly like the other 200+ on sale on the site, while the second one has a few more tweaks and spins on it. The second product seller will possibly charge more and accrue a higher profit because his/her product is unique and stands out from the rest.

When you design your products, don't be afraid to tweak your fonts, because even the simplest of tweaks and creativity can make your product stand out from the rest.

Remember this; if you create a product that looks exactly like others, you are only putting yourself in a 'price war', where no one usually wins.

Keep it narrow

Many crafters believe that creating and selling everything under the sun translates into more patronage and more money, but that isn't how it works. On the contrary, it might only result in a huge stock of unsold products, more burn out, and high costs. Rather than producing materials here and there, you should focus on being the best in your area of craftiness, so that when people need specific products in your area, they'll come to you.

It can be very tempting to want to spread your tentacles because it might seem like the more you produce, the more options you'll provide for your clients, but that might be counterproductive.

Take out time to think about your area of strength and focus your energy on making products that you'd be known for. It is better to be known as an expert in a particular product than to be renowned for someone that produces a high number of inferior products.

Thus, you should keep it narrow and grow to become the very best in your area of craft.

Be consistent

If you intend to become successful, you have to work on your Cricut craft business consistently. Some people work once a week or thereabout because they sell as a hobby; however, if you intend to make in-road in your business, you have to work every day.

If you have other engagements and can't work every day, you should create a weekly schedule and stick to it. If you shun your business for weeks and months at a time, then you will not go anywhere with it.

Apart from consistency in work and production, you also have to be consistent with your product quality and pricing. When your customers are convinced about your products, they will easily recommend you to their friends, family, business partners, and many others.

There are ups and downs; thus, you shouldn't reduce your work rate because things are not going as planned. Success doesn't come easy, but one of the surest ways of being and maintaining success is consistently doing the things you love.

Be Tenacious

It is not easy to run a business because it involves hard work, sweat, and even heartbreaks. Thus, you have to bear in mind that there will be days when you will feel like throwing in the towel. There will be days when nothing goes as planned. There will also be days when customers will tick you off. You will feel like a drowning boat because you're working hard, but nothing is working out.

However, you have to look at the bigger picture because the crafting business is not a rich, quick scheme.

Remember, quitters never win, so quitting isn't an option. Keep doing the things you love, and keep improving. Successful people never give up. They suffer many setbacks, but they don't stop.

Thus, for you to be successful in your craft, you have to be tenacious and resilient. Be willing to maneuver your way through tough times, and do not forget to pick up lessons.

Learn everyday

Be willing to learn from people that have been successful in the business. You don't necessarily have to unravel everything by yourself. Whatever it is you are doing, others have already done it in the past.

Whether you intend to learn how to build a successful Facebook group or how to go up the Etsy ranks, remember that people have already done all that in the past and are giving out tricks and tips they know.

Make it a tradition to learn something new about your business every day. At the beginning of your business, you will have to do more marketing than crafting.

When you wake up in the morning, browse through the internet, gather materials, and read in your spare time, the more you learn, the better your chances of success. They say knowledge is power. To become successful as a craftsman/woman, you have to constantly seek new knowledge in tips, tricks, software upgrades, marketing, design ideas, tools, accessories, and many others. All I am saying is that you should learn without ceasing.

Conclusion

So, you've mastered the Cricut design studio; you are a professional crafter, your trash reservation skills are legendary, now what? Why not put your abilities to work for you? Here are five Cricut suggestions that will put money in your pocket.

You're able to take custom orders and produce cut files your clients can utilize inside their die cutter. Or, hang in craft forums, find out exactly what people want and then make those cut files and supply them on eBay.

Each home-based business owner must market their site. Join networking groups or post your ceremony in forums or classified advertisements sites. So, what is this money-making idea? Begin a Cricut vinyl ribbon service. We've got all seen mywebsite.com from the rear window of somebody's automobile. Now you can produce plastic tips and assist individuals in getting clients to their site.

Cricut has incredible capabilities to improve your image as a novice or as a specialist. As a matter of course, even if you're not so imaginative in real life, this machine will help you come off as a master builder.

The circuit is indeed a firm that anticipates people's desire for vintage and designed product lines and has prepared something for people with a passion for DIY to match their imagination. It's a perfect way to be a talented crafter to find a device or partner that gives you the freedom to pursue your passion. Fortunately, for anyone who wants to design, Cricut has built an incredible machine with advanced cutting technology that enables you to cut, design, and bring to life all your gorgeous craft ideas.

It's important to understand what resources and accessories to use with your Cricut to save you many headaches and cut down on your preparation time! The Cricut machine is very flexible and can be used with many kinds of materials to assemble any project you might have in mind.

Cricut Design Space gives the crafter the power to create amazing crafts only limited by their imagination. If you run out of ideas, Design Space Ready-to-Make projects are loaded with ideas, as is the Cricut website.

Learning any new software program takes time, patience, and practice. Remember to have fun, and don't give up if you don't get a design right. The more you work on the Design Space Canvas, the more familiar you will become with it.

People are always searching for ways to include personalized accents to decor. So, this is the next money-making idea. Proceed to the paint and wallpaper shops in your area and ask to leave your business cards set up a flyer advertising your custom-made wall artwork support.

As everyone can see, the Cricut machine can run different projects. These tools have proven to cut both thin and thick materials. You can also use the Cricut design software included with your device to print images on your printer. Therefore, you can use the Cricut machine to crop clip art, printed photos, and other pictures.

Cricut machines serve a variety of tasks. It is a popular option for punching because it is versatile and useful. This is why you need a Cricut machine, especially if you are an experienced craftsman. If you are a beginner, the best cutting machine for you is versatile and easy to use.

There are seven Cricut cutting machines, and they have astonishing properties, so all of them are great. Each guarantee excellent performance and quality. It also has new features and enhancements to improve your creativity.

You love crafting, it's an excellent hobby, but it might be pricey buying those supplies. Enjoy the reading!

Cricut Vocabulary and Terms

You will repeatedly hear various words and expressions when you start interacting with Cricut owners (and even Silhouette owners) or checking them when you surf the web looking for help and instructional exercises.

Clingy Mat

This is the cutting mat that you will use to hold the material you need to cut. The material shouldn't be allowed to move while the machine is attempting to slice, score, or draw on it. The clingy tangle holds it in place. There are various degrees of "clingy" depending on the material you are working with.

Tools

This normally refers to a pack of tools used along with a Cricut machine group or that you buy independently as an accessory. These typically include a sort of spatula for pulling your design off the clingy tangle, tweezers for lifting and pulling, a pick that resembles a dental instrument for "weeding," and scissors.

Weeding

This term is quite confusing lol. It refers to pulling or removing the "undesirable" pieces out of your design, within the "e" or within a shape that you need to be vacant.

Load and Unload

generally simple. It's the process of stacking and unloading your clingy tangle into the Cricut machine.

Pressure

you will have an option to automate your machine that alters the pressure on the sharp edge, pen, or turning edge. You change this depending on your material's thickness and the speed that you choose to cut your design at.

Speed

The speed to which you set the machine to cut out the design. Often you can use quicker speeds for more simple designs. The more complicated the design, the slower you need your machine to process and cut.

Cricut Design Space

This is the application on software that you will use to change, set up, and eventually send the cut instructions to your machine to cut the materials as indicated by you your design.

Materials

These are a set of things you add to the clingy tangle to be cut. This can include paper, fake calfskin, copper sheeting, fabric, sticker paper, vinyl, slender wood, chipboard, froth center, and the sky is the limit from there!

CRICUT PROJECT IDEAS:

The practical guide to follow step by step to learn the best cricut techniques, how to use them in practice with new project ideas and how to calculate the right price.

KAYLA ARORA

Table of Contents

Introduction

If you are new to Cricut's craft, you will find easy step-by-step designs in this book. They are sure to inspire your creativity and make you eager to get started on your new craft. You will also find simple, beginner project ideas to inspire your creativity. The more you practice your Cricut craft, the quicker you will advance to the next level.

Whether you are just starting and advancing in your Cricut crafting hobby or are at a level, **Cricut Project Ideas** has you covered. You will also find amazing Cricut step-by-step projects for both the intermediate and advanced Cricut hobbyists.

Each step-by-step project will include the accessories, tools, and materials you will need to create the items. But don't limit yourself to only the materials listed in the book. Once you have mastered the design, why not shake things up a bit and get creative? Try the design with a different type of material and see if it works. The more you practice, the better you will get, and soon, you will be putting your own spin on basic designs.

But the most important thing is to have fun and enjoy yourself. That is what crafting is all about doing what you love. Don't beat yourself up if, at first, your design does not come out perfect; some of the best artwork is made by mistake. For those of you who are new to the craft, the most important thing is to learn to get comfortable with the Cricut. Learn what works and what does not work. The best way to learn is to work with the system.

You will soon be well on your way to creating great items to spruce up your home, making customized gifts and handmade greeting cards.

This machine is not just for you to make things for other people. Spice up your home with customized décor at a fraction of the cost it would be to buy it from the store, including things like prints, paper flowers, and etched glass or mirrors.

Chapter 1: Beginners Projects

Cork Coasters

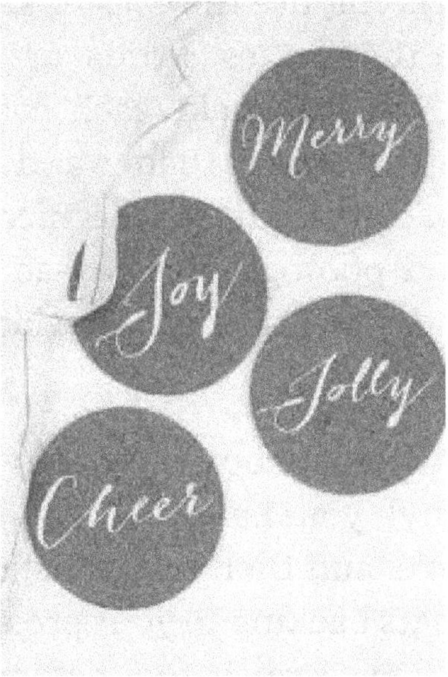

Materials Needed:

- Cork for cutting on your Cricut
- Adhesive Vinyl
- Adhesive Felt or felt tabs
- Transfer Tape

Instructions:

In Design Space, decide what size and shape of a coaster you want to create. Traditional coasters are often circular or square, but you do not need to be bound to those shapes for your coasters like the example shows. Make sure you also have the quantity you plan to make in mind.

When you have your design laid out, send the bottom shapes to cut out of the cork material.

Once your cork is cut, use the coaster shapes in Design Space to design the images, words, or other details to your coasters. You can make each coaster the same design, or you can use a theme and create custom messages for each one. It can be nice to add dates, monograms, and photographs instead of shapes and sayings. Make sure whatever you decide will fit on the coasters you just cut out.

Once you have these laid out, send your file to cut from the colored vinyl you have chosen. Weed out any unnecessary parts and then use transfer tape to move your vinyl from its backing to your project. Smooth out the vinyl with your scraper tool before removing the tape.

Using an Exacto knife, lay your coasters on top of the adhesive felt and cut around the shape. Peel off the backing and apply the felt to the underside of the coaster. If you are using felt tabs instead, make sure there is a tab at least at every corner or few inches on the bottom of your coaster. If you want a raise coaster, you could even cut designs from the felt and add it over the vinyl on top!

It is unnecessary to add the felt pieces on the bottom of the cork, but it adds a more professional touch to your project. It also adds extra protection for your furniture, where you will be using the coasters.

Embellished Shoes

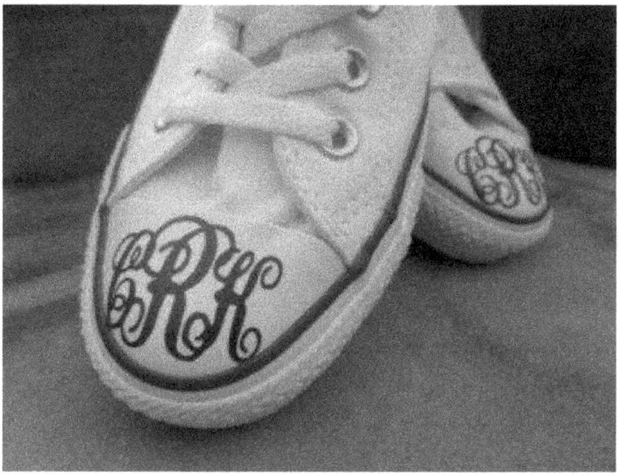

Materials Needed:

- Shoes to embellish - Canvas is not necessary unless you want to iron on something to the top.
- Adhesive vinyl or iron-vinyl, depending on your design and shoe
- Transfer tape and scraper tool
- Iron, if required for iron-on

Instructions:

In Design Space, create your image or phrase and send the file to cut out of the vinyl. You can use the phrase for one shoe and the negative vinyl for the other, or you can send the file to cut two times.

Use the transfer tape to remove the vinyl design and line it up on the shoe where you want to put it. Using the scraper tool, smooth the vinyl onto the shoe. If you add an iron-on design, heat your iron and place your vinyl on the shoe's canvas portion. Place a cloth over the top and iron it on.

Carefully peel away the backing of the vinyl, making sure it has completely attached to the shoe. You can go back over your vinyl with the iron or scraper tool to ensure everything is securely in place.

Throw on your new custom shoes and show them off to the world!

FABRIC BOOKMARKS

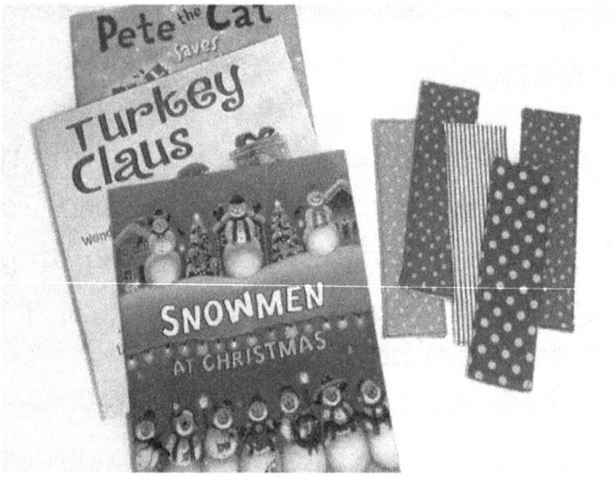

This super simple sewing venture is ideal for apprentices or children! This is the perfect task for a learner or even a child to make!

Figure out how to sew a basic bookmark with this fast-instructional exercise! Ideal for tenderfoots.

Materials Needed:

- Cricut Producer Cutting Machine (or rotating shaper and tangle)
- (2) – 7.5″ h x 2.5″ w bits of texture (a couple of various hues/prints)

Instructions:

1. Slice Textures to measure - Contingent upon what number of bookmarks you plan on making, duplicate the bookmark in configuration space and fit the greatest number of as you can on your 12×12 or 12×24 tangle! Once more, you'll have to cut two 2.5″x7.5″ texture for every bookmark. Since we would have been making a pack, I utilized my Cricut Creator. With the Cricut Producer, I can cut a pack SUPER quick using the new revolving edge highlight that the Creator has!
2. Cut Fusible Interfacing (or cardboard) - I've additionally got a Plan Space petition for the Fusible Interfacing embed! The interfacing should be 6.75″h x 1.75″ w each, and you require one for every bookmark.
3. Join the textures' wrong sides together, utilizing pins or clasps. Sew together the two long sides and the base.
4. Crease your bookmark packaging right side out. - Utilize a pencil or something little to push

the sides of the bookmark packaging out the distance. And afterward, press your bookmark packaging utilizing your home iron or Simple Press. I am fixated on my Simple Press and use it for all my warm ventures/needs!

5. Embed the bit of fusible interface into the bookmark packaging.
6. Crease the best edge down like the photo beneath. - After you get the edges collapsed down, squeeze it with warm.
7. Sew the best shut.

Make a point to back fasten the two closures!

8) Press the whole bookmark utilizing your home iron or Simple Press. - This appends the interface to the texture and helps simply press everything perfect and clean!

What's more, that is it! You're finished!

Cosmetic Bag Tutorial

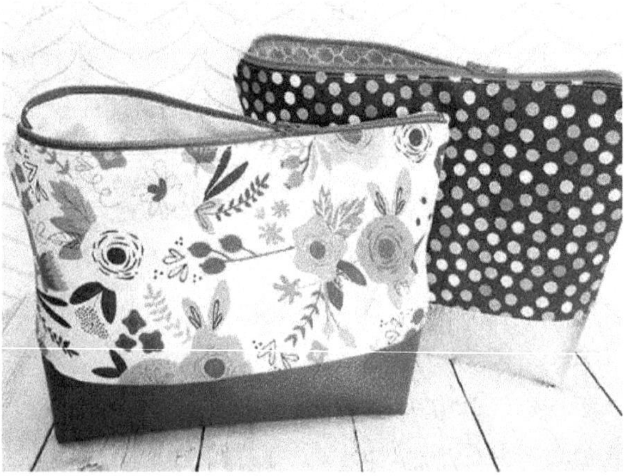

Materials Needed:

- Choose your textures and organizing string and 9-inch zipper.
- Lining: Pretty much anything works. Cotton, cloth, silk. Nothing excessively cumbersome.
- Bag Outside: Cotton, material, canvas, upholstery texture, things like that. I've been utilizing a great deal of more slender cotton, so I add interfacing to give it a tad of structure.
- Bag Base: You'll need something somewhat solid for the base like canvas, or two or three of my top choices – I utilized Cricut False Calfskin and metallic felt.

Instructions:

1) Open the Corrective Pack example and cut one full example with your Coating texture.

2) Cut the main tangle (with the two square shape pieces) once out of your sack Outside texture, and once out of interfacing, in case you're utilizing that. When I cut interfacing with the Cricut Creator, I pick the cotton setting and set the weight to "Less."

3) Cut the Pack Scrape the bottom of the stiffer material and pick the setting to coordinate. Cricut Artificial Calfskin with the Fine Point Sharp edge, on the false cowhide, for instance.

4) I have been leaving the texture marker off because there aren't generally any dubious markings. After that, I don't need to attempt to wash it out later.

Sewing Cricut Restorative Pack:

1) With right sides together, sew one Outside board to the Base piece with 3/8 inch crease remittance – utilize this estimation for all creases.

2) Repeat with the base of the Coating and one side of the Covering.

Lay the zipper look down on the right side of the Outside and top with the best edge of the Coating, look down. Line up every one of the edges and stick or clasp together.

3) With a zipper foot, sew as near the zipper teeth as you can. When you get to the zipper pull, stop the sewing machine, put the needle down, and lift the foot. At that point, pull the zipper up past where you officially sewed. Set the foot back down and continue onward.

4) Iron the texture; you sewed and sew a best line along the edge of the texture.

Rehash with the opposite side of the zipper. Outside texture lookup, zipper, Covering face down. Line up edges and stick or clasp. Sew with the zipper foot, moving the zipper haul off the beaten path when required, so you don't get a knock in your sewing around it.

Iron and best fasten the opposite side of the zipper.

5) Sew the opposite side of the Outside to the Base. Sew together the opposite side of the Coating to the Covering

Base, Yet leave an opening a couple of inches wide so you can turn the sack back to front later.

6) Make beyond any doubt, the zipper is open, not shut, and sew the two edges of the sack—the distance from the Covering end to the Pack Base end.

7) Now, the corners. Level out the opening and focus the crease. Sew shut. Rehash on each edge of the Sack Base and the Covering.

8) Trim all strings and any piece of the zipper that sticks out past the edge of the texture. Utilizing the gap left in the base of the coating, haul the entire sack back to front.

9) Sew the opening in the coating shut by collapsing the crude edges in only a little and sewing near the edge: backline and the start and end and trim strings.

10) Push the covering down into the sack, pushing out the corners, and the pack is done!

Wild OX Plaid No-Sew Reindeer Cushion

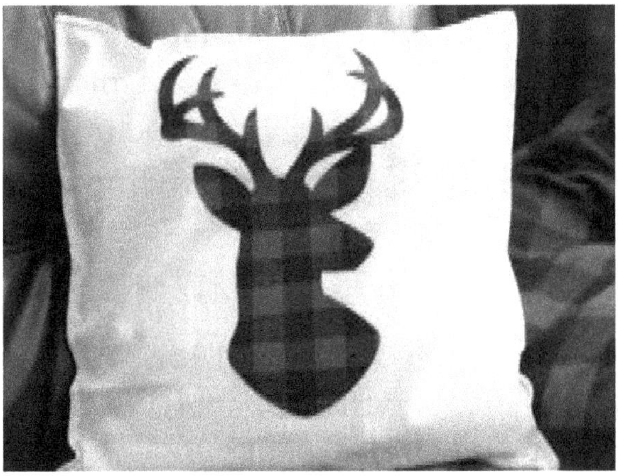

Make this fun wild ox plaid reindeer cushion in 5 minutes or less with the Cricut Producer – no sewing abilities required!

This was SO natural to make! What's more, super moderate as well

Materials Needed:

- Buffalo Plaid Texture (I got mine from Joann's)
- Pillow Cover (I utilized the Gurli Pad Cover from IKEA)
- Pillow Embed (additionally from IKEA)
- Heat'n'Bond Ultra Hold
- Cricut Creator
- 12″x24″ Pink Cutting Mat (in case you're utilizing a littler pad, you can utilize a 12″x12″ pink tangle)
- Cricut EasyPress

Instructions:

1) Open up Configuration Space and alter the measure of your reindeer if necessary. My cushion was 20″x20″, so my reindeer is around 9″x14″. TIP-when attempts to choose how enormous to influence a picture, go into Formats, and pick from more than 100 unique choices, including pads, shirts, entryways, windows, and flip failures. That's just the beginning!

2) Measure a couple of inches additional (I completed 10″x15″) and cut a bit of Heat'n'Bond. Append to the back of your texture with the paper side far from your

texture. I utilized my EasyPress set at 300° for 25 seconds to append the Heat'n'Bond to my texture.

3) Attach the texture with Heat'n'Bond to your pink cutting mat texture side up. Send the task to be cut. **Make beyond any doubt you have your rotating cutting edge in the B clasp on your Maker*

4) Preheat your cushion case with your EasyPress for around 5-10 seconds.

5) Place your reindeer on your pillowcase and utilize a ruler to quantify focus.

6) Apply EasyPress with a medium weight to your reindeer and apply (300° for 30 seconds). On the off chance that your reindeer is bigger than 9″ x 9″, you'll need to do this progression twice, once for the best, once for the base. **Make beyond any doubt you are doing this on a solid surface, similar to kitchen countertops**

7) Flip the pillowcase over and rehash past advance.

Embed cushion, and appreciate it!

MULTI-DAY TEE AND KOOZIE

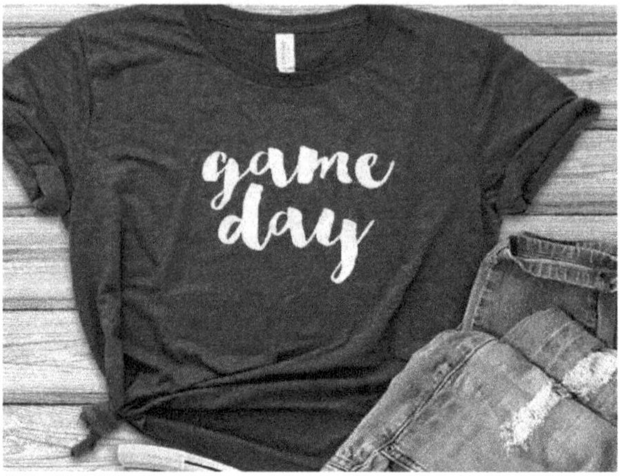

Materials Needed:

- Cricut
- Cricut Press On Vinyl
- Cricut Toolbox
- Cricut EasyPress
- Cricut BrightPad (discretionary, however super accommodating)
- Blank shirts and can koozies

Cricut cut record and Bonjour Textual style for this shirt.

Instructions:

1)Open the slice documents and change by fit your shirts. Send to the Cricut to cut; make sure to reflect cut iron-on glossy vinyl side down.

2)Weed the vinyl. The BightPad is super useful; the Toolbox is an unquestionable requirement have!

3)Use the EasyPress to apply the vinyl to the shirts and koozies. We utilized the Cricut press on the defensive sheet for the koozies and squeezed them at 360* for 30 seconds. We did likewise for the shirts, however, we rehashed the procedure within the shirts as well.

That is it! You have cute amusement day wear for any diversion you are going to!

SPEEDY AND EASY HALLOWEEN BAT NAIL ART

Materials Needed:

- Cricut machine
- Bat cut plan
- Black Vinyl
- Nail clean, Cut a minor bat plan with your Cricut machine.

Instructions:

Cut the bat structure from vinyl at whatever size you'd like. I set up the project plan at pretty much 1/2 inch.

Remove the cut shape from vinyl sponsorship and apply it to your nail.

Apply a nail clean topcoat to help secure your nail workmanship.

Note about vinyl: I've made nail craftsmanship utilizing a wide assortment of vinyl. I've discovered the vinyl that appears to follow and wait the best is slight perpetual glue vinyl. Regardless of which vinyl you pick, it will keep going longer on naturally painted, clean nails.

Monogrammed Headboard

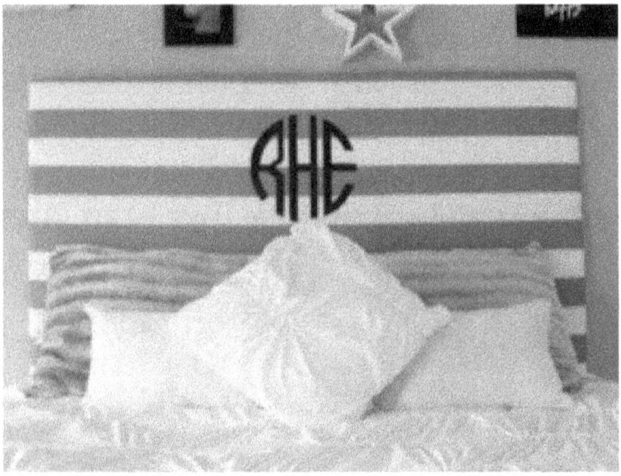

Materials Needed:

- Black iron-on vinyl
- Iron
- Clean, soft cloth for pressing
- Measuring tape
- Large striped fabric, 2 yards for a twin bed headboard
- Staple gun and staples
- Scissors for trimming the fabric
- Drill and screws
- 2 x 4's 30" long, quantity: 2
- One 56" x 33" piece of plywood
- One twin mattress topper, slightly puffy is good, kind of like an egg carton-feel

Instructions:

Spread your fabric down on the floor with the printed side facing the ground, then center your mattress topper about the center of your fabric. Place the flat side of the topper down on the fabric, so the bumps are facing you. Lay the plywood on top of the fabric and mattress topper about in the center.

Using your scissors, trim the excess fabric from around the edges of the topper and wood. Leave about 2 inches of fabric on each side.

Start on the bottom of your headboard, fold the fabric and foam topper up onto the board, and use your stapler and staples to attach the two to the wooden piece securely. Place your staples only an inch or two apart from one another. You do not want a lot of space between them. Next, move to the opposite side of the headboard and gently pull the fabric and foam tight as you staple them to the wood along the top of the headboard. Do the same to each side. Pay close attention to how you fold the corners to secure and hide well on the back of your headboard.

In Design Space, create your monogram and resize it to fit well on your headboard. Make sure to mirror your monogram! When you have designed it to your liking, send the file to cut on your black vinyl by clicking on "Make It." Once it is done, the cutting, remove the extra vinyl and weed out any pieces remaining in the small spaces you do not want as part of your design.

Measure your headboard's height and width and locate the middle of the board. Keep in mind your headboard may dip behind your bed and frame a bit, and pillows will also be stacked up against it. This means you may want your monogram to sit closer to the top or higher up your headboard's centerline than exactly center. Make any adjustments that you think would be most appropriate. When you find your spot, lay your monogram over and position it to your liking. Lay the cloth over top and press with medium pressure with your warm iron. Spend about 30 seconds per press. When the vinyl is cool, gently remove the clear backing.

Use your drill and 2 x 4's to add legs to your headboard. Measure, so each leg is placed on the bottom of your headboard a few inches towards the middle, so the legs get pinned to the wall by the bed and frame. You do not want these legs to be seen. Make sure to place your legs an equal distance from the sides, so it sits correctly. When you have your placement, drill two or three screws into each leg, ensuring the screws go into the wooden backing but not through the foam and fabric.

Gently pull your bed from the wall and position your new headboard, so the monogram is centered on your bed. When you have your headboard in place, push your bed back against the wall, pinning your newest focal point in place!

DIY Halloween Bat Treat Bag Toppers

These Halloween treat sack toppers can be redone with any hues you'd like. Essentially un-level the bat structure and change the hues. You can likewise make extravagant bat cutouts with this project. The project will take somewhat longer to make since you have to sit tight for the cut. Yet, the structure is exceptionally lovely and can be utilized for a wide range of Halloween stylistic themes and artworks.

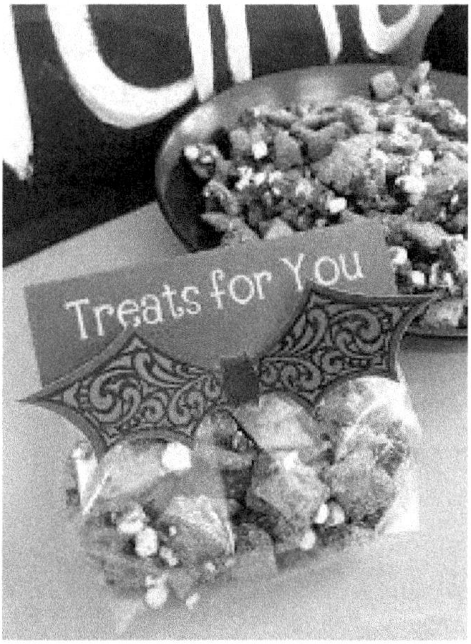

Materials Needed:

- Cricut Machine with Design Space
- Cricut scoring cutting edge
- Bat Treat Topper Project
- White paper and printer
- Stapler with staples
- Plastic treat packs loaded up with treats.
- Glue What you have to make your own Halloween Bat treat sack toppers

Instructions:

Follow Design Space onscreen guidelines to print and afterward cut the bat treat sack topper pieces.

Fold the card along the scoreline.

Fold treat pack to close. Staple shut (discretionary).

Place the collapsed card over the highest point of the treat pack collapsed edge—staple along the card's base.

Glue the bat body to the middle base of the card and permit to dry.

Optionally, adorn the bat treat sack topper with sparkle or gleam paint.

Night Sky Pillow

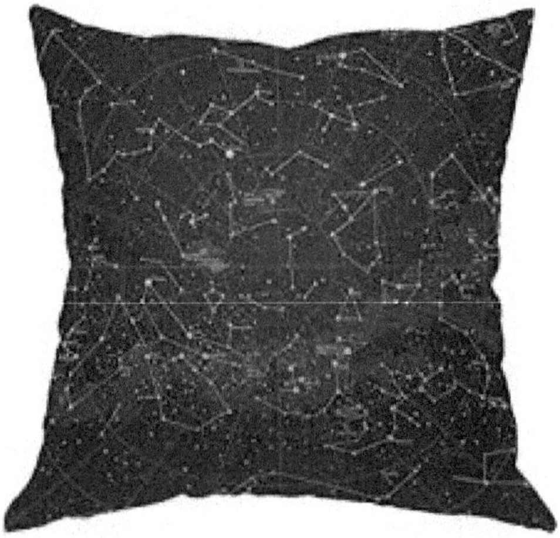

The night sky is a beautiful thing, and you will love having a piece of it on a cozy pillow. Customize this with the stars you love most, or add constellations, planets, galaxies, and more! Adults and children alike can enjoy these lovely pillows. A sewing machine will make this project a breeze to put together, or you can use a needle and thread. If you're not great at sewing, use fabric glue to close the pillow. Choose a soft fabric that you love so that you can cuddle up with this pillow. You will need your Cricut EasyPress or iron to attach the heat transfer vinyl.

Materials Needed:

- Black, dark blue, or dark purple fabric
- Heat transfer vinyl in gold or silver
- Cutting mat
- Polyester batting
- Weeding tool or pick
- Cricut EasyPress

Instructions

Decide the shape you want for your pillow, and cut two matching shapes out of the fabric.

Open Cricut Design Space and create a new project.

Select the "Image" button in the lower left-hand corner and search "stars."

Select the stars of your choice and click "Insert."

Place the iron-on material on the mat.

Send the design to the Cricut.

Use the weeding tool or pick to remove excess material.

Remove the material from the mat.

Place the iron-on material on the fabric.

Use the EasyPress to adhere it to the iron-on material.

Sew the two fabric pieces together, leaving allowance for a seam and a small space open.

Fill the pillow with polyester batting through the small open space.

Sew the pillow shut.

Cuddle up to your starry pillow!

Clutch Purse

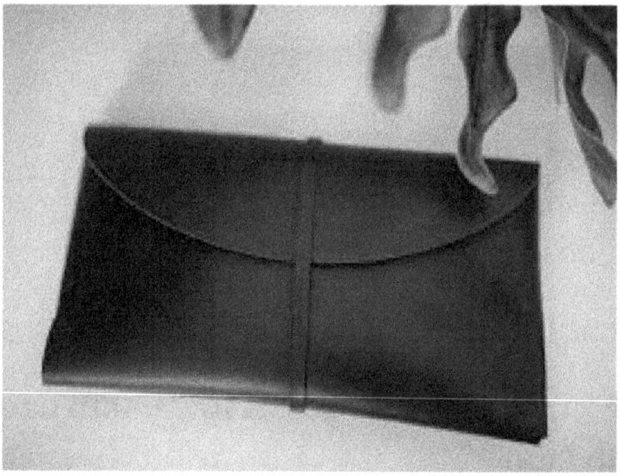

Clutches are an incredibly useful thing to have around. It is smaller than a regular purse yet big enough to hold what you need, and you can use them for any occasion. Create a few of these in different colors and patterns to match different outfits! This clutch is inspired by a project that Cricut has in the Design Space. It is the most advanced of the fabric projects in this book, and it uses the most sewing. For the best results, use the Cricut Maker for this project.

Materials Needed:

- Two fabrics, one for the exterior and one for the interior
- Fusible fleece
- Fabric cutting mat
- D-ring
- Sew-on snap
- Lace
- Zipper
- Sewing machine
- Fabric scissors
- Keychain or charm of your choice

Instructions

1. Open Cricut Design Space and create a new project.
2. Select the "Image" button in the lower left-hand corner and search for "essential wallet."
3. Select the essential wallet template and click "Insert."
4. Place the fabric on the mat.
5. Send the design to the Cricut.
6. Remove the fabric from the mat.
7. Attach the fusible fleecing to the wrong side of the exterior fabric.
8. Attach lace to the edges of the exterior fabric.
9. Assemble the D-ring strap.

10. Place the D-ring onto the strap and sew it into place.
11. Fold the pocket pieces wrong side out over the top of the zipper, and sew it into place.
12. Fold the pocket's wrong side in and sew the sides.
13. Sew the snap onto the pocket.
14. Lay the pocket on the right side of the main fabric lining so that the corners of the pocket's bottom are behind the lining fabric's curved edges. Sew the lining piece to the zipper tape.
15. Fold the lining behind the pocket and iron in place.
16. Sew on the other side of the snap.
17. Trim the zipper so that it's not overhanging the edge.
18. Sew the two pocket layers to the exterior fabric across the bottom.
19. Sew around all of the layers.
20. Trim the edges with fabric scissors.
21. Turn the clutch almost completely inside out and sew the opening closed.
22. Turn the clutch inside out and press the corners into place.
23. Attach your charm or keychain to the zipper.
24. Carry your new clutch wherever you need it!

Chapter 2: Intermediate Projects

Personalized Pillowcase

What would you say to make a personalized pillowcase without actually sewing anything? The best yet is that the Cricut machine will do all the needed cutting. Once again, you are going to be using vinyl to make a lovely personalized item for decorating your home, as a gift for someone you care about, or to take a nap! You will find everything you need to start making your personalized pillowcase below.

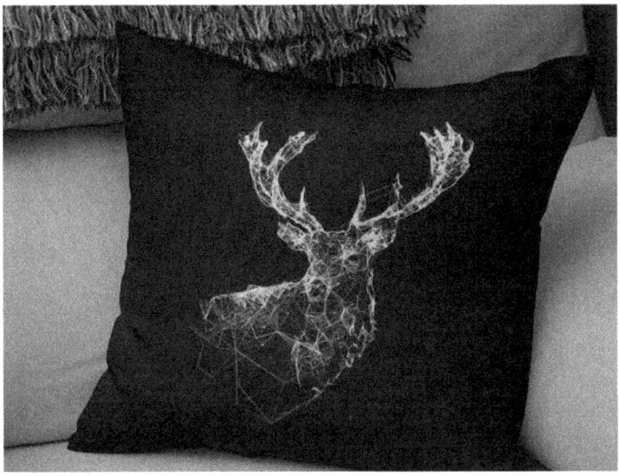

Materials Needed:

- Iron-on Vinyl
- Pillowcase
- Weeding tool
- Cricut Machine

- Easy Press or iron

Instructions:

Upload your preferred design or choose one from the Design Space image library. You can also make your own design. Make sure to adjust the size of the image to the pillow's size – you don't want the image to be too small, but you don't also want it to go over the entire surface of the pillow. You can also create a mock-up statement or a witty citation by using a font of your choice. When your design is ready, you can proceed to "Make it" – there; you will specify iron-on vinyl as your material of choice. Make sure to use "Mirror" on your design as you will be attaching the image to the pillow. Before you start cutting the image with the machine, set up your cutting mat, and arrange the material. Proceed to cut.

Your design is cut, and now it's the time for weeding. Take your weeding tool and start removing all the excess vinyl from your design until only the image you want on the pillow is left. Remove all vinyl scraps from the working surface and prepare your Easy Press or regular iron. Heat your Easy Press – you can set the timer on. The heating up will take 5 seconds. Afterward, you will heat the pillow surface for 30 seconds before attaching the design to the pillow. Place the vinyl on the pillow where you want the image to be, and then use the Press again. Make sure to apply mild pressure onto the Press and hold for 15 seconds.

Let the vinyl piece cool a bit before removing it from the pillow and revealing your new design. At this moment, the vinyl is too hot so that you can burn your fingers. Once the vinyl piece is cool or warm, you can remove it and enjoy your design.

Party Plates

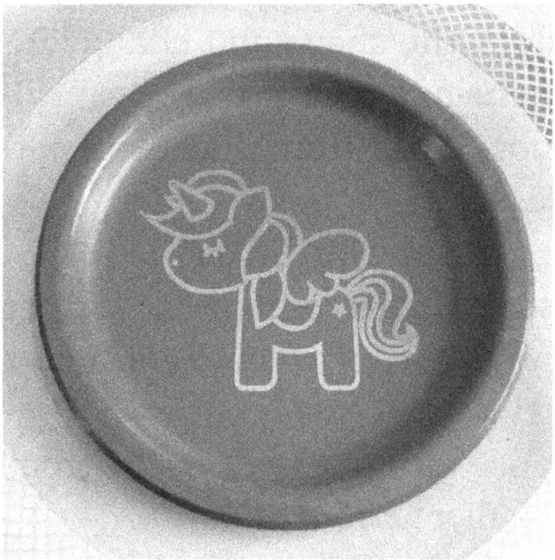

Trying to find plates to match a party theme can be challenging. With the Cricut, you can make your own to match your theme.

Materials Needed:

- Gold Cricut foil (or color of your choice)
- Transfer tape
- Paper plates in the color of your choice
- Green StandardGrip mat
- Cricut Fine-Point Blade
- Weeding tool
- Scraping tool or brayer tool

- Pair of scissors for cutting the material to size

Instructions:

1. Open a new project in Design Space.
2. Select 'Template' from the menu on the left-hand side.
3. Change the background color to match the color of your plates.
4. Unlock the shape and change it to the same dimensions of your plates.
5. Choose 'Text' from the menu on the left-hand side.
6. Type "Happy Birthday."
7. Resize the text to fit on the top of the plate.
8. Change the text color to gold and choose a font you like.
9. Choose an image you want from 'Images' or upload your own.
10. Resize it to fit beneath the "Happy birthday" and set the color to gold.
11. Select both the text and image, right-click, and select 'Attach.'
12. Save the project.
13. Click 'Make it.'
14. You may have more than one plate to make. The cutting screen is a great place to make copies of the party plate image.
15. At the top left-hand corner of the screen, you will see 'Project copies.'
16. Next to the text, there is a scroll box with the number 1 on it.

17. For a standard-sized dinner plate, you should be able to get around four images per 12” by 12” cutout.
18. Set the number of project copies to 4.
19. Four copies of the design will appear on the page.
20. Position them with enough space around them for a comfortable cut. If there is room for more, increase the number of copies.
21. Check that the fine-point blade is loaded in the Cricut.
22. Set the Cricut dial to custom.
23. Cut out the foil to size and stick it to the cutting mat.
24. Load the cutting mat into the Cricut.
25. In Design Space, select the correct material.
26. When the Cricut is ready to cut, press 'Go.'
27. When the Cricut is finished cutting out the shapes, unload the mat.
28. Foil is a bit trickier than other materials to use.
29. Carefully remove the piece that is no longer needed.
30. You can gently use the weeding tool, but some tape like soft plumber’s tape may work better.
31. Once you are happy with the cleaned-up image, cut them out into separate squares.
32. Use a transfer tape piece the same size as the image square to place over the image.
33. Use the scraper or brayer tool to smooth it out and ensure there are no bubbles.

34. Pull the backing sheet off the image and stick it to the party plate.
35. Use the scraping tool or brayer tool to make sure the image is completely pressed onto the plate.
36. Gently pull off the transfer tape.
37. Your party plate is ready to use.

Spinning Heart Card

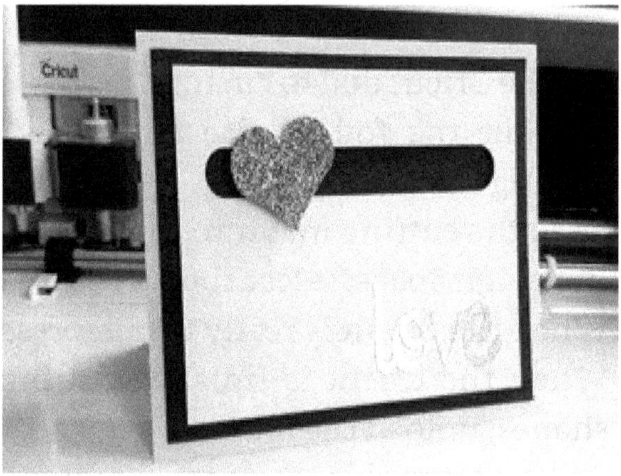

Spinner cards offer a variety of fun messages that you can send. An example is a "love" theme with a glittering heart, but you can change the message, colors, and spinning shape to be anything you want. Think of spinning images like boats, people, airplanes, flowers, etc. There is no limit to what you can do with this template!

Materials Needed:

- Two pennies
- Foam dots or circles

- Glue
- Pink and white cardstock
- Grey faux-leather cardstock or material
- Blue craft foam

Instructions:

Open the Spinner Card design file in Design Space. Cut the cardstock as instructed, following the prompts.

Using glue, add the grey, faux-leather cardstock to the pink card base, aligning it in the center of the card's front side.

Add the foam to the back of the white cut cardstock. On the front of the white part, add words or images that align with your card's theme. Do not put anything that pops out from the card close to the cut put track as it will interfere with your spinning object later on.

Lay one penny on the table and then place the white cardstock on top with the blue foam facing down to the table, lining up the penny's middle in the visible track. Glue the small blue foam circle on the penny in the middle of the track, being careful not to get any glue on the edges of the track. Carefully glue the second penny on top of the first that now has the foam dot attached. Allow drying completely before moving.

Glue the white circle of cardstock on the top of the penny on the design side of your white cardstock front, not on the side with the blue foam. Glue your spinning image on top of the white circle. Allow drying completely before moving again.

Once your glue is dry, and your spinning image is secure, glue the white part to the pink and grey card base, aligning the white in the center of the grey faux-leather background. Allow to dry completely and then test your spinner!

FLOWER PARTNER CARDS

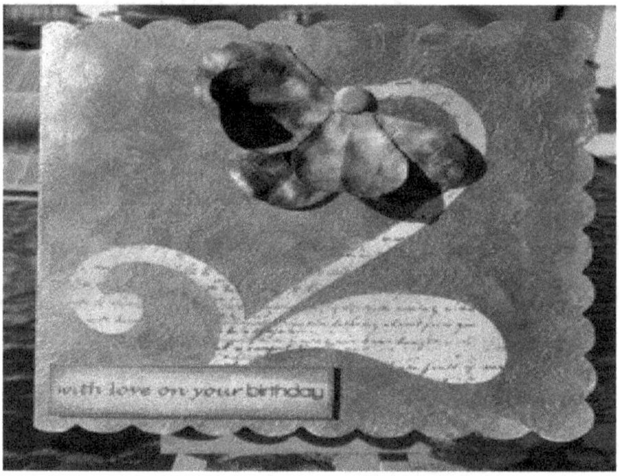

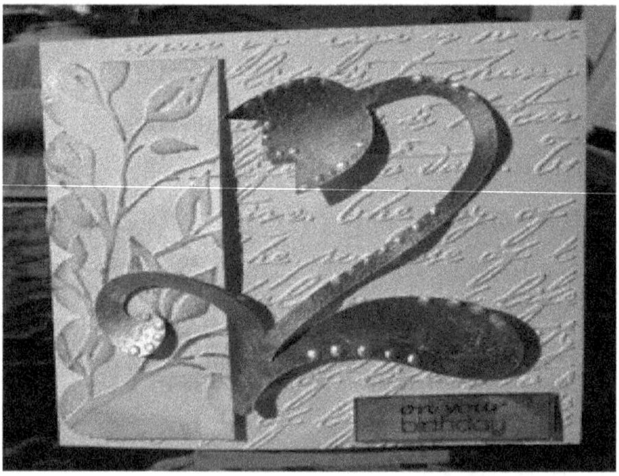

This card is a little bit of Cricut, a little bit of painting, and a whole lot of fun! Plus, it makes two cards in one tutorial, so you get two for the effort of one. Mix up the design and choose a cut out other than a flower to make it a more customized design. You can also adjust the colors and messaging to fit any occasion.

Materials Needed:

- Variety of alcohol inks, such as coral and bronze
- White cardstock
- Spray adhesive
- Stamp with a favorite saying and ink
- White embossing supplies or adhesive words in white
- White 6x6 card base, quantity: 2
- Prima flower, large
- Brass brad or two-pronged fastener
- Added sentiment sticker or quote, quantity: 2
- Embossed floral cardstock
- Liquid pearls or puffy silver paint

Instructions:

Search Design Space for a droopy headed flower shape. The Cindy Lou cartridge offers a variety of flower options that work well for the project. Cut the image 5 inches on the white, adhesive vinyl or cardstock, depending on your chosen use.

Using your stamp, add the words all over the front of the white card base. If you choose, you can print a quote or saying on the card base if you prefer instead of hand stamping it.

Attach the flower cut out to the card in the place you want it to appear. Use the spray adhesive to make sure the image stays in one place.

Using the alcohol inks, dab with a sponge applicator liberally all over the front of the card, covering and combining colors. Before the paints dry completely, while still tacky, peel off the flower cut out, revealing the stamped white base underneath. If the page appears too white for you, dab some distressed ink on top, such as the linen distress.

Use the same colors and sponge applicator to add color to the Prima flower petals. Fold the flower in half and press it onto the card base over the removed flower image's head. Use the brass brad to secure in place. If you prefer, consider using a foam or glue dot to secure the flower to the top of the image instead of the brad.

On the other card base, emboss or adhere words in white over the card's entire front part.

Cut a piece of the embossed cardstock about 5 inches tall and 2 inches wide. Scallop one side of the strip. Dab bronze ink over the piece and adhere it to the card's front with glue dots or foam adhesive dots.

Use glue dots or foam adhesive dots to attach the cardstock flower peeled from the first card to the front of the new card base. Also, attach a new sentiment sticker or label to the bottom corner of the card.

Add small dots with liquid pearls or "puffy paint" to the flower for more dimension and interest. You can do silver as pictured or a less-contrasting color like bronze or coral if you prefer.

Cupcake Wrappers

Are you planning a themed party, must make goodies for an upcoming event, or want to do something special with your family? Then this is the project for you! It creates a great visual and message for the family, friends, and guests.

- Materials Needed:
- Paper or cardstock—that's it!

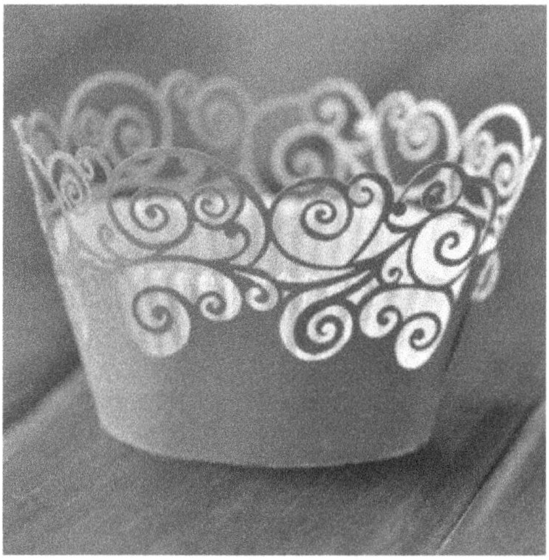

Instructions:

Open Design Space and search the library for cupcake liners or wrappers. There is a selection on the website, or you can develop your own. Set the canvas to your cardstock or paper size and make as many wrappers as you can. You do not need to make a minimal number of wrappers because you can always use them again in the future! Keep in mind that a standard cupcake needs a wrapper that is about nine inches long.

When you have your design set, place your paper, or cardstock on the mat and send the file to cut. Follow the prompts on your computer and your machine to finish cutting the designs.

Use your weeding tool to remove any small pieces that did not come out while cutting. If your design did not call for it, add a small cut on the top on one side and the bottom on the other. This cut should extend about halfway up the wrapper. If you used a pre-set cupcake wrapper, it probably already included it. This means when you wrap your cupcake with the wrapper, you will slide the top into the bottom to close the wrapper.

If you do not want to make a slice in your design, use a few glue dots to glue the design together instead.

A Bookmark

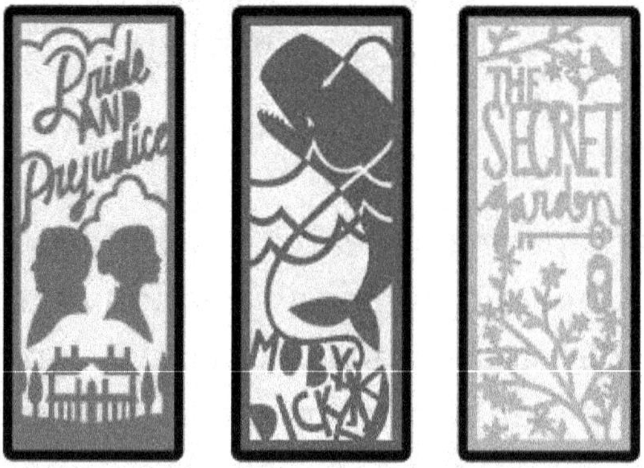

It may seem a little archaic to have or give a custom bookmark, but it is still practical and very personal. Plus, it is a simple project you can do fast!

Materials Needed:

- Vinyl
- Paper of cardstock

Instructions:

Bookmarks can be just about any size and shape you desire, so when you open Design Space, create a shape you prefer. In this example, the bookmark is about two inches wide and six inches tall. These include text cut out from the bookmark, so choose any word or phrase you want to appear and adjust the size and font to your liking. You can always add a picture or other details if you wish.

To cut the vinyl out of the vinyl of the bookmark, make sure to select your text and tell the software to set the text as a separate layer and then select "Attach."

Send the file to cut and follow the prompts on your screen. Once the bookmarks are cut and assembled, if you have a laminator, consider laminating them to help them last even longer and bring an even more professional appearance to your project.

Napkin Holders

Make your next dinner party stand out with personal and custom napkin holders. You can make them in any design you like to match your dinner party theme or season. You can also make it as simple as possible, with just a few images or words, or more complicated with multiple materials and pieces.

Choose a version based on your comfort and preference level. Also, you can also decide how you want to attach your holders. For example, you can add small slits on the top on one end of the holder and one on the bottom of the other to slide into each other or use a glue dot. You can even use a small strip of double-stick tape to enclose the holder. You could also add small holes on either side of the holder and lace ribbon or string through it.

Materials Needed:

- Colored or glitter cardstock
- Vinyl, if preferred
- Your closure method of choice: glue dots, double-stick tape, etc.

Instructions:

In Design Space, design the text or names that you want to appear on your napkin wraps. Make sure it is adjusted so that the words will appear appropriately on your wrap width. This is also the time to develop a layer with the flourishing details, like the olive branch and your napkin wrap shape. Also, think about images and different shapes you could include on your napkin holders.

With your napkin wrap base designed, repeat your patterns and words on the number you need for your place settings. This is what will tell your Cricut to cut multiple pieces and allows you the opportunity to customize each one if you desire. If you will be closing the wraps with ribbon and need holes or want to slide the ends together with slits, make sure to add those in now.

Once you have your designs laid out, send the file to cut. Weed out any small items you do not want in your design. Assemble your napkin wrap pieces and wrap your napkins or silverware for your big event! Make sure to attach them securely according to the method you have chosen.

Magnetic Paper Flowers

Adding a few bright flowers to your fridge can take your kitchen from average to extraordinary. It can help it go from a place you “have” to be to a place you “want” to be! You can create as many as you want, in any color or pattern that matches your décor. You can also come up with various flowers to suit your mood or help you keep track of your family's needs. They are also awesome gifts!

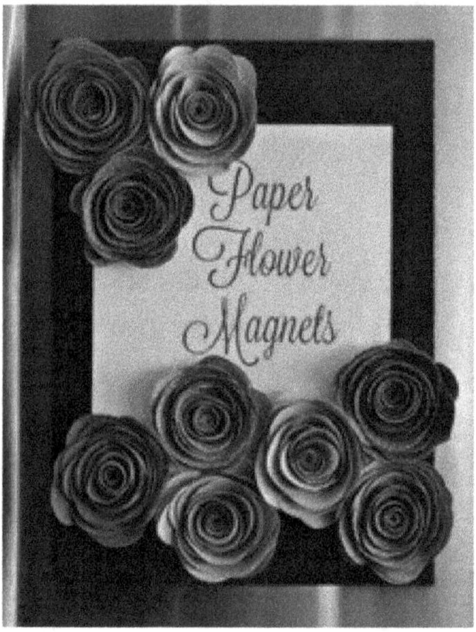

Materials Needed:

- Cardstock in a variety of colors or patterns
- Hot glue gun
- Magnets

Instructions:

Open Design Space and develop the shape of your petals. These look good as half circles or oval shapes. You can also create bumped petal shapes by stacking oval over one another. Repeat the petal shapes to make enough flower magnets that you want. A large flower typically has about 12 petals, while a medium one has about eight. Medium petals are about two inches long, while large petals are usually about three inches. Measure the size of your magnet base and develop a circular flower base. You can add a small, ½ inch long slit at the end of every petal for easiest construction if you want to.

Once you have your petals designed and duplicated, load the cardstock on your cutting mat and get it ready to cut. Send the file to cut. If you did not add the slit in Design Space, use a crafting knife or an Exacto knife to cut a slit at the bottom of each petal. Once all the petals have a cut, add a dot of glue and glue one side to the other, making them into the petal shape. Do this to all the petals.

Place your magnets down on the table, gather all the base circles, and glue them to the magnets' tops. Begin gluing the petals to the circle bases, starting on the outside and working your way in. Continue adding petals until it looks full. Large flowers will have about three or more layers, while medium may only have two. Keep playing with your petals until you have a shape and set up that looks best to you. Leave a small space in the center of the flower open.

Go back to Design Space and create smaller petals. Make them slightly smaller than the first petals. These are designed to add to your flowers' center, so adjust them according to what you want. If you are unsure, try a few different shapes to try them out. Add the slits to the petals again or wait until they are cut to add the slits with an Exacto knife. When you are ready, send the file to cut. Create the petal shapes with a little bit of glue.

Add glue to the flower design's interior and begin adding the smaller petals to the inside of your flowers. Gently pinch your flowers' edges for a more geometric appearance or gently curve them inside for something more natural. You can add as many petal layers as you like.

Art Journals

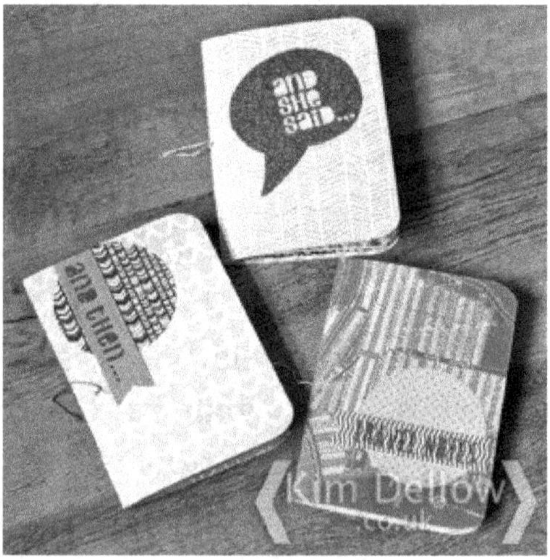

These sweet little notebooks are great for art and travel journals, but you can customize them to fit any need or desire. Choose favorite colors and patterns, personalized sayings or words, and you can even add a few more pages to the inside if you want. Get ready for some serious jealous looks the next time you pull one of these out of your bag!

Materials Needed:

- Glue
- Colored thread

- Large needle
- Paper piercer or something to poke holes in your paper
- Various cardstock in interesting prints
- Various paper in interesting colors and prints

Instructions:

In Design Space, create a square on your canvas. Round the corners. You may want to ungroup the layers and delete the bottom layer. Also, adjust the size of your square to the size of your final notebook. For example, in this example, the notebooks are 5" x 7". This means your square will need to measure 10" x 7".

Add your scoreline to the middle of the square or rectangle shape. You will find this line under "lines." Adjust the size to fit your project and then select "Align" and "Center." This should automatically adjust the line, so it is directly in the middle of your project.

Next, add notches to your center score line to tell you where to pierce your paper. You can place another scoreline at 90 degrees from the centerline and scale it down, so it is small. Alternatively, you can place a very small circle over the place you want to pierce your paper and have the machine cut the little spot out for you. Measure down about one inch from the top and bottom to place your holes or notches.

If you want to add any custom cut-outs or stickers to the front cover, you can now design those as you desire.

Otherwise, you can use shapes and stickers you already have on hand. You can always create these later as well.

Now you are ready to create the inside pages of your book. You will want to copy and paste the cover rectangle piece and make the pages just slightly smaller than the cover. Consider the size of 9.8" x 6.8". This means you will also want to re-align your center scoreline. You will also need to adjust the size. Do not move your notch or hole marks, though! Keep that one inch from the top and bottom of the cover, not the page!

If you moved the notches or hole marks, you can always group the markings from the cover and copy and paste them for as many pages of the book you are creating. Then move, do not resize, these markings, and place them over each page's centerline.

If you want to add images and cut-outs to the internal pages, you can add those now. Keep in mind that any words you cut out on one side of the page will appear back on the other side! Consider using images and shapes to be safe. You can also create vinyl stickers or drawn images to the pages if you do not want to cut into the paper. If you choose vinyl words or images, some art mediums may struggle to cover them properly.

When you are done designing your pages, send your file to print, cut, and score your cover and pages. Follow the prompts to load your paper and tools into your machine.

After your pages and cover are cut, fold on the scoreline, place the pages into the cover and line up the notches or holes. If you are using notches, use your paper punch to poke holes in the cover and paper where the notches are located. Depending on your paper, you may want to punch holes one at a time.

Thread your needle with the colored thread. Pass your needle through the holes, and tie a slip knot. Tighten your knot as tight as possible and then tie off with a regular knot. You can tie on the outside of the journal or the inside. Trim the threads as short as you want.

If you are decorating your cover, make sure you add stickers or vinyl to the cover as you prefer. Now you are ready to start journaling away!

Hologram Party Box Tumblers

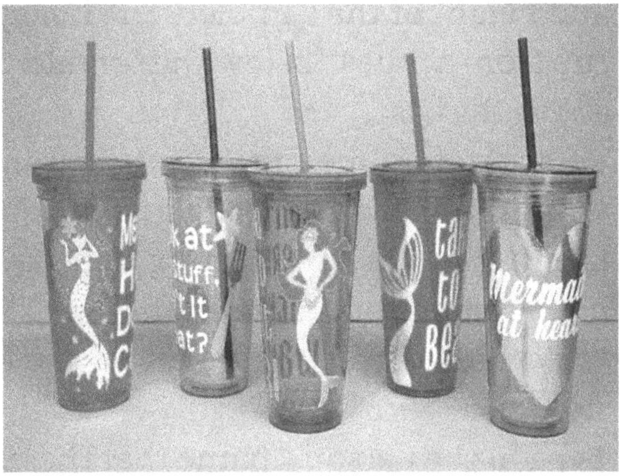

Instead of party goody boxes, why not try hologram personalized party tumblers stuffed with the goodies? The kids get their party treats inside an awesome tumbler to take home for later use.

Materials Needed:

- Hologram stick-on vinyl
- Clear tumblers
- Green StandardGrip mat
- Cricut Fine-Point Blade
- Weeding tool
- Scraping tool or brayer tool
- Pair of scissors for cutting the material to size

Instructions

1. Open a new project in Design Space.
2. Select 'Square' from the 'Shapes' menu on the left-hand side menu.
3. Change the background color to grey.
4. Unlock the shape and change it to the width and height of the tumbler. The hologram will run from about 1" below the tumbler's lip to 1" above the base.
5. To accurately measure the hologram paper's width, wrap it around the tumbler and cut it.
6. Lay it flat on the cutting mat to get the hologram paper's dimensions.
7. Select 'Text' from the menu on the left-hand side.
8. Type in the person's name that the tumbler is for.
9. Select a nice chunky font that will work for the cutout.
10. Position the font onto the middle of the square on the screen.

11. Stretch it to fit across the square.
12. Select both the square and the text.
13. Right-click and choose 'Slice.'
14. Select the first layer of the name text, move it off to one side, then delete it.
15. Select the second layer of the name text, move it off to one side, then delete it.
16. If you like, you can add an image and repeat steps 13 to 16 for the shape or image.
17. When the hologram image is ready, select 'Make it.'
18. Make sure the fine-point blade is loaded.
19. Make sure the hologram vinyl is correctly stuck to the cutting mat.
20. Select the correct material and press 'Go' once the Cricut is ready to cut.
21. Once it has cut, leave the vinyl on the cutting board and weed out the middle of the image and text.
22. Place the transfer sheet over the vinyl and use the scraper or brayer tool to smooth it out.
23. Remove the back sheet.
24. Carefully place the hologram paper around the tumbler.
25. Use the scraper to ensure it is on properly.
26. Remove the transfer sheet.

Cake Toppers

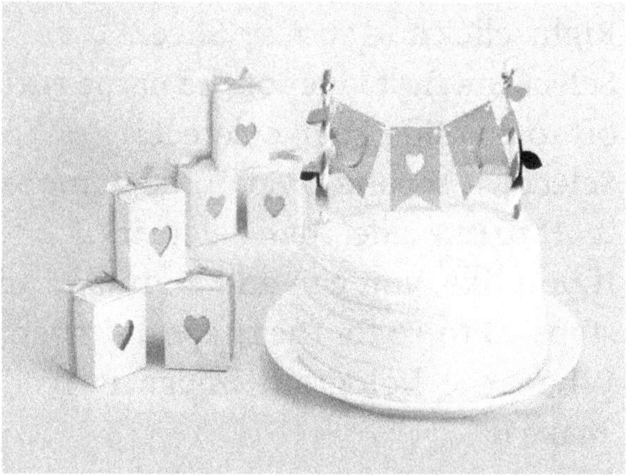

Create customized cake toppers for birthdays; gender reveal parties and any other celebration that calls for cake.

Materials Needed:

- Cricut glitter cardstock the color of your choice
- Green StandardGrip mat
- Cricut Fine-Point Blade
- Weeding tool
- Scraping tool or brayer tool
- Pair of scissors for cutting the material to size
- Wooden skewers
- Mini glue foam dots
- Glue

Instructions

1. Open a new project in Design Space.
2. Select 'Text' from the left-hand side menu.

3. Change the color to the color of the glitter cardstock.
4. Unlock the shape and change it to the required dimensions.
5. For this project, type “Golden 50.”
6. Change the font to a nice elaborate font.
7. Duplicate the text.
8. Flip the duplicate horizontally so that it is a mirror image of the original text.
9. Click ‘Make it.’
10. Ensure that the two text images have a good amount of space between them.
11. Click ‘Continue.’
12. Ensure the fine-point blade is loaded in the Cricut.
13. Choose “Glitter cardstock” as the material and set the dial on the Cricut to custom.
14. Stick the sized and cut out glitter cardstock onto the cutting mat.
15. Load the cutting mat into the Cricut.
16. When the Cricut is ready, press 'Go.'
17. When the cake topper has been cut, peel the extra cardstock away.
18. Use the weeding tool to clean up the text.
19. Use the glue to stick a skewer on each end of the one text image.
20. While it is drying, stick the foam dots on the back of the same text image.
21. When the skewer has been stuck down, carefully aligned, and stick the mirrored image design onto the image.

22. Your cake topper is ready to grace the top of a cake.

FAMILY TREE WALL DECAL LEATHER LEAF PICTURES

The family tree decal from Project 21 is going to need some heart-shaped leaves. There are many different ways to make them. The Cricut has many different materials it can cut, and you can use more than one material per project.

For this project, you are going to create leaves using Cricut Basswood and clear sticker paper transfer.

Note: Only the Cricut Maker can cut basswood because of the knife blade. You can substitute the basswood with cardstock, faux leather, or just use a vinyl decal for those who do not have a Cricut Maker.

Materials Needed:

- Cricut basswood 11" by 11"

- Cricut printable sticker paper
- Purple StrongGrip mat
- Green StandardGrip mat
- Cricut Fine-Point Blade
- Cricut Knife Blade
- Weeding tool
- Scraping tool or brayer tool
- Pair of scissors for cutting the material to size
- Quick-drying paint in leaf colors of your choice or a slightly tinted varnish
- Builder's tape
- Two-way tape
- Inkjet printer
- Good quality photos of the family to be put on the family tree wall decal

Instructions

1. Open a new project in Design Space.
2. Select the 'Heart' from the 'Shapes' menu on the left-hand side menu.
3. Change the background color to grey.
4. Unlock the shape and change it to 5.044" width with a length of 4.822".
5. Set the color of the heart to orange for the first part of this tutorial.
6. Create 5 more orange-colored hearts by duplicating them.
7. Take 1 orange heart and change the color to red.
8. Arrange the 4 orange hearts at the top of the screen in rows of 2.

9. Arrange the 1 red heart below the last row of orange hearts.
10. Unlock the red heart and change the dimensions to a width of 3.114" with a length of 3.528".
11. Duplicate 1 red heart to make 8 red hearts.
12. Line the red hearts in 2 rows of 3 hearts and 1 row of 2 hearts.
13. Save the project.
14. Click 'Make it.'
15. You will see there are two mats to be cut out.
16. One mat will have the 4 large orange leaves and the other the 8 small red leaves.
17. Set the dial on the Cricut to custom.
18. Load the knife blade where the fine-point blade is or goes.
19. Place the first sheet of 11" by 11" basswood on the purple cutting mat.
20. Use the builder's tape to stick down and secure the edges of the wood.
21. Move all of the star wheels on the Cricut feeder bar to the right-hand side.
22. Load the cutting mat into the Cricut.
23. Click 'Continue' in Design Space.
24. Make sure all the settings are correct on the next screen—select wood for the materials.
25. Click 'Continue' when you are ready.
26. Click 'Go' when the Cricut is ready to cut.
27. Cutting wood is going to take a while.

28. While the Cricut is cutting the heart shapes out, you can take the time to mark out where you will place the leaves on the tree wall decal.
29. Sort out the pictures you are going to use. They must be able to fit in a 2.85" by 2.85" circle frame. Go ahead and upload the photos into your computer or the device you use for Design Space.
30. When the Cricut has finished printing, do not unload the wood right away. Gently place your fingers beneath the cuts to ensure the wood has been cut completely through.
31. Unload the first set of hearts.
32. Pull the leftover wood from the cutting mat, leaving the heart shapes behind.
33. Use the weeding tool to clean up the hearts.
34. Gently pull them off the cutting mat, load the next board, and finish printing the smaller hearts.
35. When the smaller hearts are done, repeat steps 30 to 34.
36. When the first set of hearts is printed, you can start painting the hearts in color you have chosen for the tree. Try to use lighter color greens, browns, **etc.** as you want to have a clear image of the leaf's picture.
37. You can leave the leaves blank and apply a slightly tinted varnish to them. This will reflect the color of the printed leaf and allow for the picture to show through a lot better.

38. When all the cutting and painting/varnishing is done, go back to Design Space to continue to the project's next step.
39. With the leaves still laid out as they were on the screen, select them all and go to the top menu beneath 'Fill' and change the setting to 'Print.'
40. The layers panel will list each item as a print item instead of a cut item.
41. Select the 'Circle' from the 'Shapes' menu on the left-hand side.
42. Leave the background color as it is.
43. Unlock the shape and change it to 2.85" width with a length of 2.85".
44. Create 3 more circles by duplicating them.
45. Position each circle into the middle of the 4 large hearts.
46. This step needs to be done on each large heart individually.
47. Select the heart and circle.
48. Right-click and select 'Slice.'
49. Select the circle you have just sliced and remove it.
50. There should be 2 more circles in the same position that need to be removed the same as you did for 9.
51. There should be a hollow circle once the slices have been removed.
52. Keep 4 of the circles that were sliced and delete the rest.

53. Change the color of all the leaves to the color you want them to be printed.
54. Select the 'Images' from the menu on the left-hand side.
55. Upload the first photo.
56. Place it in the center of one of the circles.
57. Make sure it fits.
58. Select the circle and delete it.
59. Move the image to the center cutout of a large leaf.
60. Flatten the image to make it stick to the leaf 61. Repeat steps 52 to 58 for the other 3 large leaves.
61. When all the leaves have been colored, and the images inserted, select the 4 larger leaves, right-click, and 'Attach' them as you want them to print together.
62. Select the smaller hearts, right-click, and select 'Attach.'
63. When you are done, click 'Make it.'
64. Send the large and small hearts to the Inkjet printer.
65. Place the sticker paper into the Inkjet printer to print off the design.
66. Allow the images to dry for 10 to 15 minutes.
67. When dry, place the mat Design space is asking for on the cutting mat and load it into the Cricut.
68. Switch the knife blade for the fine-point blade, make sure the dial is still set to custom, and click 'Continue' in Design Space.

69. Select the correct material, which will be sticker paper.
70. Stick the sticker paper onto the green cutting mat and load it into the Cricut.
71. When the Cricut is ready to cut, press 'Go.'
72. Repeat steps 68 to 70 for both cuts.
73. When the cutting is done, weed the images to clean them up after removing the excess sticker paper.
74. After the painted or varnished wooden leaves are dry; you can stick the printed designs onto each wooden leaf.
75. Use transfer paper on each heart-shape image, then transfer it onto each wooden leaf. Line the image's shape up with the shape of the wooden leaf.
76. When the leaves are ready to be stuck to the wall, apply two-way tape, and stick them in position.

Fun Statement Sign

Materials Needed:

- Black vinyl
- Transfer paint
- Wooden pieces:
- 1×12 cut to 9 inches
- (2) 12-inch trim pieces cut from a 1×2 with 45° angles on each end
- (2) 10 ½-inch trim pieces cut from a 1×2 with 45° angles on each end

- Nails for the frame
- Hammer
- Sandpaper
- Black paint
- White paint
- Weeding tool
- Cricut machine

Instructions:

Before you start the Design Space, you will need to take care of the wooden piece and the frame. In case you already have a blank framed sign, you can skip this process and move forward with designing. Alternatively, you will want to use the sandpaper on the wooden pieces and sand them a bit before painting. The black paint is for the frame pieces, and the white paint is for the wooden board that will be the surface for your Cricut design. Leave the wooden pieces to dry and move forward to working in Design Space.

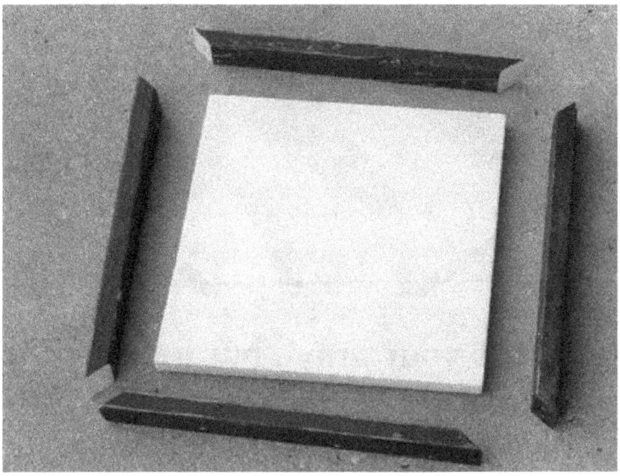

Pick an image in the Design Space from the Image library or make your design. You can use any style or font you like for letters if you are making a statement design. The library has a wide variety of images and designs, so you will probably find a perfect match for your design there. Once your design is ready, make sure to set the size to fit the wooden board you have painted white. Proceed to cut by clicking on "Make it" and set your material preferences to vinyl. Once everything looks good and ready to go, you can start cutting with your Cricut machine.

Once the paint on the wooden pieces is dry, you can use the hammer to nail the frame pieces together and frame the white wooden piece. In the meantime, you can start weeding the vinyl parts you don't need on your design.

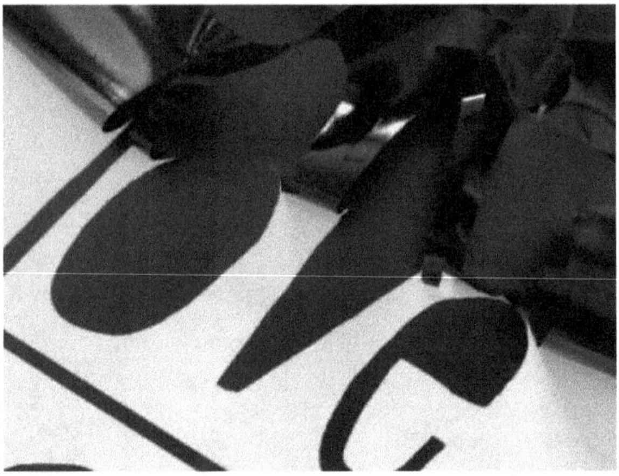

Do not try to cut your vinyl, but peel it off from one angle with your weeding tool and try to peel it off in entirety with your finger carefully. You can use the weeding tool as well if you feel more comfortable with that. Next, you will apply the transfer tape to your clean design. Cut out the tape to fit the sign's surface then apply the tape with the vinyl piece. Remove the transfer tape after carefully applying it, and you have your wooden sign ready!

FOREVER FABRIC BANNER

Materials needed

“Cricut Maker” or “Cricut Explore”, fabric grip mat, glitter iron-on (black, pink), “Cricut EasyPress”, weeder, pink ribbon, canvas fabric, sewable fabric stabilizer, sewing machine, and thread.

Instructions:

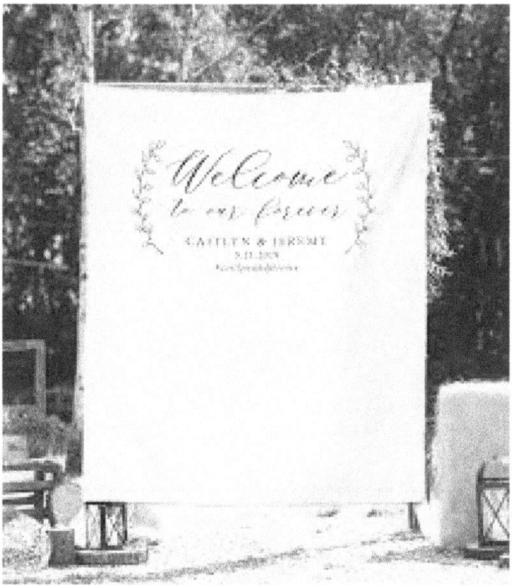

Log into the "Design Space" application and click on the “New Project” button on the top right corner of the screen to view a blank canvas.

Click on the "Projects" icon and type in "fabric banner" in the search bar.

Click on "Customize" to edit the project to your preference further or simply click on the "Make It" button. Place the trimmed fabric on the cutting mat, remove the paper backing, load it to your "Cricut" machine, and follow the screen's instructions to cut your project. Similarly, load the iron-on vinyl sheet to the "Cricut" and cut the design, making sure to mirror the image.

Carefully remove the excess material from the sheet using the "weeder tool", making sure only the design remains on the clear liner.

Using the "Cricut Easy Press Mini" and "Easy Press Mat," the iron-on layers can be easily transferred to the fabric. Preheat your "Easy Press Mini" and put your iron-on vinyl design on the fabric and apply pressure for couple of minutes or more. Wait for few minutes before peeling off the design while it is still warm.

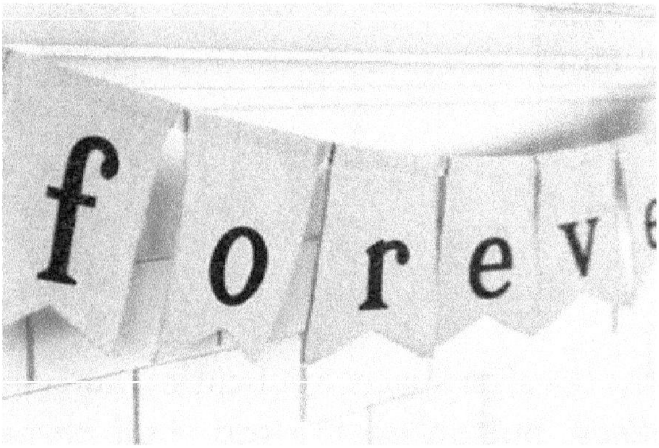

Fabric Flower Brooch

Materials needed

"Cricut Maker" or "Cricut Explore", fabricgrip mat, printable iron-on, "Cricut EasyPress", weeder, fabric pencil pouch, inkjet printer.

Instructions:

Log into the "Design Space" application and click on the "New Project" button on the screen's top right corner to view a blank canvas.

Click on the "Projects" icon and type in "fabric pouch" in the search bar.

Click on "Customize" to edit the project to your preference further or simply click on the "Make It" button and follow the prompts on the screen for using inkjet printer to print the design on your printable vinyl subsequently cut the design.

Carefully remove the excess material from the sheet using the "weeder tool", making sure only the design remains on the clear liner.

Using the "Cricut Easy Press Mini" and "Easy Press Mat" the iron-on layers can be easily transferred to the fabric. Preheat your "Easy Press Mini" and put your iron-on vinyl design on the fabric and apply pressure for couple of minutes or more. Wait for few minutes prior to peeling off the design while it is still warm.

Party Poppers

Materials Needed:

- Cardstock - 12″ x 12″
- Ribbon
- Treats and trinkets to use as a surprise for your party poppers – make sure not to use items larger than 3 inches
- Cracker snaps and glue for gluing the snaps are optional – in case you want to have that cracking sound when popping the party poppers, you can find these online in bundles Cricut machine

Instructions:

You first want to download patterns for party poppers, or you can make your own design. In case you decide to find the pattern and download it, you need to upload it in the form of an SVG file when starting a new project in Design Space. Your design is supposed to look like so on the Canvas:

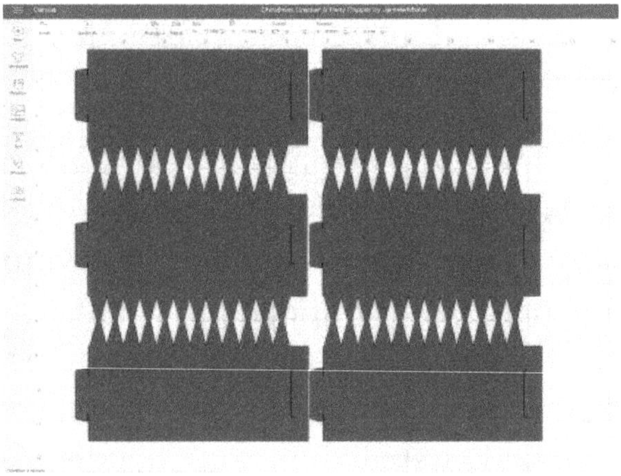

As you may notice, the design is not particularly difficult to make; however, you need to make sure that two-party poppers can fit the cardstock in the given size. This design represents the cut for two party poppers. Make sure to use "Attach" for each piece of design. Select the first three layers and attach them together. Do the same thing for the second row of layers so that these parts would be cut together as a whole. Once your design is ready, make sure to select cardstock for your material. Arrange the cutting mat and the cardstock piece, then "Make it" and cut the design.

Once the party popper designs are cut out, prepare two ribbon pieces for each and roll the cardstock designs in tubes by length. In case you are using cracker snaps, glue on the inside lengthwise instead of in the middle before rolling the cardstock. Tie one end of the tube with a ribbon then fill the tube with surprise treats and trinkets. Tie the remaining end of the tube, and you have your first party popper.

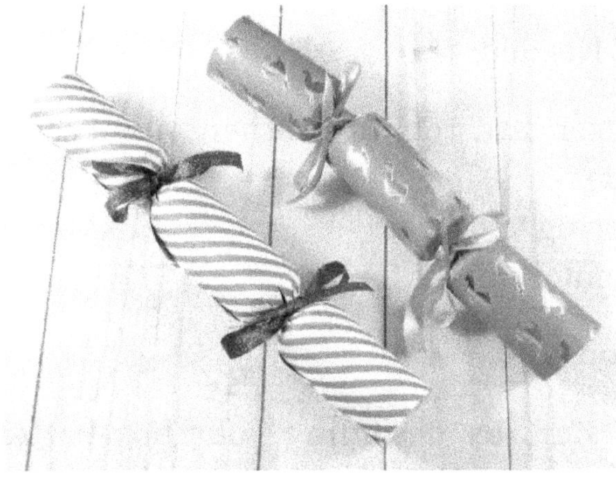

CRICUT GIFT BOXES

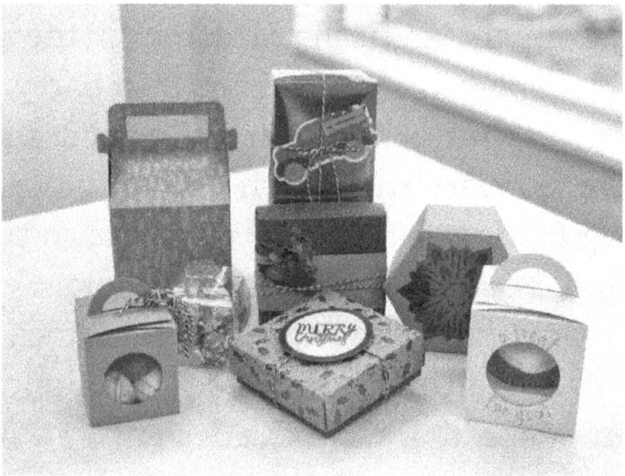

What is the joy of making crafts without gifting them to others – when we are at gifts, we would like to share some patterns for the easy making of different sets of boxes with your Cricut machine. You can also design your own box patterns once you get more familiar with Design Space tools – nothing makes one's skill better than practice. Let's see how you can start making your own gift boxes today.

Materials Needed:

- Glitter cardstock or another type of cardstock
- Glue
- Scoring Wheel
- Cricut machine

Instructions:

You will start by designing your box pattern or by uploading SVG files for box patterns. There are numerous designs for boxes found online while you can also make your designs if you are good at creating patterns that should be later assembled.

You can use patterns similar to this made for this pillow style box:

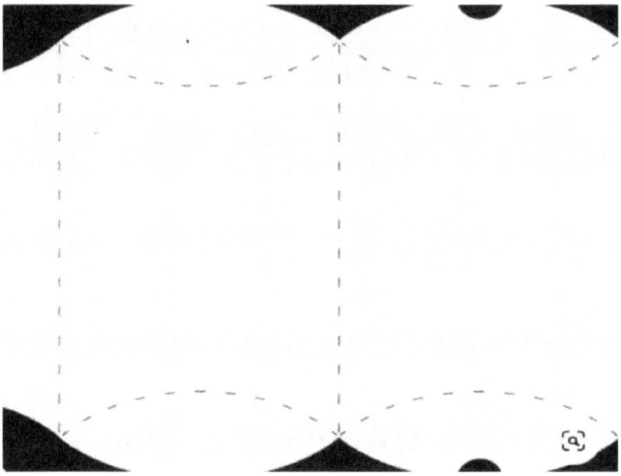

Or use some similar to these designs:

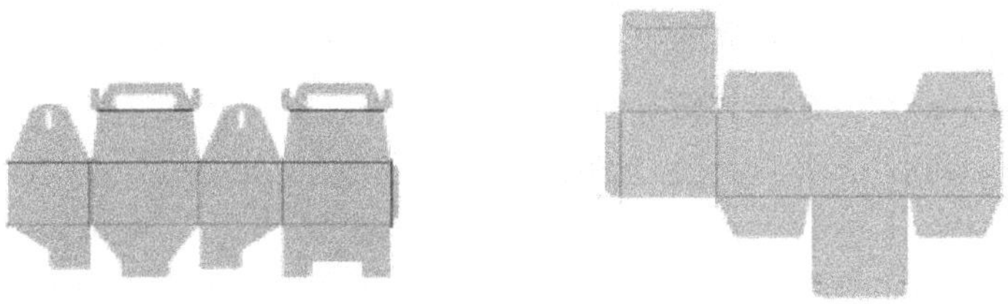

Once you access your Design Space, click on "New Project" and upload the patterns you have found and downloaded. Alternatively, start making your own patterns for boxes. You can start from the pillowcase box as perhaps the simplest to make for a beginner. Size your patterns to fit the box's intended size by using the top editing panel in Design Space. In case you are making more than a single box (perhaps you are making smaller gift boxes), make sure to press "Ungroup" to separate designs that should be cut and used separately for assembling. Make sure to change the Line type to "Score" for parts of the design that should be folded before sending your design to cutting. When you are finished scoring the lines that need to be folded, select the entire design and click on "Attach" finish the sizing if needed from this point, then proceed to click on "Make it".

Choose cardstock as your preferred material when specifying cutting settings under "Make it". Once you have prepared the material and the cutting mat, you can proceed to cut. After this step, you will assemble your box/boxes. In case you have chosen light materials such as paper or regular cardstock, you won't need to glue the box to keep the parts together. However, suppose you are using glitter cardstock and similar materials. In that case, you will need to secure the box's parts with glue – except the part that is supposed to seal (close) the box.

: Start assembling your box and glue the parts that need to be secured as you go. The best thing is to use tacky glue or glue gun to make things faster and more efficient. And, your box is ready!

Chapter 3:
Advanced Projects

CLEAR PERSONALIZED LABELS

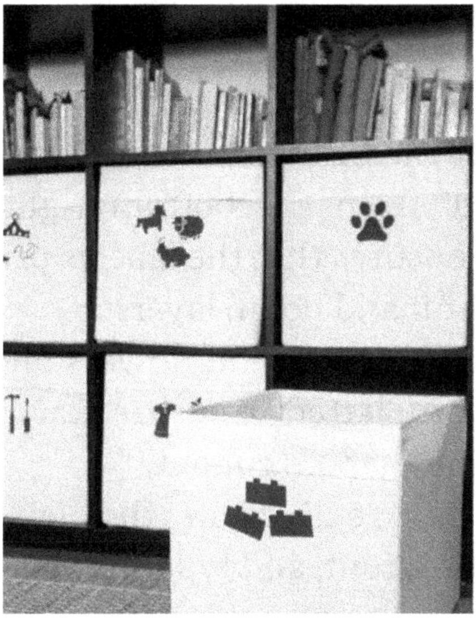

Labels are fun and can be used in many ways. These labels are designed for boxes, packets, and so on.

Materials Needed:

- Cricut clear sticker paper
- High-gloss printer paper for the Inkjet printer
- Inkjet printer (check the ink cartridges)
- Spatula tool

Instructions

1. Create a new project in Design Space.

2. Choose the heart shape from the left-hand side 'Shapes' menu.
3. Select an image from the 'Images' menu on the left-hand side menu.
4. Choose a picture of a flower or search for M1525E.
5. Unlock the flower image, position it in the top left corner of the heart. Make sure it fits without any overhang.
6. Select the heart and the flower, then click on 'Weld' from the bottom right-hand menu. This ensures that the label is printed together as a unit and not in layers.
7. Select the heart and flowers once again, then click on 'Flatten' to ensure that only the heart's outline shape is cut out.
8. Choose 'Text' from the left-hand menu, choose a font, and type the text for your label. You can choose a color for your text.
9. Unlock and move the text into position in the middle of the label.
10. Adjust the size to fit comfortably.
11. Select the heart shape and the font, then click on 'Flatten' to ensure the label is cut as a whole and not layered.
12. To not waste sticker paper, you will want to print as many labels as you can per sheet.
13. Choose the square shape from the 'Shapes' menu.

14. Position it on the screen, unlock the shape, and set the measurements to a width of 6" and a height of 9".
15. Move the first label into place at the top left-hand corner of the screen.
16. Select the label and 'Duplicate it.'
17. Move the second label next to the first one. Give the labels a bit of room between each other and the edges.
18. Fit as many as you can on the sheet then save your work.
19. Fill in each of the labels with the text you want.
20. If you have space left over when your labels are positioned, you can create smaller ones.
21. You can actually create all different sizes of labels, patterns, and designs.
22. Make sure that all the labels are for print and are flattened.
23. Delete the background rectangle.
24. Select all the labels and then click 'Attach' from the bottom right-hand menu.
25. Click 'Make it,' and check that the design and wording are correct before clicking 'Continue.'
26. Choose the high-gloss paper option and set it to the best quality.
27. Load the sticker paper into the Inkjet printer and press 'Send to printer.'
28. Choose 'Sticker paper' for the Cricut materials.
29. Load the 'Stickers' into the Cricut and press 'Go' when ready to cut.

30. The Cricut will cut out the stickers so you can peel them off the backing sheet as and when you need them.

Clutch Purse

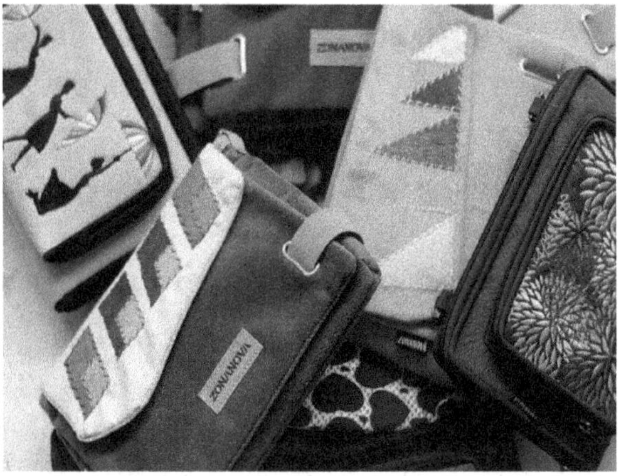

Materials Needed:

- Two fabrics, one for the exterior and one for the interior
- Fusible fleece
- Fabric cutting mat
- D-ring
- Sew-on snap
- Lace
- Zipper
- Sewing machine
- Fabric scissors
- Keychain or charm of your choice

Instructions

1. Open Cricut Design Space and create a new project.
2. Select the “Image” button in the lower left-hand corner and search for “essential wallet.”
3. Select the essential wallet template and click “Insert.”
4. Place the fabric on the mat.
5. Send the design to the Cricut.
6. Remove the fabric from the mat.
7. Attach the fusible fleecing to the wrong side of the exterior fabric.
8. Attach lace to the edges of the exterior fabric.
9. Assemble the D-ring strap.
10. Place the D-ring onto the strap and sew it into place.
11. Fold the pocket pieces wrong side out over the top of the zipper, and sew it into place.
12. Fold the pocket’s wrong side in and sew the sides.
13. Sew the snap onto the pocket.
14. Lay the pocket on the right side of the main fabric lining so that the corners of the pocket’s bottom are behind the lining fabric's curved edges. Sew the lining piece to the zipper tape.
15. Fold the lining behind the pocket and iron in place.
16. Sew on the other side of the snap.
17. Trim the zipper so that it’s not overhanging the edge.
18. Sew the two pocket layers to the exterior fabric across the bottom.

19. Sew around all of the layers.
20. Trim the edges with fabric scissors.
21. Turn the clutch almost completely inside out and sew the opening closed.
22. Turn the clutch inside out and press the corners into place.
23. Attach your charm or keychain to the zipper.
24. Carry your new clutch wherever you need it!

Wooden Airplane Décor

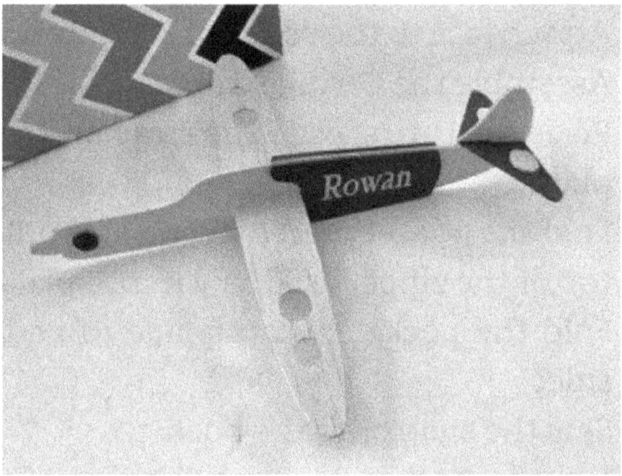

Materials Needed:

- Two pieces of 1/32-inch thick balsa wood
- Dark stain
- Ivory adhesive vinyl
- Super glue or wood glue

This is a "Make it Now" project in Design Space, so open the library, search for the project, and open the project in a new workspace. Using a StrongGrip cutting mat, lay your balsa wood pieces on and make sure to adjust your settings to “custom” on your machine. When you are ready, send your project to cut if the machine does not cut through the first time, repeat cutting, without moving your mat, three or four more times.

Gently remove the wood pieces from your mat. This is a fragile wood, so be very careful in removing the pieces not to break them. Lay your pieces to the side for now.

Go back to Design Space and write out the name or message you want to appear on the side of the plane. Make sure the size is correct for the size of the plane. Add your vinyl to your StandardGrip cutting mat and tell your machine to cut the image. Follow the prompts on your computer.

Weed out your vinyl insides as necessary and remove the unnecessary exterior vinyl that is not part of your design. When it is ready, lay the design on your airplane and use the scraper tool to transfer the vinyl to the corresponding piece.

You can offer the plane pieces with instructions as a gift, or you can assemble the plane yourself. If you are making it, use your super glue or wood glue to securely attach all the pieces and allow them to dry fully. Place this design somewhere people can enjoy your handiwork!

WOOD DANGLE EARRINGS

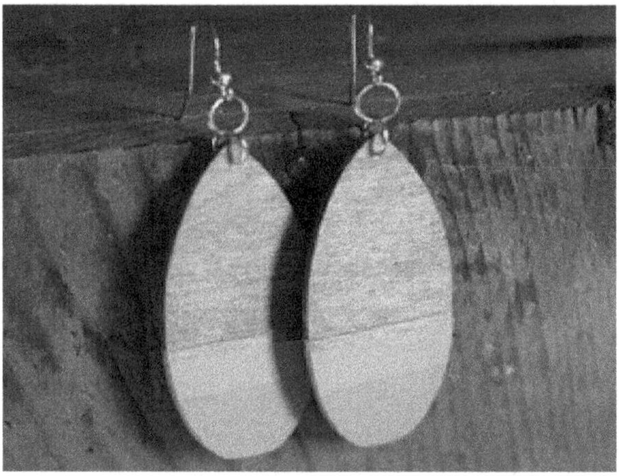

These earrings are versatile and customizable. It is easiest if you have a Xyron 1.5" sticker maker with a permanent adhesive. Still, you can achieve the same results without it. Just make sure you add enough adhesive and allow time for drying.

Materials Needed:

- Earring metal pieces
- Foam roller
- Xyron 1.5" sticker maker and permanent adhesive or another permanent adhesive
- Orange, pink, and gold acrylic paint
- Wood finishing cloths or wood stain
- Painter's tape
- Wood veneer cardstock

Instructions:

In InDesign, create a teardrop shape. If you do not have InDesign, open Design Space and look through the shapes and images until you find a shape that resembles a teardrop or surfboard. Remove all the layers until it is an outline. Repeat the outline or shape 12 times, making sure it fits on the cardstock sheet. You can tell your Cricut to cut 12 of the images when you go to cut it, and this allows the machine to replicate the image and optimize your cardstock for you! If you do not have a "wood" setting, set your machine to "cardstock," especially if your veneer is thin.

If you are using the Xyron machine, place ten of your cuts into the machine and apply adhesive to the backs. This leaves two without adhesive. Begin sandwiching the pieces together, five to each earring. Place one cut without adhesive on the back of each pile. This means each earring has six layers of veneer. If you do not have this machine, apply a thin layer of adhesive to the back of ten of your boards, working quickly as you layer each earring, ending with a sixth piece that does not have adhesive on the back.

Using your stain, apply two coats to the front, back, and sides of both earrings. Make sure to let them dry overnight so the stain can set properly. If you prefer a lighter or darker look, adjust the number of coats you apply to your liking.

Place your painter's tape over your earrings to mark where you want to paint. The tape will make sure the lines remain sharp and precise. You can hand paint without the tape if you want a more DIY look. In this example, begin with the top color, the gold color, and then move to the pink, and end with the orange. Give some time for drying in between each application. Depending on your color choices and paint quality, you may need to do two or more coats. Also, make sure to paint with the grain of your wood for the best results.

Using your reamer tool, poke a hole in the top of the earrings where the hardware will go. You can press through more to widen the hole as needed. If you have a bead reamer, you can use that, too.

Once your holes are wide enough, press your earring hardware through each earring and secure it in place! Now you are ready to wear or gift a beautiful pair of wooden earrings.

Customized Doormat

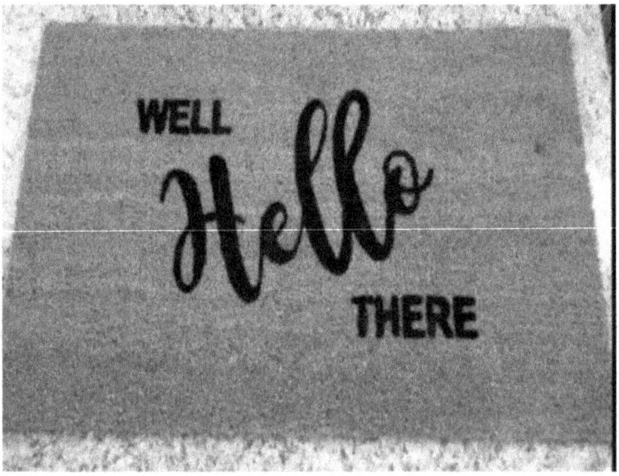

Materials Needed

Cricut Machine Scrap cardstock (The color does not matter) Coir mat (18" x 30") Outdoor acrylic paint Vinyl stencil Transfer tape Flat round paintbrush Cutting mat (12" x 24")

Instructions:

Create your design in Cricut Design Space. You can also download an SVG design of your choice and import it into Cricut Design Space. Make sure that your design is the right size; resize it to ensure that this is so.

Next, you are to cut the stencil. You do this by clicking "Make it" in Cricut Design Space when you are done with the design. After this, you select "Cardstock" as the material. Then, you press the "Cut" button on the Cricut machine.

When this is done, remove the stencil from the machine and weed.

Next, on the reverse side of the stencil, apply spray glue. After this, attach the stencil to the doormat, exactly where you want your design to be; then, pick up the letter bits left on the cutting mat and glue them to their places in the stencil on the doormat.

The next step is to mask the doormat's parts that you do not want to paint on. You can do this using painters' plastic.

Now, it's time to spray-paint your stencil on the doormat. Keeping the paint can about 5 inches away from the doormat, spray up and down, keeping the can point straight through the stencil. If it is at an angle, the paint will get under the stencil and ruin your design.

Spray the entire stencil 2-3 times to ensure that you do not miss any part and that the paint is even.

You're just about done! Now, remove the masking plastic and the stencil and leave the doormat for about one hour to get dry.

T-Shirts (Vinyl, Iron On)

To make custom t-shirts using your Cricut machine, you will need to use iron-on or heat transfer vinyl. Ensure that you choose a color that contrasts and matches well with your t-shirt.

Materials Needed

Cricut Machine T-shirt Iron on or heat transfer vinyl Fine point blade and light grip mat Weeding tools EasyPress (regular household iron works fine too, with a little extra work) Small towel and Parchment paper

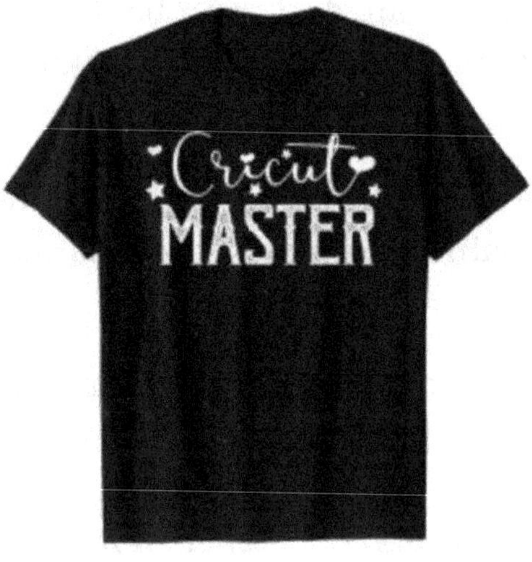

Instructions:

In preparing for this project, Cricut recommends that you prewash the cloth without using any fabric softener before applying the iron-on or heat transfer vinyl on it. Ensure that your T-shirt is dry and ready before you proceed.

On Cricut Design Space, create your design or import your SVG as described in the section on importing images.

If you are using an SVG file, select it and click on "Insert Images". When you do this, the image will appear in the Design Space canvas area.

Then, you need to resize the image to fit the T-shirt. To do this, select all the elements, set the height and width in the edit panel area, or simply drag the handle on the lower right corner of the selection.

After this is done, select all the layers and click "Attach" at the bottom of the "Layers" panel. The machine cuts everything just as it is displayed on the canvas area.

You can preview your design using Design Space's templates. You access this by clicking the icon called "templates" on the left panel of Design Space's canvas. There, you can choose what surface on which to visualize your design. Choose the color of your vinyl and the T-shirt so you can see how it will look once completed.

Once you are satisfied with the appearance of your design, click "Make It." If you have not connected your machine, you will be prompted to do so.

When the "Prepare" page shows, there is a "Mirror" option on the left panel. Ensure that you turn this on. This will make the machine cut it in reverse, as the top is the part that goes on to the T-shirt. Click "Continue".

Next, you are to select the material. When using the Cricut Maker, you will do this in Cricut Design Space. Choose “Everyday Iron-On”. On Cricut Explore Air, you select the material using the smart set dial **on the machine**. Set this dial to "Iron-On".

Now, it’s time to cut. To cut vinyl (and other such light materials), you should use the light-grip blue mat. Place the iron-on vinyl on the mat with the dull side facing up. Ensure that there are no bubbles on the vinyl; you can do this using the scraper.

Install the fine point blade in the Cricut machine, then load the mat with the vinyl on it by tapping the machine's small arrow. Then, press the “make it” button. When the machine is done cutting the vinyl, Cricut Design Space will notify you. When this happens, unload the mat.

With the cutting done, it is time to weed. This must be done patiently so that you do not cut out the wrong parts. Therefore, you should have the design open as a guide.

After weeding, it is finally time to transfer the vinyl to the T-shirt. Before this, ensure that you have prewashed the T-shirt without fabric softener, as mentioned at the beginning of this project.

To transfer the design, you can use the EasyPress or a regular pressing iron. Using a pressing iron maybe a little more difficult, but it is certainly doable. Before you transfer, ensure that you have the EasyPress mat or a towel behind the material you want to transfer the design to allow the material to be pressed harder against the heat.

Set the EasyPress to the temperature recommended on the Cricut heat guide for your chosen heat-transfer material and base material. For a combination of iron-on vinyl and cotton, the temperature should be set to 330^{0}F. After preheating the EasyPress, get rid of wrinkles on the T-shirt and press the EasyPress on it for about 5 seconds. Then, place the design on the T-shirt and apply pressure for 30 seconds. After this, apply the EasyPress on the back of the T-shirt for about 15 seconds.

If you're using a pressing iron, the process is similar; only that you need to preheat the iron to max heat and place a thin cloth on the design. The iron does not have direct contact with the design or the T-shirt. This will prevent you from burning the T-shirt.

Wait for the design to cool off a bit, then peel it off while still a little warm.

Ensure that you wait for at least 24 hours after this before washing the T-shirt. When you do wash it, be sure to dry it inside out. Also, do not bleach the T-shirt.

3D Paper Flowers (Paper)

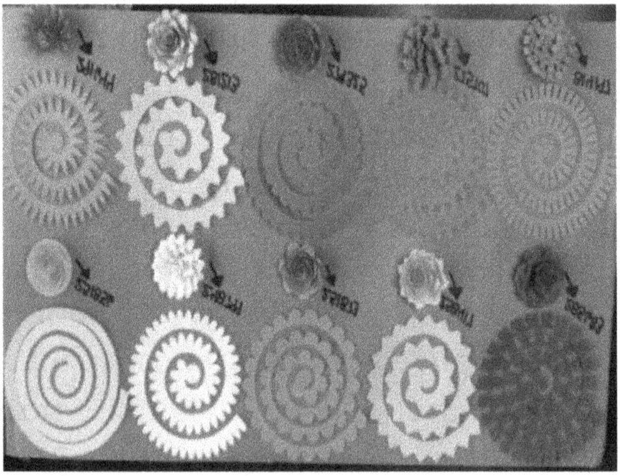

Materials Needed

Cricut Machine Cricut mat Colored scrapbook paper Hot glue gun and glue sticks

Instructions:

To make flowers, you need an appropriate shape for the petals. To make such a shape, you can combine three ovals of equal size. To create an oval, select the circle tool, then create a circle. Then click the unlock button at the bottom of the shape. Once this is done, you can reshape the circle to form an oval.

Duplicate this oval twice and rotate each duplicate a little, keeping the bottom at the same point, as shown in the picture.

Select all three ovals and weld them together to get your custom petal shape. For each large flower, you need 12 petals – each one about 3 inches long, while for each small flower, you need 8 petals – each one about 2 inches long. For each flower, you also need a circle shape for the base of about the same width as each petal. Arrange the petals and base circle shape in Cricut Design Studio.

Set your material to cardstock on Design Space or the machine, then cut the petals out depending on your machine.

After you cut out the petals, remove them and cut a slit about half an inch long at the bottom of each one. Place a bit of glue on the left side and glue the right side over each petal's glue.

The next thing to do is to place the petals on the circle base. For large flowers, you need three circles of four petals each. For small flowers, you need five circles on the outside and three on the inside. Put a bit of hot glue on the petal and add to the circle as described above.

For the center of the flowers, search Cricut Access for "flower" and chose shapes with several small petals. Cut these out using a different color of cardstock and glue to the center of the flowers.

Woodland Drink Charms

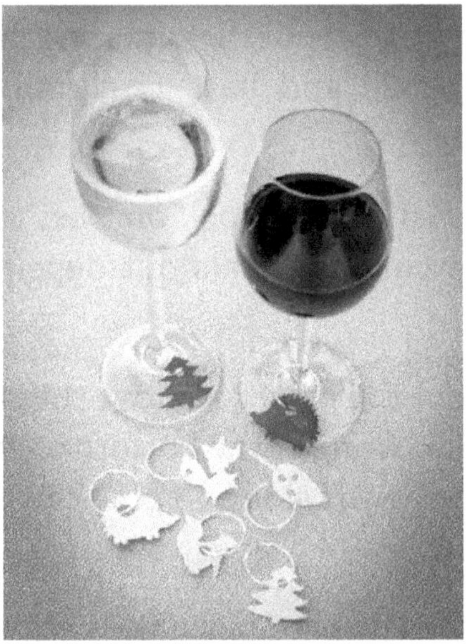

Wine charms can be pricey, especially if you want something more custom to an event or personality. Instead of spending a fortune for a sweet wedding memento or making a dinner party stand out, consider making your own! The process is simple, and the options are endless!

Materials Needed:

- 3mm thick balsa wood
- inexpensive "silver" hoop earrings in the number of charms you want to make
- Variety of paints, such as brown, green, orange, etc.

Instructions:

Open Design Space and insert various images you want to turn into wine charms. Keep the size smaller so that they will not interfere with someone holding the wine glass, but large enough to easily identify. Add a small circle to each shape that will be cut out and end up attaching the earring.

Cut the shapes onto the balsa wood. You may need to send it to cut a few times to make sure it has cut through your wood.

Remove the outside, extra wood, and weed out the circle from each shape.

Paint your shapes or stain them in the colors you want. Allow them to dry completely.

Once dry, thread one earring through the hole and get ready to dress up your next beverage! Consider adding initials, monograms, images, and patterns to the wine charms for different occasions.

Easy Lacey Dress

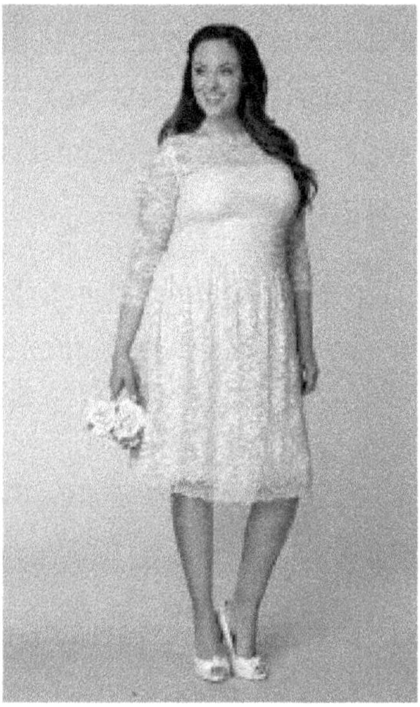

Materials Needed:

- Dress of your choice
- White heat transfer vinyl
- Cricut EasyPress or iron
- Cutting mat
- Weeding tool or pick

Instructions

1. Open Cricut Design Space and create a new project.
2. Select the "Image" button in the lower left-hand corner and search the "vintage lace border."
3. Choose your favorite lace border and click "Insert."

4. Place your vinyl on the cutting mat.
5. Send the design to your Cricut.
6. Use a weeding tool or pick to remove the excess vinyl from the design.
7. Place the design along the hem of the dress with the plastic side up. Add lace wherever you like, such as along the collar or sleeves.
8. Carefully iron on the design.
9. After cooling, peel away the plastic by rolling it.
10. Dress your child up in her adorable lacey dress!

"Momma Bear on Board Keep Your Distance" Car Window Stickers

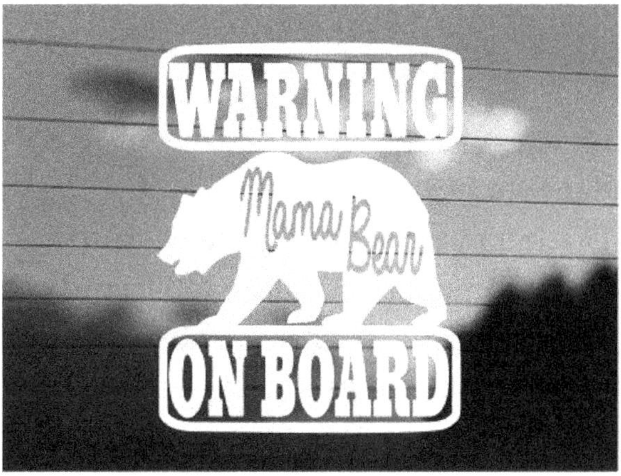

If you have ever wanted a car window decal sticker but cannot find one to suit your needs, you can make your own with the Cricut. There are so many fun things you can do with car window decals. Create fun sayings for the window, pictures of your favorite sport, different animals, and so on. If you are looking to sell your craft car window decals, they still have a following large market.

Materials Needed:

- Outdoor glossy vinyl (clear or white)
- Green StandardGrip mat
- Cricut measuring tape
- Inkjet printer
- Transfer tape
- Rubbing alcohol
- Cricut Fine-Point Blade
- Weeding tool
- Spatula
- Brayer or scraping tool
- Pair of scissors for cutting the material to size

Instructions

1. Measure how big you are going to want the decal to be.
2. Open a new Design Space project.
3. Select 'Images' from the left-hand menu.
4. Type in "bear" in the search bar and choose the black bear (Image #MF7274E7).
5. Position it on the screen and scale it to the desired size.
6. Change the color of the bear to brown.
7. Select 'Text' from the left-hand menu, and reset the font to Bernard MT Condensed. It is a nice clear font with a bit of character.
8. Type "Momma Bear on Board" on the one line.

9. Hit enter and type “Keep Your Distance” on the next line.
10. Center the text and change the color to white.
11. Unlock the text and scale it to size, then position it in the center of the bear.
12. Make sure none of the letters hang over the side of the bear image.
13. Select both the bear image and text, then click ‘Flatten’ from the bottom right-hand menu. You can also right-click and choose ‘Flatten.’
14. Save the project.
15. Click on ‘Make it.’
16. Ensure the image is aligned correctly on the page, and everything is the way you want it to be.
17. Click ‘Continue.’
18. Load your outdoor glossy vinyl sheet into your Inkjet printer. When you are ready, click ‘Send To Printer.’
19. Press ‘Print’ if you are happy with the printer setup.
20. Once the printer has finished printing the decal, unload the vinyl sheet from the Inkjet printer.
21. Stick the printed decal onto the cutting mat.
22. Go back to your project in Design Space and choose the correct material.
23. Load the cutting mat into the Cricut, and when it is ready, press ‘Go.’
24. When it is done, use the spatula, if necessary, to pull off the backing sheet of the vinyl.

25. Use the weeding tool to weed off any pieces that should not be there.
26. Cut some transfer paper to the size of the decal.
27. Place it over the decal. It is easier to work with it if it is stuck to the cutting mat.
28. Use the brayer or scraping tool to smooth the transfer tape over the image and get all the bubbles out.
29. Pull it off the cutting mat.
30. Take the rubbing alcohol and clean the car window portion that you want to place the decal on.
31. Gently pull the back of the vinyl off and position the decal on the cleaned window.
32. Once it is on the window, use the brayer or scraping tool to smooth it out and ensure it is properly stuck down.
33. Gently pull off the transfer tape, and your decal is on your window.

LARGE WOODEN SIGNS

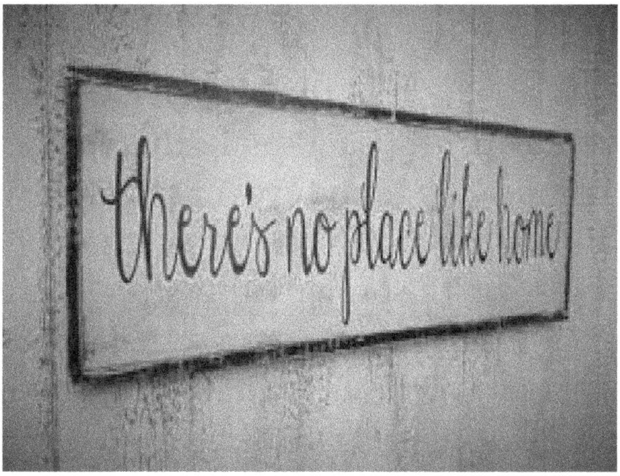

Passing messages to others can be done in different ways. This project is a sure way to express your thoughts when your visitors call during the Christmas celebration. This project is an easy craft you can make with your Cricut Explore Air 2 machine. It will make your Christmas decorations stand out. It is so gorgeous that I can't wait to share it with you. So, let me begin:

Materials Needed:

- Cricut Explore Air 2
- ¾" plywood
- Cricut tool basic set
- StandardGrip cutting mat
- The vinyl material (black color)
- Scraper tool
- Weeding tool
- Transfer tape
- Paintbrushes
- White paint

- Wood stain

Instructions:

The first thing to do is cut the ¾" plywood into 10" x 8" size, use sandpaper for sanding it, then paint it white. To make it appealing to the eye, I used Minwax Special Walnut to stain the 1x2's then allow it to dry. You will need to tone down the browns; therefore, rub gray milk paint over it. The color you can use depends on you because at the end of the day, whatever color you decide to use should first appeal to you.

Next is to design the text in Design Space before getting the Cricut Explore Air 2 machine to cut it out for you. So here is how to go about it:

First, get your text written on the Design Space

Edit your text using slice, weld, and others to arrange the words in a way that will fit the plywood and reflect your idea

Select your desired fonts for your text

Resize your text to fit your wooden plywood, of course, less than the 10" x 8" in size

When done, click Continue to show the preview

Place your vinyl material on the top left corner of your StandardGrip cutting mat with the shiny side facing you

Insert the mat using the mat guides with the mat firmly pressed against the rollers

Press the Load/Unload button on the top right corner of the Cricut Explore Air 2 machine

Insert the Cricut pen into accessory clamp A and close the clamp with the tip of the pen facing down

Go to your Cricut Design space, check the preview screen and click Go

Set the dial on your Cricut Explore Air 2 machine to iron-on vinyl

Press the flashing 'C' button on your machine and wait for the job to get done

Press the Load/Unload button when the job is done to unload the mat

Peel the unwanted vinyl from the mat then use your weeding tools to remove the tiny pieces between your letters.

Use the transport tape to pick up your design from the carrier paper.

Place the cutting mat on a clean surface face down, then curl the edge of the cutting mat up to let you peel away the vinyl from the cutting mat easily and in a way that will not mess your vinyl design.

Finally, place a ruler, as your guide, on the wooden prepared earlier, then carefully arrange the words on the wood with the aid of adhesive or glue.

This project will make your Christmas designs splendid and add color to your home.

Chapter 4:
Project Ideas For Christmas

Adorable Snowman

Materials Needed:

- Stitching cotton in snowflake white
- Stitching cotton in scarf print
- Felt in tan (This should be acceptable quality felt or the firm assortment.)
- Felt in dark
- Cricut Washable texture marker
- Iron or warmth press and press fabric
- Sewing machine
- Needle and string
- Batting
- Loads (a few marbles)
- Cricut Sewing Kit (Discretionary yet Very Helpful!)

Instructions:

This snowman is a piece of that pack, so the example is free. Simply search snowman, and you will discover the example.

Snap the image of the snowman, and you will be carried to a screen with all that you have to make the venture. You will discover the materials required and Instructions.

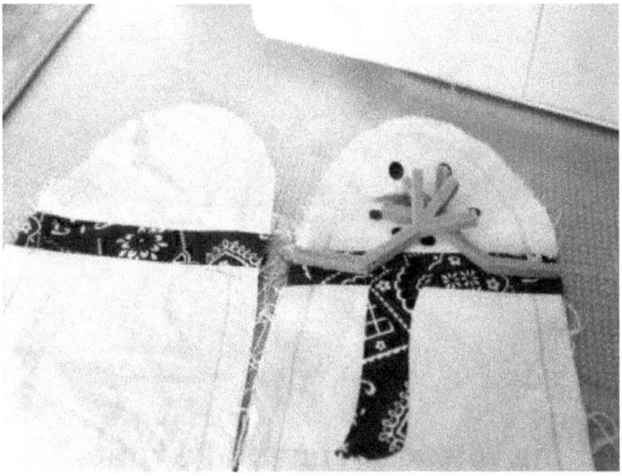

You can discover nitty gritty guidelines with pictures when you pull up the venture in configuration space.

Start by clicking "make it" in configuration space and pulling up your mats for cutting. Burden each tangle, sharp edge, and even the washable pen when incited to cut the entirety of the pieces expected to make this adorable snowman.

Configuration space will walk you through each tangle. You will be left with the entirety of your pieces superbly slice and prepared to make your undertaking.

Notice that the washable texture pen makes lines on a portion of the pieces. It will stamp the zone, so you realize where to put your face and denote your crease lines.

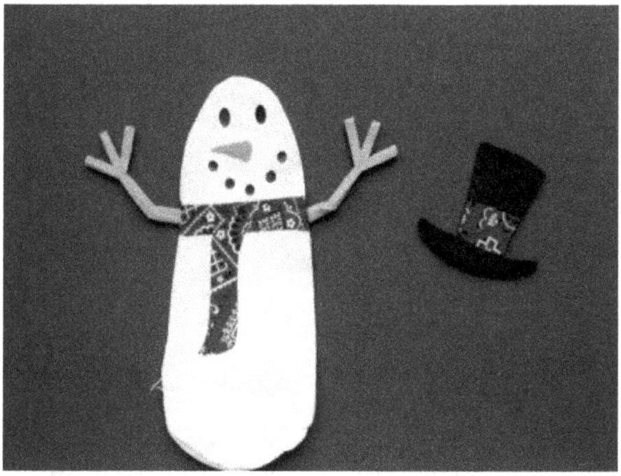

When your pieces are cut, you can start to sew them together. What's more, yes, that is a pin pad molded like a Cricut machine!

Sew the front and back of the snowman together according to the instructions.

At that point, include your face and scarf piece to the front of the snowman with an iron or warmth press.

You can pick to weave the face. Include the arms and pin the correct sides of your two sorts out to get ready for sewing.

At that point, simply stuff your charming snowman and hand sew your opening shut to finish your undertaking.

Paper Flower Christmas Gift Topper

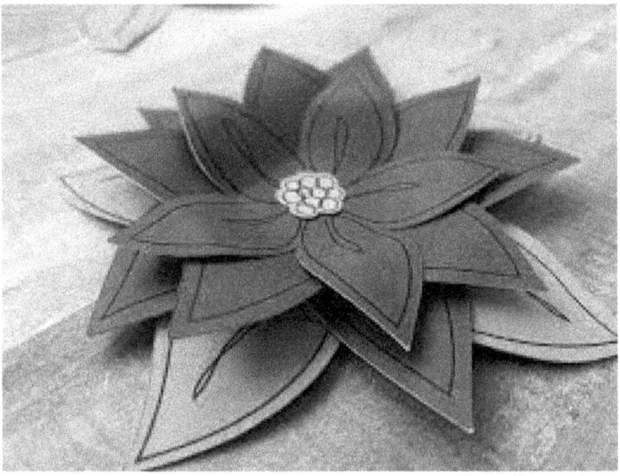

Materials Needed:

- Cricut Machine and Cricut Design Space
- Poinsettia design record from the Trim the Tree design set
- White cardstock and a printer
- Glue

Instructions

Go to the Cricut venture canvas I've recently set up for you. To guarantee the bloom's size is what you'd like, simply measure the green sprout piece for your biggest/littlest estimating.

Adhere to on-screen Instructions to print and cut the paper bloom pieces.

Paste each layer together to make a stack.

Add to your blessing! You may seize the opportunity to incorporate an unrestrained blessing tag as well.

Printing line workmanship with your Cricut

Rather than cutting all unique paper layers and including pen/drawing highlights, you can print the whole design without much of a stretch. Straighten the lines and slice, which makes a simple-to-make printed piece. Your Cricut machine will cut around the design as it would any printed design, and you can value smart undertakings with line subtleties!

For additional accents, you can likewise make a copy line layer to draw. Print with its printed line craftsmanship and afterward set your Cricut venture to draw a highlight layer. Gold sparkle lines over this printed task would look awesome!

Christmas Ornaments

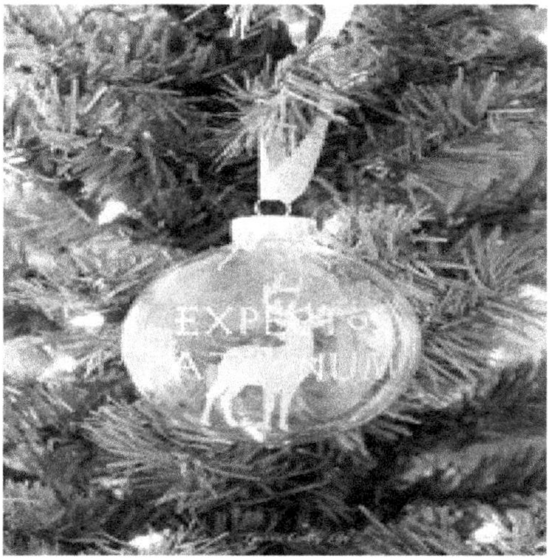

If you are not thinking about the holidays in November and December, you miss a great opportunity. It is never too early to think about gift-giving. Use your Cricut machine to make gifts and decorations that everyone will enjoy.

Materials Needed:

- Adhesive vinyl
- Adhesive foil
- Cricut Pens
- Ornaments - plain or clear are good options

Instructions:

In Design Space, upload your preferred design, image, or create your own with custom shapes.

To make a dimensional design, add various layers, and consider using different materials and colors to get a professional appearance.

If you want to cut words out and attach them to a strip of vinyl in another color, you can wrap that around your design. Or you could layer different vinyl, one solid and the other glitter.

Carefully lay out your vinyl where you want it to appear on your ornament and transfer the vinyl to the ornament. Transfer tape is best for this type of project. You can use a measuring tape or ruler and a marking pen to help you find the central location for the best results.

You can have vinyl and designs attached directly to the ornaments, or you can consider having pieces that hang on the outside or off of it as well. This can be a fun and personal gift, but the more you do it and practice working on a round surface, the better you will get at it!

Mason Jar Tags

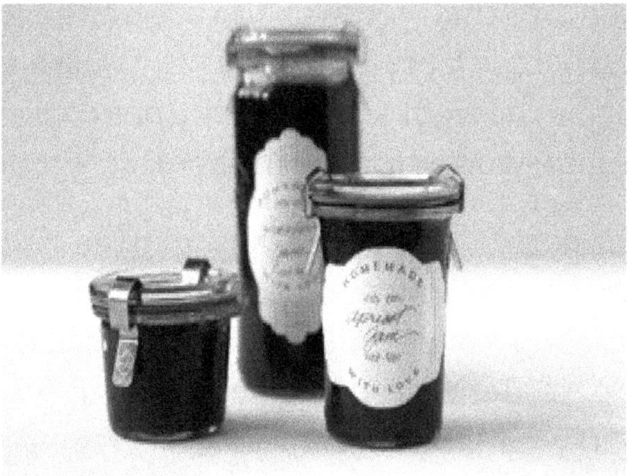

Jammers rejoice! This customized label allows you to give your homemade food creations a little extra "oomph." They are incredibly easy and can fit any jar you want to use.

Materials Needed:

- Adhesive Vinyl in lighter colors like white or yellow
- Weeding Tool
- Transfer Tape
- Mason Jars

Instructions:

Clean your jars well, especially the outside, where you want to place your label. Removing as much prior residue as possible will help your new labels stick better.

Also, measure the circumference and height of your jars. This way, you know which jar label canvas you need to create.

In Design Space, open a new canvas based on your mason jar's size that you want to create the labels for. Typically, there is a pre-set canvas. If you do not find a canvas that is the right size, open the one closest to your measurements and adjust from there.

Upload the desired images to your canvas and add any words you want to appear on the label. This can include a special message or describe the contents of the jar, etc. Make sure to detach your images so it will appear properly on your labels.

After laying out your images and words, go back and attach all the pieces and send your file to cut.

After your labels are cut, weed out any unnecessary pieces and remove the excess vinyl you do not want to use. Apply the transfer tape to the vinyl and then remove the backing. Using the transfer tape, adhere the vinyl to the clean exterior of your mason jar. Smooth it with your scraper tool and then slowly peel back the tape.

Mini Christmas Trees

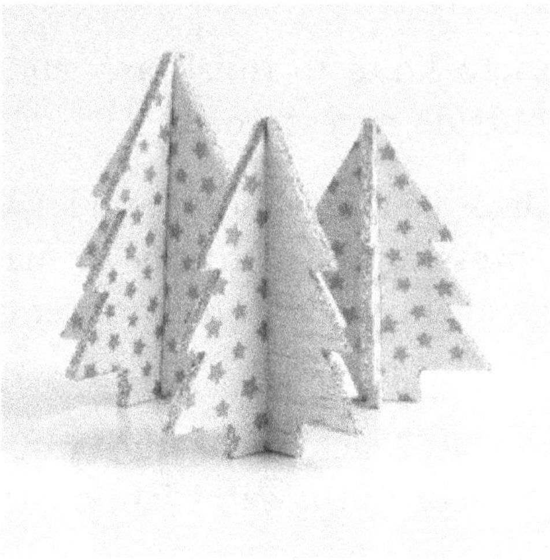

Materials Needed:

- Spray adhesive
- Ruler
- Exacto or crafting knife
- Glitter tape or glitter paint
- Matching patterned fabric
- 3mm thick balsa wood
- The predesigned Christmas tree patterns in Design Space

Open up the patterns in Design Space. Make sure to create both sizes for variety in height. Click "Make It" and follow the prompts. You may need to send it to print a few times to cut the image through the balsa wood completely. *If you are making placeholders for your table, make sure to write and add your names on your cuts now before cutting your images out. You can write to them with the pen, although it can come out a little rough depending on your wood. Another option is to print the names in vinyl and apply them after cutting.

Use your Exacto knife to finish any cuts necessary. Remove the outside, excess wood.

Spray one side of your tree pieces and lay them flat on your fabric, pressing down firmly to make sure the fabric adheres evenly to your design. Let the adhesive dry completely. *

Working with your Exacto knife, trace around your tree shapes to cut away all the extra fabric. If you want to repeat steps 3 and 4 on the other side of the trees, you can have completely decorated trees. If you do not, the trees' back side will be wooden while the fronts will have patterned, like the image above.

Using your Exacto knife, trim your glitter tape to 3mm, or purchase your tape 3mm wide. Wrap the tape around the edges of all the tree pieces, pressing to secure it. If you are using glitter paint, carefully apply the paint to the edge of all the trees and dry. If you are not steady with a paintbrush, consider doing this step before adhering your fabric so the added fabric will cover any mistakes.

Once all the pieces are designed and dry, slip the bottom cuts into the top, pressing down, so the "trunk" sits evenly on your flat surface. You are ready to decorate!

Snowy Wreath

Materials Needed:

- Grapevine wreath
- Silver berry stems
- Spray adhesive
- Silver and white glitter
- Piece of wood to fit across the center of the wreath
- Wood stain, if desired
- Drill and a small bit
- Twine
- White vinyl
- Vinyl transfer tape
- Cutting mat
- Weeding tool or pick

Instructions:

1. Thread the silver berry stems throughout the grapevine wreath.
2. Use the spray adhesive and glitter to create patches of "snow" on the wreath.
3. If you want to stain your wood, do so now and set it aside to dry.
4. Open Cricut Design Space and create a new project.
5. Select the "Text" button in the lower left-hand corner.
6. Choose your favorite font and type, "Let it snow."
7. Place your vinyl on the cutting mat.

8. Send the design to your Cricut.
9. Use a weeding tool or pick to remove the excess vinyl from the text.
10. Apply transfer tape to the words.
11. Remove the paper backing and apply the design to the wood piece.
12. Rub the tape to transfer the vinyl to the wood, making sure there are no bubbles. Carefully peel the tape away.
13. Drill two small holes in the corner of the wood and thread the twine through.
14. Hang your wreath and sign for the winter season!

Conclusion

If you have worked your way through the projects in this book, you are well on your way to becoming a Cricut pro. Like a recipe book, the projects, along with the ideas in this book, can be adjusted, adapted, and added to so that you can make each one uniquely yours.

With the Cricut, you will find birthdays, special occasions, seasonal holidays, and even school projects are a lot easier and more personalized. Everyone loves receiving gifts, cards, and so on that have been designed especially for them.

Now that I have given you several ideas of projects that can be completed using a Cricut, you should have more ideas on how to use your new Cricut machine. Each Cricut is capable of doing some super impressive creative projects.

The next step is to utilize your newfound wisdom on the cutting-edge craft project designing and creation offered by "Cricut". You are now poised to follow the detailed instructions described in this book to create your own personalized and one of a kind craft projects that reflect your creativity and serve as an exhibit of your self-expression. You will be able to turn even the most unlikely and seemingly unrealistic ideas into beautiful craft projects in no time.

Now that I have given you several ideas of projects that can be completed using a Cricut, you should have more ideas on how to use your new Cricut machine. Each Cricut is capable of doing some super impressive creative projects.

Never stop doing research. Never stop trying new things. Never, ever stop being creative. The Cricut does not make you any less creative; it makes the process easier to focus your valuable time and efforts on more important things or personalize the projects after making the cuts. It takes the tedious work out of your hands and makes everything fun, easy, and fast.

You have gone to the correct place. With this book, you will learn precisely what you have to know to make your own gathering ideal ventures in a matter of seconds and host the gathering of the year that your companions and neighbors will discuss for a considerable length of time to come.

Everything necessary is a couple of provisions and some simple guidelines. You can influence everything without exception you to can envision. You don't need to be a specialist, and you don't need to be great at makes. Give the Cricut a chance to do the diligent work for you, and love the outcomes!

The great thing about the Cricut is that you can use it with so many different materials that you will never run out of ideas for crafting and creating wonderful gifts.

The craftier you are, the more fun this new machine that you have purchased will provide you. The Cricut is not only designed to be used with multiple textiles, but you can also apply the vinyl that is used within the machine on multiple surfaces. This gives you a wide range of options when it comes to crafting with a Cricut.

You should have no questions about crafting with the Cricut after reading this book. It is so in-depth that you will be able to not only use your new Cricut but also know exactly which Cricut machine is best for your needs.

Happy Cricutting, and keep crafty!

CPSIA information can be obtained
at www.ICGtesting.com
Printed in the USA
LVHW051227200221
679497LV00007B/293